PORTRAITS OF A
SOLDIER

PORTRAITS OF A
SOLDIER

THE EXTRAORDINARY
LIFE OF
JON LIPPENS

AS TOLD TO J.W. WILSON

TCU
Press

Fort Worth, Texas

Library of Congress Cataloging-in-Publication Data

Names: Lippens, Jon, 1927-2016, author. | Wilson, J. W., 1976- author, editor,
writer of foreword, writer of afterword.
Title: Portraits of a soldier : the extraordinary life of Jon Lippens / as told to
J.W. Wilson.
Description: Fort Worth, Texas : TCU Press, [2018]
Identifiers: LCCN 2017057103 | ISBN 9780875656861 (alk. paper)
Subjects: LCSH: Lippens, Jon, 1927-2016. | Soldiers--Belgium-- Biography. Artists-
-Texas--Biography. | World War, 1939- 1945—Underground movements--Bel-
gium. | World War, 1939-1945- -Campaigns--Belgium—Personal narratives,
Belgian. |Ardennes, Battle of the, 1944-1945—Personal narratives, Belgian.
Classification: LCC N6537.L5575 A2 2018 | DDC 700.92 [B] --dc23
LC record available at https://urldefense.proofpoint.com/v2/url?u=https-3A__lccn.
loc.gov_2017057103&d=DwIFAg&c=7Q-FWLBTAxn3T_E3HWrzGYJrC4RvUoW-
DrzTlitGRH_A&r=O2eiy819IcwTGuw-vrBGiVdmhQxMh2yxeggw9qlTUDE&m=
Giac6Ehq8OzhuCnULNdlu6uOlJd4UXvora3pMeI4Am4&s=YpQ5pVmrL5GPxt1
Qodazv4O7BNKJwGyK8njdyBp4Alk&e=

Unless otherwise identified, photos in this book are from the
Lippens family collections.

TCU Box 298300
Fort Worth, Texas 76129
817.257.7822
www.prs.tcu.edu
To order books: 1.800.826.8911

Cover and text design by Bill Brammer
www.fusion29.com

*This book is dedicated to the unknown and
largely faceless men and women who hid in
plain sight and fought valiantly against seemingly
insurmountable odds to combat the spread of evil.
These underground resistance fighters gave hope to
their countrymen as well as momentum to the Allied effort.
People just like Jon Lippens. The world is eternally grateful.*

*Jon, your memory and life will be forever with us.
The world is a better place because of you. One of your
dying wishes was to see this book published. Heartbreakingly,
you did not make it long enough to see it published, but I know
you are upstairs smiling down. Rest in Peace, Jon!
Thank you for being one of the good guys—
every day of your incredible life.*

CONTENTS

Acknowledgments

I would like to thank Jon Lippens for allowing me into his home and memories nearly every Sunday for the year preceding his death to listen, question, and build this book. Thank you to his incredible loving wife, Fran Lippens, for her friendship, and for being such a wonderful influence on this project and on me. Ryder and Reese love you, Fran! Thank you to my mother-in-law, Debby Dyer, for your wonderful editorial brain and wit that turned my mess of words into a digestible story. Larry Brogdon, you are the reason this book ever happened. Thank you for introducing me to Jon, as well as being a friend and mentor to me over the years. Larry Lydick and Jack Fikes—thank you for your invaluable insight into Jon's professional life. A special thank you to Kathy, Melinda, Becca, Molly, and Dan at TCU Press for making this dream a reality. Thank you Byron Biggs and Carter Llewellyn for the invaluable story on Captain Jack. Thanks, Mom and Dad, for being unique and for the love you always gave me. Lastly, thank you to my beautiful and inspirational wife, Andrea. Your love and support from the onset of the project kept this going, and I couldn't have done it without you.

Introduction

Jon Lippens, a legal American since 1954, survived the battle for mankind, as we know World War II. Upon receiving Confirmation as a Catholic at age twelve, he was given a journal by a nun in which to record his life journey. He began making daily journal entries then that continued throughout his life, which made this book possible. Much of what he reports about the war came from his fellow soldiers and from his own personal experiences. The events of the prewar and war years occurred more than half a century ago, but most of what Jon witnessed was indelibly burned into his memory. Where specific dates and details had faded, Jon consulted books and websites for confirmation, and also to fill in important background information about events he did not witness himself. His entries document a life filled with horror and death, joy and survival. His belief in God made his survival tolerable. His life makes this story incredible.

I met Jon Lippens in May 2015. I was visiting a friend named Larry Brogdon to view and talk about his art collection. I noticed a small painting hanging alone on one of his walls. It depicted a camel and its turban-appointed rider. This piece stood out to me, so I asked Larry about it. He explained about this fine man he knew named Jon Lippens, who created that unique painting, and began to tell me about Jon's amazing story. I asked Larry if I could meet Jon, and we did meet a few weeks later. My first encounter with Jon was nothing short of jaw dropping. I knew right away that his story needed to be shared. I consider myself a bit of a war buff and thus have read many books on the subject of World War II, but this man had lived it. Jon Lippens became a dear friend, and for this, Larry, I thank you. Jon radiated his passion for the Lord and was never short of words. He was an incredible man who lived an extraordinary life. His knack for survival was uncanny, as was his ability to recall events that happened so long ago.

J.W. WILSON
August 2018

PART 1

Prewar
1927-1940

CHAPTER 1

Beginning

*"If you are scared, consider yourself
already dead. It'll make it easier to fight."*
-UNKNOWN

I have heard this said so many times, and try as I might, I could not prepare myself to die. Death was as common here as smoking cigarettes, both of which littered the battlefields of Europe. I was no stranger to death. It was everywhere and inescapable. I should have died hundreds of times over and yet never flinched in my desire to kill that monster who was trying to kill me. Youth bred naivety, which served me well when fear would have deterred a more mature fellow. The Germans had done things to people that were incomprehensible, and the ease they exhibited in killing a human, even a woman or a child, was no secret. I would not, for one split second, hesitate to put a bullet through a German's head, given the chance. Where was God, you ask? I hardly knew him then, but his presence can be confirmed in each day of my life, or it can be dismissed as mere luck. The ability to think and reason can create doubt. War not only ruined me but created me.

I was born on February 8, 1927, in Ghent, Belgium. My legal name in French was Jean Gustave Lippens. I changed my first name many years later to Jon, albeit not legally, after moving to the United States, because my mail kept coming to me as Ms. or Mrs. Jean Lippens. Waiting rooms were always paging Jean, always expecting a female.

I was born and raised in the city of Ghent but learned to love the countryside and its villagers, its farmers, and its people. Mom and Dad both owned their own businesses and had many employees and responsibilities. My dad was a successful architect, structural engineer, and in addition had a cork manufacturing company. My mother had a wholesale business

My baby picture:
Jean Gustave Lippens, 1927

in wool. They were busy parents, and mostly preoccupied with the success of their businesses. They were not bad parents but rather very driven to succeed in their professions.

I had one sister, Lucienne, who was a couple of years older than I. She was an exceptionally intelligent student who was enrolled in the best private school in Ghent. She completed her education at the well-recognized Université de Louvain in Belgium. She then graduated from the well-renowned European school of nursing named after Edith Cavell, who famously died on the Belgian front line of World War I in 1918, while assisting the wounded and dying soldiers.

I was educated in an all-male state school called Rijksmiddelabare Jongen Schule, or in French *Ecole Moyennes de L'état,* where I did well in the study of languages, geography, and history, while in mathematics and physics, I only achieved comfortable passing grades. I had the appearance of a much older boy due to my stature. My friends described me as an instigator who liked to push the limits of trouble. I was unafraid of consequences, which meant fingers were pointed in my direction when something was amiss. On one occasion during music class, we found ourselves bored with our instructor's lesson. He had left the room for a short period of time, and I had the brilliant idea to weave a metal ruler through the piano wires inside the belly of the instrument. Our instructor returned and sat down to give us his regular demonstration. The students and I waited with frenzied anticipation for him to play. He began to play and what spewed forth from that piano was nothing short of wretched.

The family in Ghent shortly before the German Invasion

He looked baffled and peered over the keyboard at the piano wires. He very quickly directed his menacing gaze toward me and ordered me to remove the ruler from his piano. I did so and began to walk back to my desk with the ruler in hand, but he had other plans. I was commanded to give him the ruler and place my hands on the edge of the piano, where he proceeded to smack them with that same hard metal ruler. I was left with a stinging pain in my hands that lasted for three days. My fellow students sat there terrified that he would summon them next.

In those days living in Belgium, surrounded by France, Holland, England, and Germany, demanded the knowledge of all four languages. My mother's language was French, my dad's was Flemish, but they both felt very at ease speaking both languages. In order to graduate high school, it was a prerequisite in preparation of higher education to also learn the King's English and German. It was to our advantage to speak all four languages fluently, and we did.

Lucienne and me as kids in Ghent, 1928

The home in which I was born in Ghent was a very large home with a full basement and three floors. The business office and my dad's drafting rooms were on the main floor. Our living quarters were on the second and third floors. I remember the rooms being large and the ceilings high. The whole building was heated with central heating and most rooms had fireplaces. On the second floor each room had a balcony facing the street. The house came unusually appointed with a large elevator in the center of the house. There was also a two-car garage. The kitchen was in the basement, and the food was brought up to the dining room by a lift. When I was five we moved to the northwest part of Ghent. In front of the house was a park right on the edge of a very busy canal. Barges and tugboats were coming and going day and night. At the end of the park was a covered and heated Olympic-sized city swimming pool. I belonged to a water polo team and swimming club, and we used that pool for our matches. This second house was larger than the first, and had a garden leading to the offices and the factory.

The factory was at the back of the house and faced the street behind us. The reason the house was attached to a factory stemmed from the problems presented by my dad's occupation. While my dad was doing well as an architect, sometimes the projects came in too slowly. There was often

Dad with two other soldiers during WWI

Dad in uniform

WWI bunker

a problem in collecting his architectural fee for designing and building certain jobs. The way my dad's business was set up, he was not protected by the building contracts he worked under. His fees were not included in the bids, and it became his responsibility to collect such fees. Circumstances periodically led clients not to pay him, or just as often, rendered them unable to pay him. Even when he received a government project, there was no guarantee he would collect what was due. Often times he was the loser, or could only collect a portion of his fee. Architecture was his dream and his first choice in professions, but after struggling financially for several years, he realized that his dream and career as an architect were not enough to regularly provide for the substantial needs of our family.

Dad had served in the infantry for the Belgian army during World War I. He was severely injured in the shoulder during the course of one of the battles and was transported to England by boat over the rough North Sea to recover. While in England, he became good friends with a Spanish businessman who was in the cork business. When the war ended in 1918, my dad returned to Belgium. His Spanish friend told him that if he ever wanted to enter the lucrative cork business, to get in touch with him.

My dad indeed got in touch with Carlos Rexach Cubero, who hailed from Seville, Spain. A deal was made that led my dad to form his own cork company, which he called Lippens-Haghenbeek, named after his and his

Dad between the wars

mother's surnames. This new cork company required a factory, which by careful planning became part of our house.

Dad's factory bought large amounts of cork, which came in large planks or boards about six to twelve feet long, three to four feet wide and about three to four inches thick. There were several qualities and sizes of cork. Some corks were for champagnes, wines, cognacs, scotch, and many others were for liqueurs. Different regions in Spain, Portugal, and Algeria produced different cork. The boards were first treated for insects, washed, soaked, and cut into long strips of different sizes. Then the boards were cut again to a certain length, to be cut again to a circular shape and size, washed again, dried, polished smooth, separated by quality through hand and visual triage, and finally stamped by branding irons. It sounds straightforward, but it required a lot of machinery and people to produce millions of corks in all sorts of shapes and qualities.

Dad worked long hours at the office and in the factory, and also traveled quite a bit. Sometimes he had an architectural commission, which he completed in addition to all his other business demands; this caused him very often to work through many nights. It was mostly through his efforts that our family enjoyed great financial stability.

I spent time with my dad while doing my homework or painting in his office. There were several large drafting tables in the drafting rooms, and

Lucienne and me

he let me use them when I wanted. It was there that I started to draw and paint with watercolors when I was five years old. A few years later, Dad showed me how to paint architecturally and three dimensionally. While on vacation at the coast one summer, I admired an outdoor artist who drew and painted while a crowd watched. The artist talked about what he called the working vacations he and his wife took through the years, and all the places they traveled to. While he painted, his wife would sell raffle tickets. When he finished his piece, they would draw a ticket out of a hat and give the winner the brand-new painting. This artist noticed that I was deeply interested in his art. He gave me pointers and even encouraged me to pursue being an artist. I remember that moment vividly. That is when I decided that I wanted to be an artist when I grew up. I began dabbling with graphite, oil, and water-based paintings. When I was nine I painted the family Christmas cards in transparent watercolors. The access I had to supplies, coupled with endless time, allowed me to develop my artistic abilities. I don't think my dad ever felt like I would stick with it. In fact, he had other plans for me. Dad had the means and the desire for me to play the violin, so he bought me a Stradivarius on which to learn. This art form didn't interest me like painting did, and I was opposed to practicing it. Dad's experiment failed, and the valuable violin was sold later on for a small fortune. Painting interested me, so that's where I played. I painted many works of people, scenery, churches, historical buildings, boats, sailing ships, planes, and animals, some of which were of great size. My abilities improved rapidly, and my collection of works began to grow.

When she wasn't moonlighting as Dad's accountant, my mother was involved in a successful business of her own, which was the wholesale of wool. She supplied the wool that was used to produce different articles such as sweaters, scarves, hats, gloves, and other clothing, as well as many elaborate rugs.

Belgium has what I call a cold climate, with rainy and cloudy days more than half of the time, except in the summer when the warmest day could reach 80°F. Since we didn't know any better, we lived with it, and life was good. Belgium was green and beautiful and a wonderful place to grow up. We never went without and enjoyed the freedoms of prosperity.

Around the ages of three and four years old, I had problems with colds, ear infections, sore throats, and tonsilitis. Sometimes it weakened my resistance to the point where it became a real health problem. Our family physician owned a special dairy farm and a large home located about twenty miles outside of Ghent, where he cared for children with the same types of health problems. His daughter was a registered nurse and took care of the kids. The farm owned by Henry De Rijke provided fresh vegetables, unadulterated milk, fresh fruit, fresh air, and plenty of exercise. A few days on the farm did wonders for the sick and often made them stronger and able to return home and ultimately to school. I was cared for many times by the family on this farm, and it helped bolster my love for the outdoors. For many years, during summer vacation and on holidays, my parents took me to the farm, where I helped Henry with the many dairy cows, horses, pigs, rabbits, and chickens, and worked the land with him. I was given chores to do from sunup to sundown. I took special care of a large Belgian horse named Julius, and a milk cow named Theresa. At harvest time, we worked in the field and in a large vegetable garden. I enjoyed it very much and consider this period of my life one of the happiest.

There was an old and rustic smokehouse where the farmer's wife Mary cooked the daily bread, pies, and cakes. Several hams and slabs of bacon hung from the ceiling being cured. Next to the vegetable garden was a separate strawberry patch, and everywhere were all kinds of fruit trees, such as apple, pear, cherry, and many vines with all kinds of berries. There was a pump house for water, no gas or electricity, and at night, we used kerosene lights. The house had a large walk-in open fireplace we sat in on cold winter days. It was my favorite place. Located on one side of the room, it was equivalent to a present-day den. The large walk-in fireplace had a sitting area for eight to ten adults. In the winter at the end of the day, we spent a few minutes there thawing out. We joined the old folks around the fire, had a family prayer, and thanked God for the day's blessings.

The pump house was the only source of water. Any water we used came from that hand pump, including bath water. Let me tell you how we bathed. It took guts to go through that experience, because there was no heat in the pump house and you had to strip naked in the cold, stand on top of the drain, pump cold water into a bucket, pour it on yourself to get wet, soap up and wash, pump two to three more buckets to rinse, dry as quickly as possible, put clean clothes on, and hurry back to the walk-in fireplace where you got over the shivers. I remember it as a cold experience, but it must have prepared me for many years later when I was in the service. The bathroom was a one-holer, which entailed a board with one hole across a cistern for all those calls of nature.

This farm and my days working for Mr. De Rijke would prove to be very precious for our family several years later, when our lives changed dramatically.

Belgium

I am often asked to describe growing up in Belgium before the war. Like most children, I was oblivious to nearly everything outside my immediate surroundings, but I loved my childhood in Ghent and I treasure the fondest of memories. I remember a proud, friendly, and hard-working people, people that have endured many hardships throughout our long history. A recession is always expected after a war, and Belgium was no exception after the First World War. Our recession was deep because of the costs of rebuilding a country utterly destroyed by the Germans. It was a long, arduous process, but by the hard work of our people, Belgium had recovered sufficiently from the effects of World War I by the 1930s. Our country had a vast and expansive collection of artifacts and treasures that had been plundered by the Germans, and little was recovered due to the fact that the German homeland wasn't invaded. Such items were nearly impossible to find and very difficult to collect after the conditional surrender. But Belgium owned many assets in the Congo in Africa that allowed for financing to recover and rebuild the country.

My Heritage

My birthplace of Ghent has a wonderful and arduous history. This is the land where medieval Europeans first rose against privilege and power. A lion rampant, shrieking out an angry challenge on a giant, silken banner of scarlet and gold, hung from a gilded Belfry Tower. Ghent, the throbbing, pounding Mill City of the Middle Ages, where tens of thousands of weavers, fullers, and dyers periodically emerged from pitched battles against each other, bloody riots, tumultuous protests and demonstrations, and wars against their rulers and would-be rulers to manufacture the heavy

A trip to the beach with Lucienne and Mom. Dad was always working.

Flemish cloth worn in every ancient land of Europe (and today preserved in paintings by Flemish masters found in museums around the world).

Ghent was the largest city of medieval northern Europe except for Paris, a monumental place by the standards of those times, with a thirteenth-century population of over sixty thousand souls, who built up an almost unique (for then) mass-volume manufacturing economy. Ghent did everything to size: its centuries-old canal houses, standing in an unbroken line along the enchanting *Graslei* (Herb Canal), are three times as large as ordinary canal structures of that age; its fifteenth-century Butchers' Hall (*Het Groot Vleeshuis*) still extends for a full city block, and the bell on its cathedral tower weighs twelve thousand pounds. Its supreme masterpiece, Van Eyck's *Adoration of the Mystic Lamb*, consists of no fewer than twenty-four panels.

But as wonderful as it was and as aged as it is, Ghent is a living city, not simply an urban museum. Because its development continued well beyond the architecturally graceful Middle Ages and into the often not-so-elegant nineteenth and twentieth centuries, it is not always a "pretty" town. It's occasionally dark and begrimed, somber and stark in spots. Ghent has seen everything, done everything, enjoyed or suffered every European triumph or defeat, and—in the period of its greatest eminence in the 1200s and 1300s—dramatically witnessed the very industrial, labor, and class conflicts that have so troubled the world in modern times. Ghent is a travel adventure that enlarges the understanding and consciousness of

My grandparents on my dad's side —Rene and Rosalie

those visitors who come prepared for it.

Ghent is often called the bubbling cauldron of Europe. Long before there was an industrial revolution, Ghent possessed many of the attributes of an industrial city. Long before the era of capitalism, Ghent enjoyed a form of capitalist organization. Evolving from an Abbey ("Abbij") founded by St. Amand in the 600s at the meeting place of the Scheldt and Leie Rivers, Ghent developed in the 1200s into Europe's largest producer of cloth from wool, employing upwards of thirty thousand persons—all organized in strictly delineated Guilds—to weave and finish and dye the

Lucienne and me with Mom

yarn they imported from England. This wool heritage found its way into my mother's career.

The Belgian motto is "Unity Makes Strength." That is why we have the Belgian Lion as a symbol of our supposed strength and unity. Yet the Belgians are now divided, but coexist, and there's persistent animosity between different groups, for one reason or another. Our constitution was set up by a great king of the past, and it was a good peaceful time for our little country that had, for many decades, good laws, good morals, great respect for the law of the land; it was a good place to live. However after the Great War of 1914-18, the existential and socialist belief of the New World Order was adopted, then reinforced after World War II, with a secular and rotten government. Even in the army, I didn't hear the foul language we hear now. In the Belgian army, our drill sergeant told us that if you curse another soldier and if he gets killed, which he most likely will be, you will forever remember and always regret what you said. Avoid cursing and insulting one another and that is an order!

Belgium was divided into nine provinces and was named "The Crossroads of Europe" with four official languages, Dutch or Flemish, French, English, and German. The western part of Belgium was predominantly Flemish, because the region was located in the Lowlands called the Flanders, and people spoke Flemish, while the eastern part of Belgium was called Wallonia, and people spoke predominantly French, German, and a dialect called Walloon. The central part of Belgium was called Brabant. They were bilingual and spoke both French and Flemish. The French-speaking Walloon and the Dutch-speaking Flemish have never liked each other, which has caused the country much unrest and turmoil.

Belgium is beautiful but small, covering less than twelve thousand square miles, and is one of the most densely populated areas of Europe. It has excellent highways, and rail travel moves in every direction at speeds of 140-160 miles per hour, with connections to almost any destination in Europe, including Russia. Brussels has one of the most modern subway systems in the world. The Belgian coast runs from the French border to Holland on the North Sea. Sand dunes, some as high as sixty-five feet above the sea level, keep the water out of the interior Lowlands. The largest of the resort towns along the coast is Ostend, which dates back to the tenth century. From its port, the Crusaders set sail for the Holy Lands. Ostend is also an important transportation center, where a major European highway begins and goes all the way to Istanbul, Turkey. A number of international trains to many parts of Europe start at Ostend. The seacoast of West Flanders is very nice and is an international playground. The beach is covered with clean white sand, free of stones, and at low tide is nearly a half-mile wide in some places.

Despite its tensions, for a long time Belgium was a good place to be.

PART 2

War
1939-1944

CHAPTER 2

Germany and War

When World War II started in the year 1939 I was thirteen years old. The Germans unleashed a plan upon the world that was cloaked in deceit and aimed at the immediate annihilation of Europe. We Belgians had long readied our country for the possibilities of attack but were still ill prepared. The ensuing daily struggle for survival matured most of us young folks very quickly. Everything I knew and did was about to change. The life I had known and loved was over.

Belgium felt the first repercussions of Nazism in the chaotic year of 1935, when German agitators urged the return of the east border towns of Eupen and Malmedy to the German Reich. These lands had been assigned to Belgium by the League of Nations in 1925 as a condition of the German surrender. When Hitler denounced the Locarno Pact, which essentially was set up to keep Germany from using future force to extend its borders, tensions grew. A second problem was that the Reichswehr, a German unified military organization, occupied the Rhineland, a mountainous water-passage area containing lands in Belgium, Germany, and France.

Following that crisis, Britain, France, and Belgium, for the first time since 1914, held staff conferences in London in the spring of 1936. However, three years before WWII began in 1939, Belgium abandoned her postwar position and returned to her old policy of neutrality. It meant the end of the FrancoBelgian alliance and withdrew Belgium from collective action and any new Locarno Pact that was concluded. "Alliances, even defensive ones," declared the Belgian King Leopold in announcing the new policy, "would not serve us because, prompt as we may be, aid could not reach us before the first shock of the invader which might be overpowering and against which we must be prepared to fight alone."[1] Belgium had the precarious position of bordering Germany, with its allies either out of position or not positioned strongly enough to come to our aid should mighty Germany invade.

During the year 1938, Belgium mobilized its troops, as war seemed to be imminent. On August 26, 1939, a few days before the Nazis launched their attack on Poland, Vicco von Buelow-Schwante, the German Ambassador to Brussels, was received by Belgian King Leopold III. Stressing the validity of the German note of October 13, 1937, the German envoy reassured the Belgian monarch that in the event of war, the Reich would respect Belgian neutrality. The King believed Hitler would recognize our neutrality and so put his trust in Germany, only to become a victim of his own sincerity.

War Machine

Belgium's stance of neutrality did not preclude being prepared. We would not attack but only defend. In 1938, Belgium drafted every single man in defensive preparation for the coming war. Belgian commerce ground to a halt. Each man under the age of fifty reported for duty and began rigorous training for the inevitable. Dad was fifty-two years old at the time and thus excused to keep running the family businesses. Some businesses had to go on to support Belgian citizens and prepare them for war should it come. I was eleven years old then, and of course all this was very interesting to me. There were soldiers everywhere, and daily I saw troops marching through the town on their way to the military firing ranges, or to the daily parades with the military bands on the grounds in front of the downtown army fort. On Sunday and other special occasions, we had military parades through the main street and boulevards while the avenues were decorated with Belgian flags. I envied and admired our courageous soldiers. In those days it was an honor to serve, and the enthusiastic and patriotic population applauded them for their bravery.

Belgium was divided into nine provinces, which were similar to our states. Every province had a large fort we called a caserne (barracks/camp) that sheltered the troops, artillery, tanks, and other supplies. Then each town had an infantry division composed of 15,800 troops. Each town or city had a parade ground and had regular parades, as if to let the civilian population know that they were there and ready to protect them. The show of force gave citizens relative comfort, or so we thought.

In August 1939, France knew that in this war of nerves she was fighting for her life against a Germany that had lost the few shreds of honor it had seemingly possessed. No treaty could be made with this unscrupulous enemy.

At dawn on September 1, 1939, German forces invaded Poland. Polish forces were aware of Germany's intent but were incapable of stopping the oncoming German juggernaut. The massive German forces easily moved into Poland unabated. The whole world was shocked by the event. The German U-boat 30 torpedoed transatlantic passenger liner SS *Athenia,* carrying 1,400 passengers off the western approach to England. Germany denied this, thinking it would draw America into the war. The *Athenia* was the first UK ship to be sunk by the Germans. Luckily most passengers and crew were rescued, but this attack alerted the world to Germany's true intentions, which were far from just regional. Germany had been conducting diplomatic relations as a smoke screen while at the same time gearing up their forces. Germany had been clandestinely building the most powerful war machine the world had yet known, with an army of 12 million men. Now, they unleashed it upon the world.

Dawn

War came to us before dawn on May 10, 1940, with the simultaneous German attacks on Belgium, Holland, and Luxembourg. Allied armies rushed across Belgium in a life-or-death struggle with the invading Germans. Hitler had made it clear that it was not up to neutral nations to decide their destiny; that people within striking range of Nazi power were no longer able to remain neutral even if they had scrupulously observed the rules of neutrality, and that one by one they had to expect the fate of Denmark, Norway, Czechoslovakia, and Poland.

Belgium, with a prewar population of approximately 8.5 million Belgians, was on the direct path of the invaders heading toward Paris and then London. Belgium had been the victim of aggression before. It was in Belgium 125 years prior that Napoleon met defeat in Waterloo, near the center of Belgium, where his conquest of Europe ended. In 1914 the Germans invaded and occupied Belgium for four years, lost the war, and surrendered. We called that war the Four Year War. Later it earned the nickname World War I.

Little Belgium became overnight part of the Allied war machine. King Leopold III assumed command of the Belgian armies and directed resistance to the invading forces. The Belgian government issued an appeal to the population to preserve calm and spot sabotage. Full mobilization took place. Bridges and roads were blown up to prevent the first German advance, and the country's flood system of sluices (locks) was put into operation.

Thirty days after the Germans invaded Denmark and Norway, the juggernaut rolled into Belgium, Holland, and Luxemburg on the road to France. Belgium, not much larger than New Hampshire but the most densely populated country in Europe, was ground under the wheels of the conquerors.

I was taught at an early age to hate the Huns because of the many terrible things they had done to Europe in World War I, when they murdered thousands upon thousands of conquered civilians. Worse yet, they killed them by torture or starved them to death.

We were well aware of the German Fifth Column living amongst us in Belgium, as they moved in well ahead of the invasion. These were Nazi fanatics who sabotaged every effort the country made to stop the Germans from advancing. There was little or nothing our little country could do to stop the Germans, but we slowed down the inevitable advance.

In World War I, Belgium had been a battlefield for four long years, and when the Germans lost the war, our country was in ruin. My dad and my uncles fought in the trench warfare and told us some awful experiences they had. I had a library of books describing every battle fought by the Allies during the 1914-18 war. The battles were often named after the regions or towns in which they were fought: Verdun, Argonnes, Sambre, Meuse, Somnes, and Yser were some of the famous battles.

The outstanding problem after the armistice of 1918 was the creation of a world molded to endure in peace. The phrase "the war to end all wars" was in part a promise. But Hitler's practice of breaking agreements, promises, and declarations made with the British and other governments had gathered momentum by 1939. Within six months after solemn pledges of non-aggression, Hitler's army marched into Czechoslovakia, annexing Bohemia and Moravia. Hitler was convinced that he had obtained the whip hand in European affairs and had a free hand in Central and Eastern Europe to subjugate smaller, and as he regarded them, inferior people to superior German rule and culture.

On that particular morning of May 10, 1940, we were jolted awake before daybreak by the eerie sound of alarm sirens. Our first panicked thoughts quickly became reality. The sirens bled off into the planes, antiaircraft artillery fire, machine gun fire, and numerous explosions that announced the arrival of the Nazis. In the air, we saw some of our Belgian planes dog-fighting in hopeless battles with the superior and modern Luftwaffe (German Air Force). I ran downstairs, where my parents were listening to the emergency broadcasting service, giving the latest news and our survival instructions.

News did not travel fast for us. Bits and pieces of information would trickle in, but we never knew what might be happening on the edge of town or in the surrounding towns. One of the first things the Germans did was to bomb our radio towers, which effectively kept us in the dark. The few who could afford short-wave radios were able to keep in touch with the ongoing events. However when the news made it in, it was not uplifting and caused unbelievable fear amongst us.

The first thing we did was to put thick tape on all the glass doors and windows in the house to protect us from flying glass should we get bombed. Next we filled our glass containers with water just in case the utilities were cut off. We filled the kerosene lamps and located the candles and matches. We completed the reinforcements in the bomb shelter, which was located in the cellar. Our family rushed to the food store to get the available food and supplies before they ran out. We weren't without company. There was absolute panic on everyone's faces. The people furiously bought everything they could carry to stock reserves, and in no time stores sold out of everything. The lingering memories of World War I informed everyone of what was necessary for survival. The mere memory of starvation instilled panic in everyone. Luckily the Lippens family had a natural well at the cork factory, so plenty of fresh water was readily available. Fresh produce—especially sweet potatoes, corn, potatoes, and carrots—were at a premium, so these were the quickest to go. Dad was smart and knew the Germans couldn't be stopped. He got us as prepared as possible. He ordered me to help him burn all the books in the house dealing with World War I. These books didn't shed a favorable light on the Germans, and it was for this reason that they needed to be destroyed should the Germans come knocking. He was educated enough to know that the Gestapo could take you away just for possessing the books. It was too risky to chance.

Ghent was bombed often, and the spotty news from the front wasn't good. The forts, canals, and bridges, which were supposed to stop or slow down the enemy's advance, didn't slow them at all. Unfortunately, it would get much worse. The battles were fierce, and the enemy kept on advancing. The Belgian air force was annihilated in a short time, and the few remaining planes escaped to England.

The invaders crossed the Belgian frontier at four points. German planes flew over the Belgian capital of Brussels and bombed the airport. They damaged the airports in Antwerp and in Ghent, destroyed the railroad yards, and damaged severely the industrial areas as well as visible communication installations. Parachuted German troops landed in the vicinity of Brussels. The Germans knew they had superiority in men and machines. They also knew that the only way to win the war was by utilizing what the Germans called the "Blitzkrieg." This warfare method exacts short, fast and powerful attacks, using speed and surprise to overwhelm the enemy. The unified armed forces of Germany, also known as the Wehrmacht, were facing in Belgium a minimum of 800,000 trained Belgian troops (roughly fifty divisions), a country weak in the air and with fortifications designed to retard the invader rather than halt him. The "Albert Canal" and the modern "Fort Ebeb Emael" didn't slow the enemy, and they were our best defenses. However, the Germans would pay a terrible price for their annexation of Belgium. A letter from a Belgian soldier on the front told the following story: "The Germans have to climb over their own dead to get to us but they still come on." They had to fight their way in, but it was obvious that we, and the Allies, were losing ground quickly. However, the Belgian soldiers, outnumbered about twenty-five to one, were fighting like lions. For eighteen days, the battle roared in Belgium, but when we ran out of troops and ammunition we had no other choice but to surrender.

The horrendous sounds of artillery shells exploding in and all around our town could not be escaped as the enemy approached our city. The Belgian army held them off for a while at the River Leie, but succumbed to the overwhelming strength of the enemy and retreated. I remember hearing the roar of guns and the crash of bombs shattering the serenity of the spring days. The initial dogfight of the Belgian air force and the vastly superior Luftwaffe was quickly followed by great fleets of German planes sowing death over our peaceloving country and cities, unloading its cargos of bombs and parachutists. It was a very scary experience, and was only a taste of what was yet to come. Initially, our family would scramble to the basement shelter every time a bomb landed nearby or each time an air raid siren went off. Our reaction to this changed after a week or two. We grew so accustomed to the bombs and sirens that we stopped running to the basement. Dad convinced us that if a bomb happened to land on the house, the bomb shelter wouldn't save us under the tremendous weight of the rubble. If a bomb struck our house we wouldn't live anyway, so we decided to keep some semblance of normalcy in the house, which really only meant not running to the basement every time a siren went off. We could feel the vibrations from each explosion and learned to sleep through many of the bombings, always hoping, of course, that our house didn't receive a direct hit.

A few days later the enemy arrived at the east end of our street, trying to reach the north end of the city. Numerous German tanks and an overwhelming number of infantry advanced toward the Belgian and French positions and trenches just west and north of us. The battle in and around our street went on for several hours, and the fighting was intense on both sides. The outcome to us Belgians could very easily be seen. The sheer number of soldiers the Germans possessed mowed over everything in their path. Our brave men, being completely surrounded by the German troops, had to surrender because they had suffered too many casualties and were running out of ammunition. The Belgians and French who had joined the defensive battle were surrounded and couldn't escape. My family was hiding as best we could in our basement. My curiosity got the best of me so I took the best seat I could on the roof of our house to witness the Germans move in. The Germans had soldiers with electronic bullhorns telling us in Flemish and German to stay inside or we would be shot. Anybody caught outside would be shot on sight. My parents didn't support my decision to go to the roof, but they couldn't talk me out of it. I was getting a front row seat to watch the Belgian defeat.

A feeling of despair washed over us. We realized that we were now prisoners and completely at the mercy of the Nazis. The great battle over our Flanders went on for many more days, and in the end, we suffered a terrible defeat with massive causalities and would now have to endure our enemy's occupation for the foreseeable future.

As the battles in Belgium subsided and confusion ensued, a friend of the family and I ventured out to the battlefields just outside of town to try and locate her brother, whose unit had been fighting on the River Schelde and the River Leie. The terrible scene I witnessed is very difficult to describe. Wasted human bodies littered the ground, marking wherever the Germans had been. The shredded remains of men lay scattered everywhere the eye could see. Thousands of dead German, Belgian, British, and French soldiers covered the battlefield, which just a few days prior stood as a beautiful iconic city.

There were many severely wounded soldiers hoping, waiting, screaming for help. Bloodied and charred remains of bodies and body parts lay scattered like trash. Everything around us was burning and exploding. The smell of death was intolerable. At the canal locks, we witnessed German bodies floating in piles and backed up against the lock doors. We searched for a good while amongst the carnage, but finding a specific man here was impossible. We never did find my friend's brother. Months later, the Red Cross found out that he was a prisoner in a hard labor camp in Germany, where he probably wouldn't have a chance to survive. Nonetheless, he somehow made it through the war and came back to his family a very sick man. He never recovered physically and died two years after his return. His body had suffered so much abuse that he couldn't heal from the damage inflicted on him.

While we still walked the battlefield, a German patrol of regulars (not SS) approached and stopped us. The officer in charge spoke in German and demanded our identification papers. My friend Madeleine, who was twenty years old, handed her ID over. I told them I was thirteen years old, gave him my name, and said that I didn't have my ID with me. We both spoke fluent German in response. He looked at us with a severe steady look, didn't say anything, and then demanded to know why and what we were looking for. He suspected we were plundering the battlefield and told us that it was punishable by death. We told him we had no intention of doing such a thing, but were looking for her brother, whose unit had been fighting in that area. He gave the order for his men to search us, and demanded to know where we lived. He asked Madeleine why she was in Ghent when her ID showed she lived in Evergem. She trembled as she told him she was employed by my dad, Mr. Lippens, and didn't make it back home because of all the fighting. He ordered us to look at him. He had a very serious and deep look to him. Then he turned to his men and ordered two of them to get us out of the area. As we expeditiously were led away, he yelled at us in German in such a way that left no confusion. "You better stay home! Walking the battlefield was a very stupid thing to do! Go home and stay home! It was a stupid decision to walk the battlefield! Next time you will not be so lucky!" This was my first encounter with the enemy and what very easily could have been the end of this story.

The battle of the Schelde River and of the Flanders delayed the German advance, which needed less than three weeks to complete its victory over our country. This delay in advancement played a pivotal role in the escape to England of nearly 340,000 troops who were pinned to the ocean by the Germans at the seaside town of Dunkirk. These British, Scottish, French, Belgian, and Dutch soldiers were part of one of the largest sea evacuations ever conducted: Operation Dynamo. In nine days, 861 mostly private volunteer fishing vessels and yachtsmen pushed their vessels as close to shore and harbor as possible. The docks were badly damaged, which required the ingenuity of many to rescue these soldiers from capture by the massive German army. Many of the evacuees had to wait hours in shoulder-deep water to climb aboard a vessel. This came to be known as the Miracle of Dunkirk. The evacuating soldiers left behind on the beaches enough equipment to outfit eight to ten German divisions.

Toward the end of May 1940, King Leopold III of Belgium surrendered with his remaining troops and became a prisoner of war. He and his children were kept prisoner in the Castle of Laeken for the duration of the occupation. The king refused to get into political negotiations with the Germans throughout his captivity. His firm stand was contrary to German interests and indicative of the state of war that continued to exist between Belgium and Germany.

The loss for Belgium was all-encompassing. The loss of life and property was the most critical aspect of it but not close to the end of it. Belgium paid the price the Germans demanded for the Nazi conquest with an imposed general contribution of $100 million in francs, or the equivalent of $1.67 billion in today's currency. This was immediately followed by requisitions for the German army and homeland. They appropriated every month eight thousand head of cattle and four thousand pigs; in certain coalmines they took up to 70 percent of the production; they requisitioned 45,000 railroad cars and demanded from the Belgian National Railways a monthly war indemnity of $30 million ($500 million in today's figures). Most of the horses were taken; the textile industry had to hand over 80 percent of its production, the leather industry 84 percent, and the tanning industry 75 percent. From the population, their systematic robbery or plunder included requisitioning cars, motorcycles, mattresses, pillows, wool blankets, copper, brass, bronze, lead, silver, gold, and whatever else they needed or wanted for their war machine. Many beautiful and rare art pieces disappeared or were melted down for Hitler. Every citizen of Belgium suffered from the effects of the Nazi pillaging in the most severe and crippling manner. The common ordinary things that normally were easily obtained or purchased were now exorbitantly priced and more often nonexistent.

There was destruction everywhere and in their retreat, the Belgian army added to the chaos by blowing up many remaining bridges, railroads, locks, ships, and anything else the Germans would be able to use or that would slow their advance.

The Nazis implemented an immediate civilian registration. It was not an option for young or old, no matter what age, gender, nationality, color, or race. All Belgians made their way to the nearest public building, which had in most cases been repurposed as a Nazi command center. Our family walked to my school to be registered. This was done not only for identification but also for the rounding up and separation of Jews, Gypsies, the handicapped and mentally retarded, whom they separated and shipped off as a priority for disposal.

The Germans tried to gain the cooperation of the Belgians but realized quickly that the majority of the population detested their presence. We made a stand by resisting the crippling demands, and almost overnight things turned from bad to worse. Their initial terror wasn't dispelled, but many citizens resigned themselves to accept the conquerors rather than succumbing to tortures or execution by the Nazis. However, these naïve citizens soon found out that they had been deceived, as their cooperation with the Germans led to more crushing demands from their oppressors to support their war effort.

Through large posters that were glued to outside walls and trees, we were informed of their new laws. We were to obey without fail new decrees, rules, laws, and terrible warnings. Excuses were not acceptable, and just about any disobedience was punishable either by beatings, hard labor, imprisonment coupled with severe punishment, or death. The signs weren't uniform, but made clear to us that registration was a priority. Weapons and communication devices were forbidden. A curfew was now in place. Any rebelliousness wouldn't be tolerated.

Before the Germans took control of Ghent and us, we experienced a total blackout as the power plants got bombed and destroyed. The Belgian government had orchestrated the initial blackouts to keep the invading Germans in the dark for navigational purposes. Once Germany took control of Ghent, we learned of a new brand of blackout. All windows had to be completely and immediately covered with double-thickness opaque black curtains, and all homes or business would be inspected. Offices, factories, and plants had to have all the windows painted in dark blue and all exits also covered with thick black double covers. The punishment for refusing to comply was the immediate arrest of the head of the household or business manager and said individual would be sent to a hard labor camp somewhere in Germany. This usually meant a slow, tortuous death.

All Belgians were ordered to turn in their weapons immediately to the nearest Nazi command center. We were not a family who had any arms worth reporting, but those who did would receive a receipt from the administrator. This receipt was proof that your house did not carry weapons should the Nazis come knocking on your door. These receipts didn't always keep them from searching again. The Belgians seemed very aware that the receipts did not mean that these weapons would ever be returned to their rightful owners. It was the total confiscation of all firearms, including shotguns and all black powder guns. If you were found guilty of possessing any explosives, guns, or rifles, your arrest was immediate and followed by a public execution. Dad kept a .38 caliber breach Enfield revolver that we were able to hide in the attic, where in one of the many large timbers supporting the slate shingle roof we had a small hiding place. On many occasions the Germans searched the house but never found the hiding place. Dad felt that this particular hiding place would never be discovered, so keeping this revolver for an emergency was okay. When the Nazis showed up for a random search of our house, they always brought a team. These soldiers were extremely thorough and detailed while searching the entire house, yet they were surprisingly courteous. They respected the house and the items of which they had no need. They didn't break anything or destroy any of our property. If a door was locked, they would ask us politely to unlock it so they could search its contents. If they did find something they wanted, then they would take it. They didn't ask permission for their thefts. The items they sought were items useful to their war effort. We lost all our brass, copper, and metal items that were of size, which I presume went to be melted down and repurposed. All of our mattresses, pillows, and sheets were seized and used to bed the Nazis elsewhere. The search party also took a few items of gold and silver that were of some value. We did have a very large brass lion that was carried off as well.

The Nazis immediately imposed a strict curfew, which was from 1900 hours until 0500 hours. If you had a reason to be on the street during that time, you had to apply for a special permit. Anyone on the street without a permit after the curfew was usually shot or arrested and immediately hauled to prison. The punishments for this crime and a multitude of others could vary depending on the mood of the attending officer. Some arrestees were gathered and sent to a triage area where they were given the choice of which labor camp they would be shipped to somewhere in Germany. None of the optional destinations would be regarded as a better choice.

We were ordered to turn in all the radios without exception. If you didn't comply, the Nazis arrested the head of the household, who was sent to a triage area and shipped to a hard labor camp.

In exchange for our radios, our occupiers, utilizing prisoner labor, began installing cables to each house, which became our legal source of news. A German company called "Telefunken" manufactured these direct radios. Telefunken would years later pioneer the FM broadcast. When we first received our cable system, it came with a box giving us choices of twelve stations totally controlled by the Nazi propagandists. Each home was connected to their programs, which kept us informed of any changes or new orders. They programmed everything that went over the cable with precise planning. The news we were fed often claimed that the Nazis were winning on every front and told about the enormous Allied losses. While this news early on may have been correct, it failed to keep us apprised of Allied progress as the war developed. Each and every news story heralded the Nazis for heroism and bravery in the face of a terrible and barbaric enemy. Allied victories never made the broadcasts. Except for the beautiful concert music, which was exquisite, the news they programmed consisted solely of lies and propaganda.

Large homes were inspected and surveyed by the Germans for their military usefulness. They checked the number of family members versus the number of rooms, bedrooms, and bathrooms. The size of the kitchen, bathrooms, and washroom were very important. They determined how many officers and orderlies could occupy the bedrooms and how many troops could occupy the rest of the house. If satisfactory to their needs, the Nazis would move into a house. They occupied bedrooms, hallways, garages, dens, living rooms, and whatever else they wanted to occupy. Our house being of considerable size was quickly short-listed. Once the house was occupied, the Germans had the run of it, and we lost all privacy. They could circulate where they wanted, go through our reading and study books, go through my dad's office and business, and always welcomed the opportunity to do so. The selected homes were marked with plaques on their exteriors indicating they were requisitioned for military occupancy. Several days after the occupation began, German officers came by to meet with my dad. They investigated the house, his business, and the factory, and found them to their liking. We would now be sleeping with the enemy. They immediately set up a time schedule for the use of the dining room, kitchen, bathrooms, washroom, etc. They provided the coal or fuel needed for the central heating and gas for the water heater. The coal was a welcome luxury from which both parties could benefit. Coal became a luxury for most families, as its primary destination was to German interests. When German troops moved in, we had enough coal for the central heating throughout the house and benefited from the heat provided for them. I once counted forty Nazis living under our roof. We learned quickly how to coexist with them. Survival was the most important goal for us. This new working arrangement caused the neighbors to become suspicious of us because we had the German brass constantly in and out of our home and business. We were caught in the midst of a very precarious situation. We may have been living with our worst enemy, but we were aware of those who had far less.

Captain Heinrich Muller was installed as the highest-ranking officer living in our house. He occupied the room next to mine and as it was, we shared a communicating door that I kept locked. However, the captain knocked quite often, asking questions about my family and me. He wanted to know if I had read *Mein Kampf* yet and what I thought about it. I answered that I hadn't read it yet but that I probably would when I went back to school in September. I felt brave enough to discuss Hitler with Captain Muller. I told him that I had heard on the radio and read in the newspaper that Hitler had a rough start in politics and had spent some time in prison. I continued that I hoped that if I got arrested, that I would get the same treatment he received, which was very lenient. The captain found this comment funny and he laughed. He said I was a real comedian and that I should count on it. My future seemed to be very important to Captain Muller, or at least he seemed interested in helping me become a Nazi. I often told the captain that I was happy with my life before the war and that I loved my family, my town, my school, sports, and my beliefs. I questioned him on why the Gestapo and SS were beating and torturing people who hadn't yet been tried in court. He replied that I was too young to have such thoughts and opinions. The captain sensed my rebelliousness and suggested that I needed special training with the Hitler Youth. I should attend the meetings and then I would understand the error of my ways. The captain even offered to take me personally to the meetings, where I would hear speakers who would open my eyes. "To what?" I asked. He answered that I needed to listen and obey instead of questioning him. I should consider thinking before I responded to his message. The captain told me that he would speak to my dad about my dangerous and hateful attitude. He did indeed talk to Dad and instructed him to teach me about my lack of respect and obedience or else I would end up in serious trouble. These encounters occurred often for the short time the captain stayed with us, and I was always encouraged to attend a Hitler Youth meeting. He reaffirmed that my country belonged to Germany now and that I was a German. As we were still in the process of restructuring our society to the Nazi model, school for us was not yet in session. Had the Nazis never arrived at our border, we would have been on summer break for the months of June, July, and August. When Captain Muller inquired, I always made excuses to not attend the meetings saying that I needed time to study. Due to the summer months, my excuses finally wore out, and one day Captain Muller ordered me to put on my school uniform and go with him to a big Hitler Youth rally that was to take place in downtown Ghent. This particular rally was very crowded and very orderly. Everyone was lined up and standing at attention. We were given a decent vantage point due to Captain Muller's rank. What I witnessed horrified me, yet I showed no signs of indifference. I listened for two hours to all the great things that Hitler was doing and had done. Germany was ridding Europe of its enemies. We were given instructions on what we needed to do to further the spread of the empire. The young men such as myself were encouraged to participate through the Hitler Youth programs. A headline speaker concluded the rally. This was the first time I had heard the fervent preaching of Germany's Minister of Public Enlightenment and Propaganda, a monster known as Joseph Goebbels. On the car ride home with Captain Muller, he asked me many questions and carefully applied further pressure on me to join the Hitler Youth. I always politely assured him that I loved the life that I had known and was not ready to make that kind of commitment. Deep down I drew further away by the day. The second rally would come the following month, and again Captain Muller escorted me, against my guarded will. The scene was very reminiscent of the previous rally. Everyone in attendance seemed to hang on every word the speakers would emit. This second rally gave me the chance to hear the political styling of the Reich Commissioner for the Strengthening of German Nationhood. This man would later ascend to sit next to Hitler himself and was the person most directly responsible for the Holocaust. Heinrich Himmler's words had little to no effect on me, and again I kept my outrage bottled up. The final rally I attended that summer was without escort, as I was merely walking the street and happened upon a crowd-lined street. I inquired of some people waiting on the sidewalk about the cause of the commotion. I was informed that the Führer himself, Adolph Hitler, would be driving by these busy streets in his motorcade as he made his way to give a speech. I had no intention of hearing him, let alone saluting him as he drove by, as I knew to be the custom, so I ducked into a large department store. Unbeknownst to me, a German soldier saw me leave the street and head into the store. The next thing I knew was I was being yelled at and chased through the store. I was not able to get away and the soldier smashed me in the shoulder with his rifle butt. He demanded that I follow him back to the street front and participate in the *heiling* of *our Führer.* Several minutes later the motorcade drove by to tremendous fanfare. Under the eyes of the soldier, I raised my right arm and mouthed the words *Heil Hitler.* This would be my one and only encounter with Adolph Hitler.

Captain Muller's platoon moved out after a few weeks and left their spaces perfectly clean. A day later a new squad moved in, and from then on this would be the routine. Every few weeks the house would empty, then repopulate with new personnel. We had no choice in the matter but surprisingly, our unwanted guests never caused us any harm aside from the constant pestering about visiting a Hitler Youth rally. These guests seemed to really enjoy reading all of Dad's unburned books as they were always asking Dad questions about them. One lieutenant was interested in artistic ambitions. He would bring me his weekly *Adler* magazines, which showed fantastic military drawings and illustrations. The illustrations were beautiful and elaborate, but they always seemed to show the Germans as conquering heroes and saviors of the human race. I knew better, but still enjoyed the magazines.

Hundreds of thousands of homeless were living in the ruins of bombed-out Belgian towns. Most of them were cold, hungry, and sick. Our hospitals were requisitioned by the Germans for their military casualties, and if not used for that purpose, knowing that they had a big red cross on the top of the roof, the Germans stored their ammunition and other military supplies in them. All public buildings were occupied for military use, and only a few small private clinics were able to help the civilian population. Insane asylums and institutions for mentally ill, handicapped, and retarded people were closed and their patients systematically murdered in haste as the buildings were reoccupied by German troops. When public questions ever surfaced regarding the missing patients, the Germans claimed they all died of pneumonia. We knew the horrible truth.

The Red Cross had a daily soup line. Our family utilized the Nazi-issued coupons to fill our large container with our ration of soup. You didn't want to analyze it, but it was fairly edible. It consisted of lots of mixed vegetables, but the meat content was always in question. Our family may have had heat, but food was always a concern. We often visited the Red Cross food line. I assumed it was nutritious and thought it tasted good, mainly because we could taste some type of meat. We never knew if it was bacon, chicken, rabbit, horse, cat, dog, or possibly some fat rats. We were never made aware of the source of the meat, but at the end of the war, we noticed that very few animals like cats, dogs, and rats had survived. We suspected they ended up at our dinner table, but the thought of starvation caused little hesitation when food was offered. The famous Belgian breads we had grown up with had morphed into a concoction of wheat and sawdust. The bread ration required a substantial soaking in one's soup just so it could be chewed. I have never understood how sawdust became filler, but needless to say, I had consumed my share of sawdust.

Food, clothing, heating fuel, and coal were all rationed to us Belgians, and were available in very small quantities. Unless you had other means to procure clothing, you had very little chance to acquire the necessary warm clothes. We actually lived in one room and used the fireplace for heat when we needed additional heat, but the central heat normally was sufficient. Germans assigned rationing tickets to each family, allowing a certain amount of food for each person per family, which wasn't close to the required minimums. If you had some money or something to trade and if you knew a farmer, then you could sometimes buy expensive black-market food. Once or twice a week, my mother and sister went to different farms on bicycles that had small saddlebags. Many times they came back with too little to make a difference, but bought what was available such as bread, ham, bacon, eggs, cheese, milk, potatoes, and a few vegetables. Not quite enough to feed a family of four people for very long, but we were always grateful with what we could manage. Many times during our occupation we were able to receive help from Mr. De Rijke's farm, where I had spent so much time working and recovering from my childhood maladies. Mr. De Rijke and his wife let us buy cheaply some additional food items that they could spare from their farm. This same farm would also serve me as a wonderful hiding place when I reached the German draft age. During the occupation, each farm had 80 percent of their produce and harvest requisitioned by the German army. Mr. De Rijke took serious chances helping us. If the Germans found out that he helped us, his family could have been executed and the farm burned to the ground. But they helped us out as they could from what they could keep for themselves.

The food allowance during the German occupation was a starvation diet by design. The Nazis had their military to feed, and our well-being was not part of the plan. It was very hazardous to smuggle food into town because of the restrictions and the many checkpoints around the town. If the Germans searched you and found smuggled food, anything was possible, but most of the time it was confiscation or a fine. We traveled separate routes home so that one of us might make it through with something to eat.

The German army took control of Belgian industry and requisitioned the necessary manpower and machinery. They supplied the raw material needed for the fabrication of their war machines. If you owned a business you could remain the owner of it, but you were expected to collaborate fully and meet their approval and quota. If you disagreed or interfered in any way, you were removed and replaced by a German equivalent. Should you have the misfortune of being removed from your position, then you were likely not around long enough to meet the incoming personnel. The Germans demanded the retooling of our cork business to produce life jackets and life rafts made out of cork for the German navy. My dad explained to the Germans that retooling was impossible because the factory simply wasn't set up for it. They said they would pay for the new equipment or machinery, but Dad showed them that he would require a larger plant with much more room for the additional equipment. They replied they would finance the expansion and provide the necessary machinery. This went on for some time and for some reason, without explanation, they dropped the whole idea and didn't return. Later on we found out they gave the contract to a competitor. Needless to say we had something to celebrate.

Our first personal experience with harsh and brutal treatment by the Germans came shortly after the German invasion in 1940, when I was still thirteen years old. I needed urgent tonsil and adenoid surgery at the hospital. Much of my aforementioned youth was spent at the farm of the doctor trying to recover from the many ailments with which I was afflicted. My tonsils had endured all they could handle and became very inflamed and infected. The hospital was located quite a distance from our home, which made it difficult since we had to travel by foot. Surgery was scheduled very early on this particular morning. My parents had to apply for special travel permits because we had to cross the town before 0500 hours, and streetcars were not available until 0600 hours. As we walked the distance, we went through many checkpoints at which we were ordered to stop and show our permits. When we arrived at a pontoon bridge that we had to cross, German guards yelled at us to stop. We stood very still and waited for them to approach us. We were ordered rudely to raise our hands and explain the reason we were out during curfew. Our explanation wasn't sufficient as the Nazi guards, all the while yelling at us, ordered us to cross the next bridge a half-mile down the river. We were terrified as they pushed and screamed at us. Dad pleaded with them in German that we had a scheduled surgery at the hospital that was right across the river on the other side of this bridge, and that we wouldn't make it in time if we took the long detour. They said they didn't care if we made it or not, but that this bridge couldn't be used by civilians during curfew. They ordered us off the bridge immediately. We were just about to turn around when we heard a voice speaking in French with a German accent: "Attendez!" (Wait!) "Let me see your papers!" He took out his flashlight and looked at the permits and looked at us, then gave us our permits back and told us to go on and cross the bridge. As we walked away, we could hear the guards talking with what must have been a high-ranking officer because there was a lot of heel-clicking and a lot of saluting going on.

In the month of June, as the Nazis were in the process of impressing their will and ways upon us, many of us former Belgians wanted to assist in any liberation effort should it come to life. Although we were cognizant of the idea that we could remain under Nazi control forever, we truly believed that one day we would be rescued. The boys under the age of fifteen had virtually no school because it was being reorganized by the Nazis and would open September 1. These summer months found us looking for ways to help in the resistance effort.

As soon as the Germans wrested control of our country from us, the Underground Resistance sprang to life. My desire to assist in the resistance grew with every terrible German activity I heard about. My close friend and blood brother Bernard and I decided we needed to find something important to do to help our country. We immediately started to experiment with our own primitive explosives. I wanted so badly to play a role in the resistance. We weren't ready for a confrontation with the Nazis just yet, so we decided on sabotage as our foray into the resistance effort. We began eagerly by assembling the components for Molotov cocktail incendiary devices. This type of bomb was simple to produce and easily concealed from our occupiers. The construction of these crudely made bombs gave us confidence that we could offer some level of resistance against the Germans. Our bomb-making enterprise gained steam a few weeks later when Bernard and I made an important discovery. While riding our bicycles through a wooded area outside of town one day, Bernard and I found an abandoned and well-hidden Belgian army anti-aircraft ammunition dump that still had live ammo in it. We noticed a mound of earth that had a peculiar shape to it, and several bushes grew out of this mound. On closer inspection, we discovered a small metal door hidden on the backside, away from curious eyes. The Germans were apparently unaware of its existence. The door was half open, and we entered. Inside the ten-by-ten single-room bunker, we discovered anti-aircraft bombs stacked on wooden planks in a pyramid shape filling a quarter of the room. We immediately looked at one another with an idea. We devised an exciting plan to take these bombs and repurpose them in our secret lab, which was on the third floor of Bernard's house. Bernard came from a wealthy family and thus had a very large house with much room at his disposal. We were very careful whenever we worked there. We would visit the abandoned ammo dump and remove the heads of the artillery shells and transport them to Bernard's house and our upstairs lair. Then from the heads we removed the silk bags containing the explosives, which was probably "Pentolite," PETN, or TNT. The windows were covered, and we worked by candlelight when the light outside wasn't sufficient. Bernard had access to metal cans about 5 inches in diameter, and 8 inches long, with a metal cap, in which we drilled a hole to force the fuse. The final step was sealing the cap. We had created a whole arsenal of bombs, but missed adequate fuses. We hid the cans until the right time, when we could procure the fuses and make a suitable plan. Our fuses, which were always hard to come by, were unusually short, which demanded a lot of planning for a quick escape. We were acutely aware of the danger we faced should we get caught, but our ambitions got the better of us. Our plan was to blow up the large German transport trucks that we came across. These trucks were typically used for hauling soldiers or ammunition and weren't in short supply. Our bombs would slide almost perfectly into the tailpipes of these vehicles. We would always make sure the scene was safe as could be, and normally this was during the day, because of the curfew placed on us. We would quickly walk by one of the German trucks, light the fuse, and slide the device into the truck's tailpipe. Then we quickly exited the scene. The noise was incredible. Our bombs were loud, and though the damage was light much of the time, we kept the Huns nervous and confused. We were thinking big, but we had a lot to learn. A few of the trucks sustained heavy damage because of the ammunition in the rear of them, which sometimes blew apart the entire vehicle. During this summer, Bernard and I estimated we blew up fifty to sixty trucks in this manner. Our homemade devices often met their goal and damaged, disabled, or destroyed their intended targets. Night bombings, although rare, gave us a better chance to hide and more importantly, escape. The true impact will never be known, but we imagined the local German truck drivers had to stay on their toes.

One particular day, my sister Lucienne was doing some bookwork at Bernard's father's office. Bernard and I were in the loft three floors up from Lucienne. Bernard and I had disassembled several antiaircraft shells on the worktable. The pieces and respective contents were lying across the tables. Bernard had the bright idea to have a smoke. He obviously had become too comfortable around the TNT, which would expose his carelessness. He struck a match to light his cigarette. The air must have been full of TNT dust, because the instant the match ignited the whole room flashed in a blinding glare. We checked ourselves for damage, which turned out luckily to be only singed hairs. We then realized this mistake could quickly lead to our discovery, and we needed to avoid any detection. We didn't dare open a window to fumigate the smoke because the German police would have immediately investigated. We needed to remove the smoke somehow, so we cracked the window as slightly as possible in order to allow tiny traces of smoke out and precious fresh air in. The smoke was so thick that it took three weeks before the room was usable again. We were extra careful in the future.

The Nazi "penetration" of our culture began in earnest and followed a pattern applied elsewhere. It started with the German attempt to Nazify the Belgian educational institutions. Regimentation of boys and girls was modeled after the Hitler Youth organization. Private schools were closed if they didn't comply or fall in line with German teachings. If they refused to obey orders, they were shut down. We would still learn foreign languages, but the German language would become the primary language in the country.

School was still required for all children, albeit under a much different methodology. The months of June, July, and August were still summer months and still vacation months from school, according to the Nazis educators. I would attend an all-male German State School where regimentation was pushed to the extreme. The school supervision was reorganized as Nazi and pro-Nazi and was controlled by the German government. Every four months we were assembled in the gymnasium for a so-called health inspection. This was a coverup for a physical examination, which we later learned was part of the Nazi belief system called eugenics or *Selective Breeding*. This is set of practices that culled the weak from the strong in an effort to improve the genetic quality of the population. They measured your features to see if you had the Arian profile. If you had Jewish facial features or any deformities, you were set aside and would most of the time never be seen again. They asked questions about your family, your health in general, your favorite sport activities, and your beliefs. They carefully took record of all your answers. You wouldn't have dared tell a lie because of their impressive records in which they corroborated your statements each time they questioned you. If you did give a different answer, you were detained until you could explain your mistake. The Germans were very impressed if you mentioned a member of the family who had or was of German background. For instance, when I mentioned my mother's maiden name was Haghenbeek they were very interested, and when I mentioned that she had half-brothers named Hoffman, they were even more impressed. They expressed to me a value that they attributed to my background. It didn't really make any difference and didn't exempt me from their questioning. The sole benefit of having an appreciated heritage was to be treated to a slightly more relaxed atmosphere, and I was shown a bit more respect than my other classmates. I was not naïve enough to believe that these Germans wouldn't end my life on a mere whim should I give them reason.

The whole school system was also reorganized and now had new pro-Nazi teachers for each class. The Germans believed in strict obedience, respect, and discipline. I don't know why we owed them respect, because their attitude toward us showed they didn't know the meaning of it. They wanted schools to be regimented, where each class was like a platoon with an assigned leader. The first day of school was in September, which we were under strict orders to attend to learn our new curriculum. As we eased into our desks, we were presented with our own brand-new personal copy of *Mein Kampf*, in German of course. We were ordered to read it daily and give a report to the class once a month discussing what we liked and disliked about the book. We knew better than to emphasize our dislikes. We learned of the Nazi plans for expansion, the Nazi belief systems, and our new role in the Nazi way of life.

The structure of the classroom was simple. They believed that if anyone in the class made a willful or accidental mistake of any kind, the whole platoon (class) would pay the consequences. Childish behavior was not allowed. We were threatened with deportation to hard labor camps if we didn't act obediently. There was a punishment for failing grades, which wasn't a huge threat but would warrant additional grueling assignments by the pro-Nazi teachers. Another punishment would entail being subjected to intense lecturing. There were no physical punishments to us at that period of our lives. We were not yet men and so were treated as children. The Nazis believed they could train us children to think like them, and physical punishments were counterproductive at this age. We had several classmates who were deemed exemplary students by our German teachers. They were given special treatment and exceptional privileges over the rest of us. These were given the honor of becoming Hitler Youth. These boys were especially frightening because they had been our friends and classmates just prior to the invasion. Now they walked with the devil. One of my best friends at the time was Guy Versmessen, and he was lured away by the promises of becoming a Hitler Youth. He was an easy sell since his dad had become the principal of our newly remodeled pro-Nazi school. Ademar Versmessen had been installed as principal of the school due to his pro-Nazi stance. He also happened to be my dad's longtime backgammon partner. Seemingly overnight, my friend became someone I could never trust again. He could have easily caused a serious change of fortune for me had he overheard any of the numerous anti-Nazi conversations that some of us had. I had to behave in a very guarded way around him for fear of reprisal. My friends often warned me of this fact. Our friendship had been severed and had become a relationship based on fear. Guy constantly begged me to join the Hitler Youth. He explained how much fun it was and that I would be sorry one day if I didn't join. I also had to maintain a positive relationship with him so that he didn't report me. The Hitler Youth were exempt from the same strenuous work schedule as the rest of us. This situation would be comparable to empowering a school bully and giving him the authority to further his cause.

Even sadder was the fact that my parents played backgammon with Mr. Versmessen every Saturday. Before the war, the game was a pleasurable weekly experience. After the Nazi takeover, my parents were obligated to continue the weekly game so as not to upset Mr. Versmessen and elicit a possible visit from the Gestapo. Early after the invasion, I remember watching my dad and Mr. Versmessen argue about the Nazi belief system. Both men held to their beliefs as tempers flared. Dad knew better than to push too hard and thus was able to end the disagreement without eliciting potential trouble. The backgammon game kept Mr. Versmessen returning weekly as much as Dad wished it over.

Obedience was the most important lesson taught in the classroom. An order is an order. Right or wrong had nothing to do with it, just as long as it was executed as ordered. Our school had been located in the old remains of a castle, which came complete with medieval architecture and castle towers. They used the towers for punishment, where the guilty party spent most of his classtime hours in one of the six towers with the regular prisoner's diet of bread and water. You had to keep up with your homework and were expected to think about your mistake and had to write an essay about it. When released you had to show it to the teacher first, and eventually during the following week, if acceptable by the management, you presented it before the class.

No matter how hard I studied, I never received a grade higher than a C in any of my classes once the reorganization happened, and it made me angry. I complained about it to my teachers, but they said that I knew how to correct it, and it wasn't by extra studying. One of my teachers told me that I continued to make wrong choices and that my stubbornness to obey was the source of my problem. They encouraged me to do something about it.

I had spent a good amount of time growing up with a cousin named Jaque Kaplan, who like me was very tall for his age. We attended school together and got into trouble together. Sports were something that came easily to both of us. He enjoyed the trouble we caused and spent a good deal of time paying for our mischievousness. Jaque helped me when we found a dead rat in the schoolhouse and decided to have a little fun. I approached Dr. Deanen, a professor of mine, at the urinal. While he was relieving himself, I slipped the dead rat into his coat pocket. His finished his business and made his way back to class. Once Dr. Deanen discovered the contents of his coat pocket, he immediately called for a schoolwide assembly. He addressed the assembly and demanded to know who placed the rat in his pocket. He demanded that the offender be a man and step forward. "Accept the responsibility!" There was not a word from the mouths of our student body. Again, Mr. Deanen commanded the perpetrator to step forward. Not a word came out. Then one of the kids who had joined the Hitler Youth spoke up and pointed to me. I was summoned to the stage and interrogated in front of everyone. Dr. Deanen asked me why I did this, but I didn't have a sufficient excuse. I did confess my guilt, and my sentence was carried out. I was sent to the school's tower for solitary confinement. Luckily for me, the Nazis didn't believe in strict punishments for boys under the age of fifteen as they felt they could still be reached and drawn toward the Nazi belief system. In the tower, I was made to read my copy of *Mein Kampf* and prepare a presentation for my teacher and my class. Jaque was not implicated that day for his minor role. He did share that he was very impressed with my presentation to the class.

Shortly thereafter, the Gestapo paid a visit one night to Jaque's house. His family was arrested and taken away; their crime of being Jewish would have a much harsher punishment. His parents were reportedly shipped off to a concentration camp, and we never saw them again. Jaque's grandmother had made arrangements before the invasion began for Jaque and his sister, should anything happen to the parents, to be taken to a Catholic convent by the nuns and hidden away from the Nazis. The grandmother, who was very elderly and frail, was also arrested with the family, so her plan would never be carried out. She was deemed unable to travel and therefore was shot in the head in front of her family at their home. Jaque and his sister disappeared from our lives instantly. I was very sad for Jaque and did not think I would ever see him again. I often wondered what had happened or where he might be, even though I knew the probable outcome.

We had regular inspections and drills that aimed at teaching us to work together to follow the orders set before us. Each class was considered a platoon with a minimum of thirty-four male students and one platoon leader. There was a flag and a bearer for each platoon. Each flag had a different color and insignia. If you wouldn't follow their orders then you were drilled until you wouldn't think of disobeying again. The rule was: Obey! Submit! Comply or we will break you! At the age of thirteen, I was not built like a child. I stood six feet tall, which found me towering over most of my classmates. My never-ending regimen of sports had developed me into a muscular young adult. As students under the age of fifteen, we were treated better than most Belgians. We were fed considerably more than the populace, which helped me to maintain my growing body. I ate much better at school than my family did at home.

Lunch was not a break time that you could enjoy; it was timed and was done in an orderly and quiet fashion. Break time was not a relaxing time either; it was a time to be used for personal needs such as going to the men's room, which only was allowed at these times and had to be done quietly and orderly.

Everyone twelve years old and older was required to carry an ID card, which was numbered. It showed your age, date of birth, address, and phone number, which gave the Gestapo all the necessary information they needed for identification. The Gestapo bullies enjoyed harassing people and loved using their authority to exercise their sick minds. The newly formed Belgian and relocated German police as well as the Gestapo stopped me many times during my youth for no reason at all, always asking me for my ID. Several times they brought me into the headquarters to investigate and interrogate me just because they suspected I might be a Jew and because they could. They figured that since I had brown curly hair, an olive complexion, and brown eyes, I was a candidate for the extermination camp. In short, I don't think they liked my looks very much, and I didn't care for their looks either. They were street trash that enjoyed bullying, torturing, and executing anyone, young or old, it didn't make any difference. I somehow managed to get released each time, but I never knew why. Nothing the Nazis did made much sense to me.

Gestapo

The Gestapo was the brainchild of veteran ace fighter pilot and second-in-command of the Nazi empire, Hermann Göring. His creation unleashed a horrific machine of death that the world will never forget. This secret state police force of the Third Reich was eventually wrested from Göring by

Heinrich Himmler, who made the Gestapo the most powerful police force the world had ever seen. It had carte blanche to operate without judicial review, which essentially put it above the law. The Gestapo had the authority to investigate cases of espionage, sabotage, treason, and criminal attacks on the Nazi party and Germany. The Gestapo was free to do as it wished as long as it carried out the will of Nazi leadership, which was anything but law-abiding.

My first encounter with the Gestapo was on my way to school one day. I didn't get off the sidewalk when two German officers and their bodyguards approached me, coming from the opposite direction. We had been told and warned to yield the sidewalk to them and were to walk in the street when approached by the victorious conquerors. But since I was just thirteen, I thought they might make an exception. I knew better, but I gave in to the temptation to disobey. I quickly found out the hard way that it was a big mistake. As the officers approached, their bodyguards saw what I was doing and pushed me off the sidewalk and hit me in the back with their rifle butts. They screamed at me in German, telling me that I'd better learn to obey. One of the officers stopped and approached me in the street. He asked my name, my age, and the school I attended. His orderly wrote it all down. Then he asked me why I decided to disobey the order. I answered him in German that I forgot, but he yelled back that we were warned sufficiently and that their orders didn't have to be repeated but simply obeyed. He yelled there was no excuse for disobedience and wanted me to answer again why I had disobeyed orders. I told him I wasn't feeling well and I wasn't paying attention. He didn't like my answer and slapped my face and knocked off my hat. He ordered me not to pick it up. I remember becoming acutely afraid for myself then. The sting of his hand on my face set in and the shock of the hit transformed into anger. I began to turn to walk off with my head in my hands when one of the soldiers picked up my hat and threw it into the sewer. Then, one of the officers cursed me and yelled at me to come right back. He continued to say he hadn't dismissed me and that I failed to salute them before I walked away. He told me to stand at attention and salute him as I was taught in school. I robotically raised my right arm as straight as I could and saluted, "Heil Hitler." I certainly learned a lesson and regretted my action because I was humiliated in this bad experience. The hate for these people raged inside of me. The officer enjoyed the sight of me standing at attention. I hated Hitler and his servants with all my being. All this could have been avoided, but it wouldn't be the last time I would make the Nazis mad and have to bear the consequences. My hate for them worsened even more as time went by. When the Germans were acting out against us, no one dared to interfere or speak up, as we knew what the Germans were capable of. We were helpless in the presence of these monsters. The Germans believed in scare tactics, and utilized them most effectively. I guess it made them feel superior. Fear was certainly a powerful motivator.

One of the rules on the boards posted to trees and walls ordered the civilians never to walk in groups. The Germans were leery of groups of people walking on the street, and ordered all civilians when traveling to walk two by two or singularly and six feet apart. Failure to obey meant you committed a rebellious act of disobedience. If you were rebellious to that order, you would almost always pay for it. The consequences generally were all determined by the mood of the Nazis at the time. On our captive King Leopold III's birthday, we decided to celebrate with a gathering of Royalists walking the Main Street of downtown Ghent singing the National Anthem in his honor. This was a form of protest for us against the Nazis and certainly an act of rebelliousness. Suddenly, as could surely be expected, we were rudely interrupted and surrounded by several truckloads of German army soldiers putting an end to what we thought was just a little fun. But the Huns had other ideas about it and decided to jail us. They loaded us in trucks and took us straight to Gestapo HQ.

Most of us were beaten with their German batons. Some beatings were worse than others. I was hit repeatedly in the head, the jaw, the gut, and my back. Each blow would have been a sufficient punishment but we were to be made an example of. The guy next to me had his face beaten bloody and repeatedly punched in the stomach. They called out several more names to step forward and beat them also. We were not released yet, and after our beatings, were told to join the others in the holding cell. The commandant in charge of our punishments reminded us of the weekly meetings, which were Nazi propaganda meetings, and he ordered us to attend.

Then he ordered us to stand at attention, salute the Nazi flag and repeat after him in German, of course: "I will obey and pay attention to all the German orders. Obey! Always obey!" We saluted Hitler and then he released us two by two from the jail.

I found myself in serious trouble one evening as I rode my bicycle around looking for food. It was getting late, and I wasn't paying attention to the clock. Without being aware, I had missed curfew but continued to ride the street. My bicycle was a roadster with balloon tires that could handle the rough roads. I was wearing knee high white socks, which likely made me an easy target. A German guard saw me and opened fire from across a great distance. I immediately jumped off my bike and got on the ground. I pulled my bike onto the sidewalk behind me. The tracers from his rifle flew by me in rapid succession and I don't know how I wasn't hit. I removed myself from his vision and firing line. A kind neighbor saw what was happening and told me to come inside his house. Luckily, the distance must have been too great for the soldier to warrant a chase. This was a warning to me and I learned my lesson. To him I must have been something to break up his boredom.

Fourteen

As my fourteenth birthday drew near in 1941, my German hosts informed me that I had to get a job after school. It was a German law that everyone had to be employed from the age of fourteen and older. If you couldn't find a job they would find one for you, but the job they provided wouldn't likely be a pleasant one. I wasn't able to secure a job due to the lack of opportunities and was ordered to report at the Krupp Steel Plant in Ghent. I worked a short shift after classes, from 1700 hours to 2000 hours, five days per week, and from 0700 hours to 1500 hours on Saturday. The steel plant was manufacturing tanks, trucks, ball bearings, and engines for the enemy war machine. I pushed a cart with steel parts to different assembly stations, and I didn't like the end products or the job I was given. I felt like a traitor to my country every second I was there. I decided I needed to find a different type of work; especially since we believed that plant would sooner or later be bombed, and I had no intention of being present for that.

A friend of the family, Charles Gossens, had been by the house many times over the years. He was well connected in Ghent and suggested a safe solution for me in regard to my job search. He was an engineer employed by the old and now new government in the Highway and Bridge Department, whose job was to repair and maintain the bridges and roads for the Nazis. Mr. Gossens drove a Nazi-issued Citroen car and also a BMW motorcycle. He was a man who had some power and to our luck was not a friend to the Nazis. He would propose a repair job to the Nazi brass that wasn't of real importance, but which regularly received approval. He would do this so the important repair jobs that would have been much more advantageous to the Nazis went neglected. He was a member of the local yacht club where my dad and I spent so many days prior to the war. He confided in us by telling my parents and me that my best and safest occupation would be to volunteer in the Red Cross Rescue Services. It is thanks to him and his connections with the Red Cross that I wasn't drafted into the German army when I became fifteen. I had worked for less than a month at the steel plant when Mr. Gossens saved me. I had my plan in place, so I spoke with my steel plant supervisor and told him I had found another job with the Red Cross. He thought that it wasn't a good idea, but gave me three days to prove it. I was to report back to him and show proof of employment within three days, which I did.

As per German rules, I went to my school and made an appointment to speak with Principal Versmessen, tell him what I was going to do, and obtain his approval. He was, of course, opposed to my decision to leave school. However, considering my options, he wished me well. He said I could always catch up later on and take the necessary courses for a Certificate of Completion. I had the permission I needed to work for the Red Cross, which promised a much longer life expectancy than being drafted into the German army.

Pearl Harbor

America to me was an interesting faraway place that only became reality through some of the movies we watched. Aside from that, I knew very little. I remember hearing talk about America's neutrality because Belgium had been of the same stance before the invasion. My parents tried to explain this America to me, but a fourteen-year-old could only handle so much geo- and political-speak. Little did I know how truly remarkable and courageous that country would be. Belgians generally liked Americans and the image they projected to the world. I had at that time an uncle who lived in New York City, and he would send us letters that described how beautiful the country was. He expressed his wishes for us to come to New York, but he knew we couldn't. After the German invasion, the Nazis began to censor our mail. My uncle would receive letters from us detailing how wonderful the Nazis were and how great they treated everyone. We would describe how happy we were to be living under Hitler's rule. We did this to ensure our letters made it out to him. He knew that we were making it up, but more importantly, he knew we were alive. Any mail merely suggesting that the Nazis were anything but angels never left the country.

On December 7, 1941, the American people were awakened to the full realization of the danger that confronted them. The newspaper headlines on December 7 proclaimed: Japan Wars on the United States and Britain—Makes Sudden Attack on Hawaii—Heavy Fighting at Sea. I was told later by one of my coworkers that during the night hours after the attack, something had happened to the people of the United States. Every sign of division, every internal conflict had disappeared. The nation faced the dawn with determination—America had united itself. Instantly they stood steadfast together. Hitler sneered at the Americans as a nation of cowards in the last gasp of civilization. But through his wisdom, President Franklin D. Roosevelt, who had been taking steps within the limits of US neutrality to meet whatever emergency might arise, said: "Yesterday, December 7, 1941—a date which will live in infamy—the United States of America was suddenly and deliberately attacked by naval and air forces of the Empire of Japan....I ask that the Congress declare that since the unprovoked and dastardly attack by Japan on Sunday, December 7, a state of war has existed between the United States and the Japanese Empire." This attack claimed 2,403 dead Americans in Hawaii.

I was unaware of what was going on in the United States prior to the attack, but read that during the ten years leading to Pearl Harbor the American people, with the rest of the world, had been fighting a war against an economic depression, which was the direct result of the costs of the first World War. We know that all wars must be paid for. Millions and millions of dollars cannot be squandered in destruction without meeting the losses. Payday cannot be postponed for very long, and ultimately it must be met out of the pockets of the people. They pay first in lives, then in taxation, depression, and unemployment. It was during this period of world depression that Hitler found his opportunity to arouse the spirit of revolution in the German people, and Japan laid her plans to overthrow the economically "depressed democracies." German treachery was clearly evident behind Japan's violent action, abetted by Italy as an Axis partner.

It was a very sad and dark day when we heard about the attack by Japan. For a while we had the same feeling as when the Germans attacked us. We didn't dare discuss it with anyone because talking about any kind of news or information would have been a giveaway of the source. No one could be trusted in those days. The Gestapo had ears everywhere, and their rewards for ratting were tempting for people in need. The tragic news we heard coming out of Pearl Harbor was received with tremendous sadness, but I must admit the Belgian community let out a collective sigh knowing that the US had declared war on Japan and its ally Germany.

In late 1941, Winston Churchill spoke to the world in one of his many legendary speeches, which my parents secretly listened to on their tiny crystal radio at the 2100-hour broadcast. This particular speech gave many in the occupied world hope that rescue was coming. My parents carefully shared the details of this speech with us the next day. The 2100-hour broadcast of the BBC became the time for all those associated with the resistance and those seeking hope to tune in. Every available precaution was taken to allow for the opportunity to listen at that hour. Our family, who lived with the enemy, had means to get the news they so desperately needed. My parents used locked doors, a multi-room buffer, and a pillow over their listening heads to secretly catch the daily news. The tiny crystal radio speaker was easily muffled by an ear and pillow. Unbeknownst to my parents, my sister Lucienne and I shared a similar kind of radio that we often hid beneath our pillows. News, at that time, was so very important to everyone. The use of illegal radios was indeed a problem for the Nazis, and they developed mobile search groups equipped with special radio-detecting capabilities to search them out. These specialized Nazis would drive around at night homing in on the signals that illegal radios produced. If caught, the arresting penalties were always much harsher than the crime warranted. I am not sure if our tiny little crystal radios were powerful enough to emit a signal that would draw in the Nazi search groups, but we never got caught. My dad felt that we were passed over by the search groups because our house had a military designation on its door due to its Nazi inhabitants. We were well aware of the developments of the war as the BBC broadcast them, and heard the words of Churchill on the invasion of Russia: "The Nazi regime is indistinguishable from the worst features of Communism. It is devoid of all theme and principle except appetite and racial denomination. It excels all forms of human wickedness in the efficiency of its cruel and ferocious aggression. No one has been a more consistent opponent of Communism than I have for the last twenty-five years. . . . But all this fades away before the spectacle which is now unfolding. The past, with its crimes, its follies, and its tragedies, flashes away.

"I see advancing (upon Russia) the hideous onslaught of the Nazi war machine, with its clanking, heel-clicking, dandified Prussian officers . . . the dull, drilled, docile, brutish masses of the Hun soldiery plodding on like a swarm of locusts. . . . behind all this storm, I see that small group of villainous men who plan, organize, and launch this cataract of horrors upon mankind.

"We have but one aim and one single, irrevocable purpose. We are resolved to destroy Hitler and every vestige of the Nazi regime. From this nothing will turn us—nothing.

"We will never parlay; we will never negotiate with Hitler or any of his gang. We shall fight him by land, we shall fight him by sea, we shall fight him in the air, until we have rid the earth of his shadow and liberated its people from his yoke. . . . if Hitler imagines that his attack on Soviet Russia will cause the slightest divergence of aims or slackening of effort in the great democracies who are resolved upon his doom, he is woefully mistaken. On the contrary, we shall be fortified and encouraged in our efforts to rescue mankind from his tyranny."

I was too young at that time to fully comprehend the enormity of Churchill's words, but my parents briefed us as best they could. I heard this speech in its entirety many years later, after hearing from many of the soldiers of its impact on the world and the way it gave the oppressed people hope. The German Distribution Cable Radio, which the Germans had graciously installed for us, celebrated the tremendous surprise victory of the Japanese over the Americans. The Germans never admitted to a loss and still were gaining on every front. They continually told us about the terrible setbacks and losses for the Allies. Lies, lies, and more lies were all we heard for four years.

The need for unbiased news was great indeed. Not everyone had access to a little crystal radio as we did. Just knowing that the Allies were fighting for us gave us all a world of hope. No fewer than two hundred "Underground Newspapers," the largest secret press in any Nazi-subjugated country, were circulated in occupied Belgium throughout the war. These small and rudimentary newspapers were printed in old factories, houses, or buildings that appeared closed down or were hidden from easy detection. These papers would contain the most recent available news from people who had access to radios. They would deliver only to persons who were absolutely trustworthy. Each subscriber had to pay for his newspaper. The distribution utilized loyal students to distribute the news weekly. The publisher had to worry about getting the news, first, and not getting caught, second. They operated in a very efficient manner that stressed minimizing their risk. The penalty was execution or deportation to a slave labor camp if one was caught distributing a newspaper. Just having possession of one of these newspapers could easily lead to your death. Trust was the ultimate factor in the success or failure of each newspaper. One person could lead to the death of a multitude of people by getting caught or by talking to the wrong person. Should the Gestapo catch you, then you could be sure they would torture you to get information. If you spilled, the names you gave would summarily be rounded up and interrogated just the same. A great many people faced extreme risk to keep trusted citizens informed and renewed with hope.

Red Cross

One day in January 1942, about a month before my fifteenth birthday, Mr. Gossens stopped by my house unannounced early in the morning. He told me to pack up two pair of underwear, two pair of socks, two shirts, and two pair of pants only into a small bag. He told me that I was leaving home with him and that I had a few moments to say goodbye to my parents, which wasn't easy. We embraced each other very firmly and hoped that this wasn't for the last time. My parents knew that this plan was risky but might save my life. I then got into Mr. Gossens's car and we headed away to initiate my new role as a volunteer in the Red Cross Rescue Service (RCRS). Mr. Gossens made the connections and arrangements ahead of time. The people who were in command of the RCRS welcomed me and informed me that my job would be to search through the rubble of bombed-out buildings and locate survivors, or what was left of victims. It would be a very difficult and dirty job, and unveiled things to me that most fifteen-year-olds shouldn't see. My uniform consisted of a Belgian World War I dark khaki army helmet, light gray heavy-duty coveralls, matching shirt, a white armband with a red cross symbol and RCRS in black letters, black work shoes, a wide black belt, a raincoat, a twenty-five-foot rope, a very impressive three-foot long steel crowbar, and a shovel. I knew going in that it wouldn't be an easy job but had helped in rescuing and recovering some victims previously. Just having this job wouldn't guarantee my safety from the draft, but it created quite an obstacle for the Germans. The prospect of locating someone like me on the job was almost impossible. Rescue and recovery missions went on daily and constantly in different locations and towns. I was essentially hiding in plain sight in an ever-changing environment in the midst of a war. Locating a fifteen-year-old boy wasn't an easy job, nor was it a priority for the Germans. I didn't dare call home to let them know where I was or how I was doing. I had to be careful with everything I said because no one could be trusted fully anymore aside from immediate family and close friends. The temptation to turn someone in was too great. Nearly every family was poor, starving, and cold, so neighbors were leery of each other. The reporting of anyone was an opportunity to be rewarded with basic needs. People knew that they could receive food, clothing, and/or coal if they turned anyone in to the Gestapo. The Gestapo had made it known that those who reported anti-Nazi activity would receive much-needed help. Worse, the Gestapo maintained a free pass in killing anyone, at anytime, anywhere, and didn't have civil courts to protest the accusations. As a result, thousands of innocent people were turned in, tortured, beaten, and killed on sight, in jail, or in a concentration or hard labor camp. Your life meant nothing to the Gestapo, whose members took pleasure in killing because they had lost their conscience through their existentialist belief and practices. Once someone had made it into the Gestapo's file, they were in considerably more peril from arrest and subsequent punishments.

During 1941 and 1942 the Allies began bombing the harbors, railroad yards, and industrial areas of German-occupied areas regularly. With every bomb dropped, there became work for people like me. Work for Red Cross Rescue Services was never-ending. We were always on duty and due to constantly changing jobs, we had to reshuffle the crews often. We worked in small teams, as manpower was always limited. My job was to locate the bombed-out structures, sort through the rubble that I was able to move, locate any humans alive or dead, and retrieve them. The survivors were few but always a priority. Most of the time the recovery involved deceased persons where I would try to piece together and identify the victims. Once identified, the bodies and body parts were put in tar bags and tagged. The bodies and body parts were never easy to pair up, and many were unidentifiable. We recorded a file of what we found and where we found remains. Survivors were transported to the nearest medical center for help. The Red Cross had doctors and nurses on staff that were always busy. After I had found a survivor, which was rare, I almost never saw them again.

Occasionally, I was called back to disinfect a damaged shelter or building where I had found bodies or body parts that had been decaying for several weeks. The smell of these jobs remains with me to this day. The decaying smell of blood, guts, and body parts would fall under the category of indescribable. We covered our faces with scarves against the toxic smell. One particular cleanup job involved the bodies of a mother and her two children, who were found impacted together from an explosion and had to be scraped off the ceiling and from behind the supporting timbers. This was not a happy time in my life. I don't think a boy can remain a boy after such an experience.

As the Germans continued to expand their reach, the Allies had begun to mount a formidable counteroffensive. The Allied plan began with the bombing of locations that fed the Nazi war machine—such as power plants, refineries, weapon manufacturers, and equipment factories. The constant bombings by the Allied forces killed hundreds of thousands of civilians in industrial areas where these key targets were located. Some bodies near the impact sites were never found. Innocent men, women, and children were killed or injured day after day by the very forces charged with saving us. Everyone knew that civilian losses were part of the deal, but knowing that these deaths came from your rescuers was slightly unnerving. We knew the Allied bombs were not intended to kill our people but that those bombs had a purpose greater than the deaths they caused. Very few survivors of bombings were found once we arrived, and most of the time we were too late. Some wished they hadn't survived because they were now the only survivors left in their families, and others were so badly injured that each day of life was painful agony. Our biggest problem in the RCRS was the lack of equipment, medical supplies, doctors, nurses, and hospitals, not to mention food and water. We needed moving equipment to reach and transport buried victims and usually only had a few mules or horses and wagons. At night during the frequent total blackouts, the only way we could locate anyone was by using tracking dogs that could guide us to survivors or bodies. Unfortunately, most of the victims trapped in cellars, basements, and bomb shelters could not be reached in time because of the amount of rubble that had fallen on top of them. Most trapped victims suffocated or drowned before we could get to them. Picks, shovels, crowbars, and a lot of muscle were our tools. The Nazis wouldn't allow us any equipment unless we reported Germans among the victims.

Most workers of the factories in industrial areas had apartments located nearby. The purpose was to keep the employees from having to travel back and forth to work in inclement weather. But when the factories were targeted, civilian losses were enormous. The machines that were used to manufacture weapons of death for the Nazis were destroyed, along with the civilian workforce who were there against their will. Whole families were often killed instantly and disappeared from existence.

During my Red Cross days, I tried to utilize my precociousness and assist the Allied effort in creative and helpful ways. Our German occupiers were generally everywhere, and on occasion they grew bored of their dealings with us. I was approached more than a few times by a Nazi seeking directions to a museum, the Palace of Justice, a city pool, or others areas of interest. I had the look of an older kid so was approached as someone who knew the lay of the land. My RCRS designation allowed me a certain level of anonymity against interrogation from the Germans. This position held some definite perks. I took great pride in giving the German soldiers very detailed directions to the wrong destination. If the soldier wanted to visit the bathhouse, which was close by, I would suggest he board a particular nearby streetcar, then make a transfer at such and such a place to another streetcar, then walk for a few blocks which would take him to the other side of Ghent. This trip would have taken him roughly forty-five minutes to an hour to arrive, when he would finally learn that he had been duped. I was always sure to be absent if that soldier happened to return to find me. I can only imagine the anger this must have caused him, and it gave me tremendous pleasure.

During the early years of the war, things for us Belgians seemed hopeless. We struggled daily with the thought of Germany ruling us the rest of our lives. The sheer thought of liberation was almost as far-fetched to us as the thought of finding enough food to last the week. The starvation diet we had to subsist on created an entire black market for items that previously were acquired without effort. Although my family shared residence with the Nazis, we were always scrounging for enough food to stay alive. Being in the Red Cross afforded me the paltry luxury of a steady diet. We weren't fed a lot, but we were fed regularly. My absence from home and the overwhelming workload kept my mind busy and away from the immediate troubles at hand.

I knew I was biding my time until I reached the age of sixteen. I sure as hell wouldn't be volunteering for the German draft. I had my sights set on joining the Underground Resistance however I could. They wouldn't touch me until I reached sixteen years old, so I busied myself with my Red Cross duties. I was privy to news from the war around the world during meals and encounters with other Red Cross members. The fighting in North Africa, the German advance in Russia, then the attack on Pearl Harbor . . . the losses in the Pacific, the horrible fire bombing of London, things were looking very grim for us and the Allies. I never saw my parents during my time working for the Red Cross. I spoke to my dad but one time. He called the Red Cross command center to wish me a happy fifteenth birthday. I told him how happy I was that he called and that I loved him, but we collectively decided he shouldn't call me again for my own safety. Officially, I was now eligible for the German draft, and my ability to remain off the grid was extremely important to my survival. Dad and I wished each other the best and said some heartfelt goodbyes. It would be years before I had an opportunity to hear my dad's voice again.

I remember hearing my parents talking about the war and my dad, being the optimist he was, always finding positives about our situation. He would say "The Germans have got themselves spread too thin to hold and control all their occupied territories and front lines. The tide will be changing soon. Germany is beginning to hurt and is suffering terrible losses on the eastern front in Russia and in Africa. We will make it! It will not be too long, maybe a few years." He hated the Communists and so hated to see the Russians on our side. Dad was convinced the Bolsheviks were as bad as the Nazis, if not worse. As much as he disliked the Russians, they gave us Belgians a ray of hope. Dad believed the Russians were going to beat the Germans just as they defeated Napoleon, in a massive campaign with terrible losses.

Black Brigade

The Nazis had a massive army, but didn't have enough manpower to watch over everything they conquered after they moved on to their next battle. The Black Brigade was placed in positions of power to help the Nazis keep an eye on their flocks. As horrific a group as our Nazi occupiers were, they paled in comparison to the Black Brigade. This German tool of terror also went by the name *Milice* in France. The French considered the Milice more dangerous than the Gestapo or the SS because they were native Frenchmen who understood the dialects, the towns, and knew the people. These Milice had turned on their country to serve the Nazis. They were traitors of the highest order. In Belgium these men, called the Black Brigade, were the most despicable wretches of humanity, and those in a position to act sought out their deaths without hesitation. The Black Brigade were traitors to their own country and, as per German design, were filled with Belgian outcasts and criminals whose viciousness surpassed that of the German Gestapo and SS. They were Belgian fascist fanatics given extraordinary liberties by the Gestapo to spread fear amongst their countrymen and weed out anyone offering resistance.

Technically, the Black Brigade was a Nazi branch of the Belgian army, but the most hated and feared people that ever existed to us. You hoped never to have to deal with them, except to execute them. The Belgian Resistance fighters would stop at nothing to kill a member of the Black Brigade. The Brigade's members were notorious for showing off for their Gestapo leadership by being extremely violent to us civilians. The most terrifying part was that often the Black Brigadiers knew you and your family. They could have you killed for as much as looking at them wrong. If these people didn't like you before the occupation, then you weren't alive very long after the occupation. The Germans set up checkpoints to get in and out of town after the invasion, and the Black Brigadiers typically were the ones manning these posts. They stopped everyone of interest and checked them thoroughly. They were impossible to deal with. If caught with illegal items such as extra food, they confiscated all you had, and you were lucky if they didn't fine or arrest you. You never knew what was going to happen, but their attitude was consistently rude and very disrespectful.

In 1942 and 1943, the biggest question that kept the Axis powers under tension was when and where the Allies would attack and attempt to land on the Atlantic wall. It was not a question of if, but rather when. Germany expected the Allies to strike across the English Channel at France or Belgium, and thus had frantically built the so-called Impenetrable Wall along the coast, which was heavily defended by a huge army. A branch of the German army called Organization Todt, which used approximately 1.4 million civilian prisoners, constructed the wall. These men suffered unspeakable horrors in their special slave labor camps. They would be pushed to their physical limits on a daily basis, and if a man perished, his body was discarded and replaced by someone living.

Around the time the Impenetrable Wall was being hurriedly built in 1942, and following the miracle at Dunkirk, the Allies had come up with a daring plan referred to as Operation Jubilee to test the German's strength on the Atlantic coast. The test tube was the town and harbor of Dieppe, located on the northern coast of France along a long cliff that overlooks the English Channel, and which through the centuries had been a battle port from the days of Norman conquests. The Allies hoped to seize and hold this major port for only a short period, simply to prove it was possible. This would effectively boost morale for the Allies and demonstrate the British capability and desire to open a western front. But German intelligence had somehow learned of the Allied interest in the area, which ruined any potential of surprise. In the Dieppe sector, the Germans had placed artillery batteries in hillside caves and on the crests of hills so that the crossfire could sweep the entire beach area. All the guns were within range of one another. Before and behind them were machine-gun nests at frequent intervals, with intricate barbed-wire barricades. The streets of Dieppe, which ended at the beach, were outfitted with formidable tank barriers. Every house in the shorefront area of the town was made into a defensive stronghold.

The odds were against them, but the Allies were overdue for a break. The invasion force had hoped to make their way onto the beach itself without observation. If this could have been accomplished, the whole result of the attack might have been different. But this unfortunately was not to be. The invaluable element of surprise was destroyed before the shore of France was in sight. One group of landing crafts was approaching Berneval and was sighted by a German patrol boat that immediately flashed a signal for help. E-boats rushed to the enemy scout's assistance, and the alarm was spread along the whole French coast. Out of this ill-fated squadron of landing craft, few returned; many of the men aboard were slaughtered at sea. The Canadian troops engaged in the operation made up virtually the entire force, which had numbered over six thousand when they left the coast of England. In seven hours of fighting in hostile waters and onshore, nearly 60 percent of the force had been killed, wounded, or captured before a retreat was ordered. The operation was a dismal failure and a blow to the Allies.

But the Germans knew that someday soon the Atlantic assault would be perfected on a larger scale. Where and when the assault would be made was now their constant worry. It was later discovered by the British War Office that just prior to Operation Jubilee, a crossword clue appeared in the *London Telegraph* with the clue being "French Port," and its correct answer, "Dieppe," which suggested a spy working at the *Telegraph,* alerting the Nazis to the invasion. The subsequent investigation, however, determined it was merely a striking coincidence.

Two years later, in 1944, the Allies would have their redemption at Normandy.

CHAPTER 3

United We're Strong: The Belgian Resistance

The Nazi juggernaut had obliterated our Belgian national defenses in 1940, which had been less than robust since our neutrality pact had given our country a false sense of security. The battle lasted a mere eighteen days, and Belgium surrendered on May 28. Our armed forces, which comprised nearly 20 percent of its male population, became prisoners of war and detained in camps in Germany. The total and complete occupation of Belgium began immediately. Belgian resistance was slow to develop at first because the feelings were that a total German victory was imminent. The first members of the resistance were former soldiers who had been released from POW camps back in World War I and who wished to continue the fight against the Germans. More and more civilians joined the resistance as an alternative to forced labor camps and in response to inhumane German policies that were enacted upon the Belgian people. Many of these civilians did not qualify for such duty and were turned away. The resistance needed men of a certain caliber who were willing to die for their country.

During World War I, the Belgian community had learned the importance of strong networking through underground groups, and increasingly used these same strategies once the Germans conquered them for a second time. Passive resistance was the most widespread form of resistance, and the officially prohibited broadcasts by Radio Belgique reached a large majority of the Belgian passive resisters. Striking was the most common form of passive resistance. The Germans always repressed the large-scale strikes.

The more active participatory citizens of the Underground Resistance grew from humble beginnings. Early efforts entailed random acts of sabotage. Once

The bridge I helped destroy with explosives, circa 1941

these groups became organized, their efforts instantly grew more coordinated and began to elicit fear among their unwanted guests. The resistance fighters intended to confront the Nazis with their own reign of terror. The French Forces of the Interior (FFI), which was created in France, was also called the Underground Resistance. They were divided in two kinds of operations and were commanded from England via a central headquarters in Belgium. One operation was a battle-hardened and highly organized group, while the other operation consisted of men with considerably less experience and which tended to be a more spontaneous movement. The job of both these groups was to distract, confuse, delay, repel, and kill the enemy by any means available. Both operational groups were trained and equipped. They knew their goals would be accomplished at great risk to their lives because they were operating in enemy territory, albeit in their own country. They ambushed German patrols, laid booby traps and mines, disrupted German communication systems, sabotaged production, and blew up factories, railroad tracks, and switches, and utilized every possible method to slow down the transportation of enemy troops.

The reliable BBC radio network out of London didn't show favoritism in their daily news and communications, which reported the true facts of the war in progress. But the network was definitely pro-Allies. Sometimes the BBC broadcast French poetry that no one could figure out because they were intended solely for the Allied Underground Forces or SOE (Special Operations Executive). These poetic broadcasts relayed detailed coded messages that instructed the resistance fighters on what needed to be accomplished.

Winston Churchill had famously ordered the SOE to set Europe ablaze. The SOE went by the moniker of Churchill's Secret Army. This Secret Army instructed the resistance fighters, equipped them, and provided the necessary explosives to perform the tasks they commanded us to perform. The supplies were often dropped by the *Moon Squadron*, which were incredibly brave and resourceful air shuttle pilots who typically flew single-engine Lysander planes that dropped six-foot-long metal canisters with rifles, machine guns, TNT explosives, ammunition, knives, medical supplies, food, and clothing. Occasionally, the Moon Squadron dropped SOE agents who brought us new intelligence, new sabotage techniques, and trained us in new skills. The written instructions we received went by the inscription of "A Curriculum Of Deadly Skills" and taught us such new things as hand-to-hand combat, use of new small arms, sabotage techniques, installing mines, and deactivating explosives, as well as specific instructions on how to make a variety of booby traps out of everyday objects or food.

The Underground Resistance Fighters existed in World War I, and we admired their exploits and legendary stories. However, many paid with their lives in their effort to repel the Germans. Much wartime experience gained from WWI assisted the Underground Resistance in our fight against the Nazis. Within a few weeks after the Nazi invasion, our underground forces were organized; we were the envy of the small amateur saboteurs.

Two or three months after we organized, the FFI took over coordinated resistance efforts and reorganized our units. There were no uniforms, no armbands, and they gave no medals. They operated in strict secrecy with one goal in mind: the liberation of our country.

With the anti-German tide rising around the continent due to the use of inhuman wartime practices, the invaders resorted to terrible methods of vengeance. The Nazis dealt with resistance amongst their controlled territories with immediate action that included, but was not limited to, shooting and burning living innocent hostages, torture, and inflicting the death penalty for just about any infraction. The Nazis created a *Roll of Honor,* which was a working list of those executed by the Nazis for acts against the German empire. This list was made public as a reminder to those who were considering such actions.

The Germans knew we hated them and that we were very opposed to their presence, but as with anything else, the Germans had ways to deal with it. Their show of force could be massive when provoked. They had the power to kill anyone opposing them, and butting heads with them was like signing your own death warrant. This deterrent wasn't enough to stop the resistance from churning along. Rather, the efforts increased as the months progressed, and hope slowly reemerged.

Enraged by the increasing activity of the resistance in France and elsewhere, coupled with the high-profile kidnapping of a German officer by

CROIX ROUGE
DE BELGIQUE

ROODE KRUIS
VAN BELGIE

Par décision du Comité
exécutif de la Croix-Rouge de
Belgique les

Palmes 1940-1945

sont décernées à

Bij besluit van het Uitvoerend
Comité van het Roode
Kruis van België worden de

Palmen 1940-1945

toegekend aan

Mijnheer Jean Sippens

de Gent
van

en récompense des services
rendus pendant la guerre
1940-1945

als erkenning voor bewezen
diensten tijdens den oorlog
1940-1945

Bruxelles, le 18 mei 1946
Brussel, den

Le Directeur Général,
De Directeur Generaal,

Le Président,
De Voorzitter,

Brevet N° D. 1707

Service Award I received from the Red Cross

French resistance fighters, the Germans viciously destroyed and burned to the ground the town of Oradour, France. They separated the women, children, and elderly into a church where they were told to wait. The men were marched to a nearby position and made to watch as the church was set ablaze. The men, helpless to save them, witnessed the cries and screams of their families. After the reality had sunk in, these men were marched to another building, machine-gunned, and then set on fire. Hundreds of lives slaughtered, just for the unsuccessful deterrent effect, and apparently for the sadistic pleasure of it. These mass murders were repeated in retribution for any successful act by the resistance.

Hitler decreed that for every assassination committed by resistance fighters, the Germans would execute fifty civilians. The Germans didn't follow international laws of warfare. They killed at will and performed the same way in Belgium, Italy, Sicily, Poland, and Ukraine, where in retaliation they shot, hung, and tortured to death hundreds of thousands of innocent civilians. With the aid of torture-induced confessions or denunciations, they shattered many resistance networks. Yet even as the civil death rate spiraled, the Resistance reacted with still more violence.

Meanwhile the situation in the occupied countries was worsening. There was increasing famine, and no one was immune, not even the privileged. Children often were not capable of helping their families because of physical weakness they suffered due to a lack of nutrition. Begging in the streets became a necessity. The black market was the only way to obtain additional food. Poor people exchanged goods instead of paying. Shoes were available for only 4 percent of the inhabitants, and rationing of clothes was even extended to infant wear. Some of the food available for purchase with Nazi-issued stamps, like bacon and horsemeat, was usually rancid. Vegetables were wilted and much of the food, whether black market or legally purchased, was spoiled. I am surprised we didn't die of food poisoning of some sort. The only source of good food was from farmers, also through the black market, and even that came to an end when the Germans enforced strict controls at the city perimeters and checkpoints.

Mass executions didn't resolve the problem with Belgian political prisoners. Prisons were soon too small to hold the great number of men and women condemned for political crimes. In 1943, additional concentration camps were opened in Belgium at Huy and Breendonck. The latter became a replica of the infamous Dachau Camp and was placed under the sole control of the mad and brutal Gestapo. Forced labor and slave gangs became a valuable weapon of the Nazis.

Growing Up

The date of February 8, 1943, loomed on the horizon as I would turn sixteen years old, and I faced the even greater possibility of being drafted into the German army. The Red Cross had protected me when I was fifteen and hid many others who lived on the run. With the Rescue Service, we were constantly moving from one bombed-out area to another and from one city to another. Hundreds of rescue volunteers were spread out in several towns, and it was difficult to track us down. But our chances to escape the draft worsened over time, and despite our necessary work, many men caught on the job were forced to join the German ranks. Every time a German stopped you, the possibility of enlistment emerged.

As prisoners in our own country, Belgian young men were required to report on their sixteenth birthday to the German draft board in their hometowns. These terrified young people would be sent to basic training sites located throughout the German-occupied lands. The Nazis required more and more bodies as the war progressed. Many of these young men were fast-tracked through basic training so they could be raced to the front lines. Several of my close friends from school who weren't as fortunate as I reported to the draft board, and they were never heard from again. Often these young and inexperienced kids were shipped off to the Russian front, where they had little chance of survival.

One day I was inexplicably summoned to the Red Cross operations office. There I was handed a coded message from Mr. Gossens, the same man who used his influence to get me into the Red Cross. I was told to meet with him at a specific time at a specific intersection nearby, where two unknown persons would make contact with me. I was nearing my sixteenth birthday and was well aware of the implications here, so I made sure to be there when I was asked. I arrived early and waited. Two men showed up when I expected them and asked me by name to get into the car. I did as I was told. We drove for forty-five minutes until we reached a nondescript house in the town of Lathem. I was ushered quickly inside, where Mr. Gossens was waiting for me. After a very brief chat, he introduced me to a man who worked for the railroad and also worked for the Resistance. Mr. Gossens said his goodbyes and was gone like that. I would be staying in this house for three days with this man and his wife. There were no names exchanged as an added layer of protection. The couple explained to me in great detail the way things operated and instructed me in the ways of the Resistance. I learned how the SOE in England commanded the operation. I learned how the Nazis hunted us, and should we get ourselves captured, no information should ever be leaked. We must be willing to suffer immense torture or die for this cause. The cause was the most important thing. The cause was the defeat of evil and the future existence of the human race as we knew it. We were all fighting the same battle, and every piece, however small, was needed for victory against the Nazis. I had to sign papers to create a paper trail, which seems contradictory to our desire for secrecy. It was referred to as the receipt of fresh flesh. There had to be a record of the underground force so as to eliminate spies and potential mistakes that could result in all our deaths. After three days of training and validation, I was picked up at the house by more unidentified personnel. They took me to a central railroad depot in the industrial section of Ghent. There I became an employee of the railroad, if only as a cover.

Railroad

As part of the Resistance we required secrecy, but we all needed jobs to cover our clandestine activities should the Nazis ever stop us outside of our Resistance missions. Mr. Gossens, who had saved me from the German draft, was instrumental in my acceptance into the underground. He made sure I had a forged ID card and a fake work permit with the railroad. I was instructed on protocol by the underground for matters of extreme importance. My instructors taught me how to act if I was stopped on the street by anyone pro-German. The Gestapo was trained to detect anything unusual, and to stay alive I was trained to have convincing answers and ready paperwork. I was taught how to answer their questions and above all how to remain calm and in control. Once I had learned enough, I was introduced to a large railroad depot and repair yard where I was hired by the railroad. My phony job with the railroad was as a waybill employee and grease monkey. When questioned, I claimed that I attached a waybill-identifying tag to each train car and repaired switches along the track. I had an official badge, and as an official employee of the Belgian railroad, I had fraudulent documents to prove it. I was allowed out around town as long as I had an explanation for being away from the rail yard. When I wasn't sleeping, I was expected by the Nazis to be working on the railroad. The railroad was in on the cover-up and was a front for many Resistance fighters. The Gestapo could question my employer, who would corroborate my story. The irony in my situation was that I was constantly blowing up the railroads that impacted German movements. By day, I was fixing them.

One day a Gestapo soldier, seeking to find out the legitimacy of my employment, dropped in on me at the railroad office. He found me quite easily and demanded that I answer his questions. His first question was his mistake. He asked me to explain the waybill to see if I really understood it. I explained it from the beginning: the waybill was the method in which a rail car was tracked, anytime and anywhere. The destination could be changed while in route and certain railroad cars could be reassigned to another destination, but the number or waybill didn't change until the present load was unloaded. When the railcar received a new but different load, the waybill was changed and the railcar would most likely travel to a new destination. The waybill employee could locate another train, call the next train station to stop, disconnect certain railroad cars, reassign trains to another destination, and be given a new waybill anytime along the way. This rambling sounds as it was designed to be. I could ramble on like this for as long as it took, because the Gestapo soldier finally ordered me to "Shut up!" He had reached his limit. The Gestapo hated to be told anything, especially when they didn't already know it, and I had begun to overwhelm him. He asked to speak to my boss, who corroborated my employment and my dealings with these waybills. The Gestapo had quickly grown weary of this interrogation, which appeared to be leading nowhere. He abruptly ended the questioning and left.

I was now on the inside and considered part of the Resistance. I was taught how to lubricate the many moving parts of a train, as that was part of my railroad job. I was also trained to apply abrasive lubricant to the vehicles of the enemies in order to render their modes of transportation useless. This would be one of my jobs in the Underground Resistance. This huge railroad depot would now be my home. I received a bed in a shared dormitory room, which wasn't half bad considering the other option had a large room with thirty beds in a row with no privacy to speak of. I didn't have much time to settle in because I was sent on a mission very soon after I arrived. I would get to practice my craft of applying the abrasive lubricant or goo as it was commonly referred to. The initial mission was made easy, and I was given a railroad switch to lubricate and render useless. I had to earn my reputation by destroying things effectively. I spent the first week destroying switches, then train parts, and moved up quickly into communications. There was nothing on earth that I would rather be doing than this. All of the resistance fighters around me felt the exact same way. At the depot, we received regular pop-ins by the Germans. We might be working on some part of the railroad when suddenly the Nazis would come storming in and we were commanded to come together for roll call. The Nazis were hoping to catch someone missing when they weren't supposed to be. They often would show up to ask questions in their effort to catch underground fighters. We always knew the answers to their questions as part of our training.

I was still fifteen years old when I killed my first Nazi. New recruits coming in after being heavily vetted and vouched for would need to be schooled quickly to keep them alive and to keep them from getting the rest of us killed. We, having never killed anyone, needed this experience to help us when it really mattered. The leadership told us that we had four men to kill that morning. This was only for first-timers. These four traitors to Belgium were captured by FFI while they were on patrol and kept hidden away for just this purpose. These arrestees were worse than the Nazis to us and were treated accordingly. They were held at the secret FFI headquarters in an old factory outside of Ghent. Their hands were tied behind their backs and tied to a pole to keep them standing. They knew very well they were going to be executed. These men showed little remorse as they awaited their sentencing. They had believed the Germans were their salvation, but now they realized the price they would pay for their treason. Ten of us new recruits were to stand in a line similar to a firing squad. We were ordered to raise our rifles, aim, and fire one shot each on command. The traitorous men were felled quickly. We buried the bodies shortly thereafter so as to not leave the stench of death in our hideout. The experience for me happened so fast that I don't recall feeling anything. I knew we had killed men who had brought harm and deceit to our country. We learned as we gained experience and forced our captives to dig their own graves to save us the time.

Now with our initiation complete and our oath to defend our country against the Nazis pledged, we looked for opportunity. Opportunity to resist the Nazis came very quickly for me. Most of the bridges in Belgium had already been damaged or destroyed. The Belgian army, in their retreat, weren't able to destroy them all, and the Germans guarded the few remaining. Only one bridge was of great interest to us, because when the Belgian army retreated, they dumped cases of rifles and ammunition right off the bridge into the channel so the Germans wouldn't acquire them. This particular bridge was close to the sailing club where I had spent so much time prior to the invasion. One of the members of the club had witnessed firsthand the retreating Belgian army dumping these weapons off the bridge. He was nice enough to share this info with a cousin of mine named Theo Hoffman, who served with me in the Underground Resistance. Our source suggested that the weapons lying at the bottom of the canal were likely brand-new FN rifles from the Fabrique Nationale Factory, which was considered one of best manufacturers around. My cousin Theo and I had a daring plan to retrieve these valuable weapons from the water beneath the bridge. This particular bridge was of secondary importance for the German traffic, and the FFI had planned on blowing it up for some time. German guards were stationed at the entrance to the bridge. One day several of us resistance fighters began diving off the bridge into the river. To the Germans, it appeared we were just having some summertime fun, and the guards quickly lost interest in watching us. As soon as we knew they weren't paying close attention, we would dive in and swim to the bottom of the canal and grab a case of rifles from the bottom. We would swim it up, which did require a great effort, and place the case on the supporting beams directly under the bridge. A second distraction was a group of men playing water polo just underneath the bridge. Then a tugboat appeared on the scene that looked as if it needed some repairs. The next day a much smaller boat arrived to feign these repairs. When a signal was given, the cases were loaded onto this repair boat. The cases were loaded as quietly as we could and quickly covered. The small boat casually motored away with a cargo that would assist us in our fight. We were successful in retrieving around fifty cases from the bottom, each containing five brand-new FN rifles. We recovered scores of ammunition, hand grenades, and mortar rounds as well. A few nights after our treasure hunt, several older FFI operatives, using the canal, installed several explosive charges on this same bridge while the Nazis lazily guarded the road entrance above. The bridge was blown the following day, and its entire structure crumbled into the river below.

As we were full-fledged members of the Resistance, our orders poured in from the SOE in England. Each mission was a deliberate attempt to slow or disrupt the German advancement. No mission was ever too small or not taken extremely seriously by us. We weren't always coordinated with other resistance groups throughout Belgium, but our efforts were nonetheless aligned. When my commander gave us an order, we were expected to follow it no matter how dangerous or risky. The majority of my training took place in real-world missions. There simply wasn't time to train. Secrecy was always a priority. By design, no one aside from our group ever knew where or what we were doing. This protected us as it did all others.

At first, I had to learn to fight the silent way as learned by paramilitary soldiers. We were instructed by the SOE in methods of hand-to-hand combat, silent killing, use of small arms, sabotage techniques, plastic explosives, and installing mines as well as deactivating mines. We didn't rest much; there were few good hands to do a lot of work, and very few places to get any sleep. I learned to shoot the Enfield 30.06 without a scope for targets at a distance. I was taught to use the Enfield breach revolver for close combat. When a mission was assigned to us, we typically walked to get to it. We regularly carried the explosives in neutral tourist camping backpacks, and we dressed like day workers or in civilian clothing. We never wore uniforms, as this would give us an identity we didn't want.

One of the more requested sabotage missions given to us by command was the destruction of a segment of a rail line. The Germans used the railroads regularly to transport supplies to their many fronts. When the location for our explosives was determined, we carefully checked the immediate environment for Nazis. Germans very often checked the rails and the switches ahead of the train's arrival. We were the reason for the advance search party. By listening to the rail, you could guess the distance of an approaching train and thus estimate the distance and the time left to place the charges. We detonated our explosives with a pencil timer or fuse. One man could install the explosives by himself, but I didn't mind having a lookout watching for the enemy. We typically had great access to TNT and plastic explosives through the SOE. We became very effective in derailing German trains with our explosives. As in everything we did, there was a risk factor, but at no time did the risk outweigh the reward. I decided going in that I would give my life for this cause. On one such mission, I was told to go to a specified point on the outskirts of a town near a large bridge. The bridge was used by the railroad and lay at the bottom of a hill. We wired the incoming high side of the tracks with TNT and hid in nearby trees awaiting the upcoming train. As the train approached, we lit the fuse on the tracks. Going downhill without time to stop, the train derailed at near full speed as it hit the blown section. The sound was enormous as car after car smashed into each other, sometimes bursting into flames. The incline of the slope was steep enough to cause many train cars to roll into the river. The cargo of artillery and tanks created massive wreckage that surely took months to clean up. We were nowhere near the area to witness the Nazi reaction.

Before I go any further, I must explain that there is an unexplainable joy in blowing things up. Not for the amount of killing involved, but for the absolute carnage you create. A German train traveling pulling over fifty railroad cars and traveling at high speed will make an unbelievable mess should its tracks develop an unexpected gap in them. One could expect a parade of anti-aircraft bombs, tanks, fuel, equipment, supply trucks, and if we got lucky, a full load of Nazi troops smashing into each preceding car. The noise of such an event is heard far and wide, so we were careful to quickly disappear once the explosion went off.

Our resistance force felt tremendous inner joy in destroying bridges, buildings, trains, trucks, and anything else for that matter. As enjoyable as an explosion was for us, each one put us at considerably more risk the next time. We were hunted by the Gestapo. We would stop at nothing to accomplish our missions, but the preferred method when killing a human target involved silence, and thus a knife.

Killing Softly

The knife, if used properly, could render its victim instantly mute. We learned that when executing a Nazi in close quarters, a knife thrust to the abdomen and then an upward lift would typically do the trick. It would always disable the enemy and thwart his ability to fight back. In a more controlled situation, meaning fewer people, we would slice the German's throat to keep him from screaming out. Again, silence was our major advantage.

My experiences in the underground were always geared toward defeating a terrible enemy that didn't seem to have a weakness. Some of the things that happened during war would be considered unconscionable acts in a peaceful, civilized society. In the context of the twenty-first century, some would suggest that killing another person in the manner that we did on occasion wasn't necessary or that it was excessive. In the minds of our countrymen and those who had been defeated by the Germans, the death of anyone associated with the Nazis was legitimized by our unbending goal to defeat this enemy. By removing a Nazi from this planet, we felt one small step closer to our freedom. We were not barbarians as were our oppressors: we were people under the heel of the devil.

One evening the German curfew was in effect, so being out of your house without a permit was not allowed. As my Resistance cover job was as a railroad worker, I had a permit to be on the street after curfew. I was returning to our safe place at the rail yards with a co-resister named Gibb. Gibb and I saw a car approaching and hid under the cover of some nearby trees and bushes in the south part of Ghent. We watched as the Citroen stopped near an outdoor restroom. The car had a plate above the front bumper reading "Abwehr," which signified a high-ranking Nazi counterespionage agent. This Nazi would be high-value target. The driver should have known not to venture out without an armed escort. While he was talking with the woman in the car, Gibb and I made a decision that should he venture from his car, our duty was to kill them. He proceeded to leave the relative safety of his car to enter the roadside restroom. I swiftly moved in behind him as Gibb headed for the car. The officer caught my movement out of the corner of his eye and turned to see. He reacted instinctively and went for his gun, which was holstered on his belt. I reached him before he could retrieve it. I plunged my knife into his neck as Gibb performed roughly the same routine on the woman. Neither of them had time to make a sound. We checked the bodies to make sure they were on their way to hell and departed expeditiously. Even though I was carrying out my oath to the Resistance, I felt terrible about that event. My conscience was very hard on me. I felt like a coward about the manner in which they were killed, but I was very content to dispatch an Abwehr officer. They were usually very hard to take out because they were normally well escorted and protected. This was an important man in the Nazi hierarchy. This lone event haunts me to this day. The woman in the car may or may not have been a soldier, but she was aligned with the Nazis and therefore considered an enemy.

I preferred to be alone when on a mission. I had gotten quite effective at moving around clandestinely. The more men involved in a mission, the greater the risk of mistakes or detection. We were nothing if not quiet in our movements. If I was carrying explosives and saw Germans approaching, I was trained to quickly pull out small farming tools, which would disguise my true purpose. Inside my backpack would be bags of seeds, which concealed the TNT underneath. I also carried a slingshot for killing birds, which I also kept in my bag. I was stopped several times by German soldiers who questioned me. I showed them my slingshot and then the dead birds, which seemed to satisfy their curiosity. A man found carrying explosives for a covert mission would be dealt with in the harshest way. The Nazis would beat you to death, torture you, or dismember you in the most public way to discourage further sabotage. This is why I carried the L–Pill, which was concealed and easily accessible in the lining of my clothes. The L-Pill was a cyanide pill that guaranteed a quick death when its contents entered your mouth. This was the same pill containing prussic acid that ended the lives of Hitler's wife Eva Braun, Heinrich Himmler, Erwin Rommel, and Hermann Göring. I also carried a hand grenade for this same reason. Capture was not an option.

We were empowered by leadership to complete our mission in any manner that found success. The Resistance wanted solid results without any excuses. Our abilities to take out our enemy without using guns increased our successes. One FFI fighter with whom I worked became an expert with his blowgun. He killed more than a few German soldiers with a noiseless dart to the neck. Another man in my outfit could throw a knife and plant it on target. This man, according to stories I heard, was responsible for killing over thirty Germans with this method. After a kill was made, the dead Germans were always hidden from view, then left to rot.

Nork

One night we were given the mission to rescue one of our fellow FFI fighters who went by the name "Nork." A roaming party of Nazis had captured him and taken him to their base. We all knew how dangerous this mission would be, but rescuing a fellow FFI was our mission and we intended to follow orders. With information from our intelligence network we located the building in which he was held. Our team assembled to rescue him. We each were provided with the uniform of our enemies, not all matched, to help us in our mission. We pulled off the entry into the building with precise technique, and no one was alerted to our presence. Several of our undercover FFI fighters got close enough and killed two guards silently with a knife thrust to the back. We maneuvered around the building quickly, quietly, and found our comrade shut into a temporary cage, barely alive. Nork had been brutally tortured and beaten. We extricated him from his cage and as quickly as we got in, disappeared with him into the night. However, someone must have seen us escaping with Nork.

I was surprised the next day when the Gestapo showed up in force at the railroad and arrested me along with several others. The witnesses they brought in claimed I was seen at the Gestapo base the previous night. Other witnesses were there from the railroad, who claimed I hadn't left all night. The Gestapo reviewed my file and yelled at me, saying: "You are unwilling to conform to the laws from our Führer!" I was taken up to the Commandant for his ruling. Knowing how to perform from our training didn't stop my knees from trembling. He asked me why I was having such trouble understanding the orders given by the Führer. He questioned, "Did you actually help the man escape?" I answered, "No, Sir, I didn't!"

The Commandant asked the Gestapo if they could prove this severe accusation. They admitted this was all from hearsay, with conflicting witness testimony. A file was created on me labeled as *Pending*. Nork was in fact saved by us and shipped secretly off to England. I was guilty as charged, but somehow my streak of luck continued, and I was released.

Kissed by an Angel

A morning in April 1943 found our squad on a reconnaissance mission in the town of Zelzate, just southwest of Antwerp near the river Leie. We were executing a sabotage mission on a particular rail line that had been used in the Nazi war effort. We had orders to detonate a small portion of the line, in effect shutting it down. Our squad was sixteen strong and experienced men. Due to spotty intelligence, we got lost and crossed through a thick wooded area en route to the target rail line. Following the provided intelligence, we walked straight into a clearing, which was under watch from a well-hidden bunker that concealed several SS soldiers manning a large machine gun. We had mistakenly walked into a Nazi ambush and had no time to take cover. Machine gun fire erupted on us at thirty to forty yards. We had no time to run but only fall to the ground. The shooting lasted for a full twenty seconds, then ended as quickly as it began and went deathly silent. I dared not move a muscle and lay as motionless as a man could. Shortly after the shooting ended, I could hear the sound of approaching footsteps and muffled German voices. The footsteps grew nearer and became so close, I was sure they were right on top of me. I remember the crunch of ground under their boots. In between the confusing sounds of footsteps and talking, I heard the piercing sound of bayonets plunging into my wounded friends. I heard just one scream, which meant surely that most of my squad was already dead. The solitary scream I did hear lasted but a mere second. I experienced fear unlike anything I can possibly describe. I tried with all I had to prepare myself for the inevitable thrust of a bayonet into my body. Each second lasted an eternity. I became very angry with myself for walking into this trap. My mind searched for a way to mount a defense and kill one more Nazi before my end came. Please give me a chance to fire my weapon at them. My face-down position left me defenseless and completely vulnerable. I knew the bayonet was coming, and I knew I had to make a move, but I froze and clung motionless to the earth. I tensed each muscle in my body to hold the position as I lay. The footsteps I heard came from every direction. The voices had a celebratory tone to them, and I understood the congratulations they were throwing around to each other. Laughter broke out as one of the Germans teased another for being a poor marksman. I waited to die. My body would rot here and my parents would never know what became of me. My story would end as helplessly and gruesomely as I could imagine. Then, without cause or reason, the footsteps became softer. The voices grew fainter and more distant and finally faded. I kept my head down for several minutes so as not to make a deadly mistake. Then after several minutes of silence, I carefully lifted my head to peek out at my surrounding world. Everything was quiet. I slowly scanned the clearing and the surrounding woods for movement and confirmed the departure of the enemy. I quietly and quickly checked my squadron for signs of life. Blood was everywhere! Shredded bodies were scattered around me. There were bits and pieces everywhere. I found but one man still breathing, so I helped his head into my lap to comfort him. He was not able to communicate with me. He was too far gone and lasted only several minutes, then quietly died in my arms. I laid him on the ground and stood up. I looked around me and bowed my head. I had no one left to help. No wounded to assist. Twenty minutes ago

The site of the German bunker where my platoon was ambushed
I was the only survivor.

I proudly walked beside these brave, dedicated men. Now I stood alone as the sole survivor. My immediate thoughts were to get help. I knew I needed to remove myself from this environment, so as quietly as I could, I darted out of the clearing and then from tree to tree, working my way west. I was numb inside as I worked my way toward where I came from. I knew I was heading in a safe direction, which was away from the Germans, who I guessed had left to share their good news. The report I put in was met with anger, sadness, and congratulations on living through that nightmare. I was a very lucky man that day but had lost some friends and trusted allies. We had revenge on our minds, and no one more than I, but our orders were not to meet our enemy head-on, as we could easily lose the numbers battle. As much as I wanted to find those Germans and make them pay, I was reminded that I was part of a more important mission. My angel smiled down on me in that clearing that took nearly everything. My resolve grew stronger, but then war did that to us. Retribution wasn't part of the Allied strategy. Our enemies could afford to exact retributive measures against us due to their overwhelming manpower, but we had to be very strategic and resourceful.

Tired

Wartime involves many struggles, and getting enough rest is among them. I often was so tired I found rest by simply closing my eyes. At times it didn't matter how many shells exploded around me. Bullets didn't seem to matter either. Going three or four days straight without sleep was commonplace for most of us. These were the longest days of my life, and I fought with every ounce of my being to keep alert. We learned that the German brass utilized drugs to keep their soldiers alert for long periods of time. The Nazi military doctors distributed *Pervitin*, which was prescribed as an alertness aid. It is suggested that the Nazis passed out more than 200 million of these pills to their soldiers. The Nazi soldiers experienced increased endurance, alertness, and strength when taking this drug more commonly known as "Panzerschokolade," or tank chocolate. This alertness aid is known today as methamphetamine, or more simply as crystal meth. The Nazi soldiers would go on to report side effects that included dizziness, sweats, depression, and hallucinations. Many reports of heart failure and suicide came from the Nazi front. Hitler was even reported to utilize an intravenous methamphetamine to keep his aging body going.

In May 1943, we received good news when we desperately needed it. The nightly 1700 hours BBC broadcast told of the losses of the German Afrika Korps and the Italians in North Africa. The Allies' communiqué relayed over the commander's crystal radio the message from the Allies that reached our ears and hearts and did wonders for our morale. "No Axis forces remain in North Africa who are not prisoners in our hands." This gave us inspired hope. What a victory! This specific radio time was also a strategic time for the underground forces to receive their coded orders from the leaders in London. We would follow the instructions from our boss, who had a team of men who listened every night to get our orders. The messages were always in French to complicate the Germans' ability to decipher them.

In July 1943, the Allies announced the landing in Sicily—the doorstep to the continent of Europe. We were overjoyed because we knew it was another great step toward victory and freedom. General Patton proclaimed that the American Army had outstripped the Germans at their own invention of "blitzkrieg." With due allowance made for the vast difference in terrain, the General said that in the first ten days of the Sicilian campaign, the Americans had made greater progress than the Germans had done in their sweep through the Low Countries and France in 1940, or even in their invasion of Poland in the fall of 1939.

We followed the war in the Pacific and the conquest of the Atolls as much as our underground newspapers and radios would allow us. We could easily see the victories of the Allies and their strength and power. A few weeks after the landing in Sicily, the BBC announced over our crystal radios that Sicily had fallen and Mussolini had been deposed. The Germans, though, were not about to retreat without a fight.

The conquest of Sicily had been accomplished in thirty-seven days, and the Allies started the battle on Italian soil on September 8, 1943. The Forty-Fifth infantry division of the US Army was an outfit made up largely of men from the Southwest US—from Arizona, Colorado, New Mexico, and Oklahoma—and was one of the first national guard units activated in World War II. They were tall, tough fellows, with more than one thousand American Indians among them. The bravery they exhibited in Sicily and Salerno was a major factor that led to the Allied victories there. Of note, the Forty-Fifth's original insignia approved in 1924 and worn on their sleeve was in fact the swastika. This symbol quickly was abandoned when the Nazi rose to power in the 1930s. The swastika originated in Asia as an ancient religious icon. In the western world prior to the Nazis, it was a traditional Native American symbol of well-being and good luck. The Allied capture of Naples was accentuated by refugees who reported that besides sacking the city, the Germans were killing its residents in wanton butchery. We heard reports of them machine-gunning women and children. Italian soldiers and civilians were being forced into slave-labor battalions to dig defenses, with death the penalty for refusal. Italy had signed a treaty with the Allies, but the Germans intended to fight it out and did just that.

On October 5, 1943, Corsica was liberated. The Allies could now slowly fight their way along the roads from Salerno to Naples. It was reported that there were nearly 110,000 casualties in the American Fifth Army alone, while the Germans lost nearly 500,000.

In February 1944, I understood the Germans in Cassino experienced nearly 52,000 incoming Allied artillery shells, and were attacked on the ground by tough Indian mercenary troops from New Zealand. They were described as knife-wielding Gurkhas who were brought in to fight in Italy. They had a reputation as battle-hardened and ruthless fighters. They also had a reputation for carrying a terrible smell with them. The Gurkhas had a custom in battle in which they would cut off the right ear of an enemy they killed. They would then wear this severed ear on a necklace around their necks as a badge of honor. These ears would become many throughout the battles and begin to decompose over time. This would give off the smell that they were known for. The Allies were very happy to have these soldiers fighting with them and not against.

The Germans had dedicated many resources to improving their technology. When a new Nazi weapon was let loose, it became front line news quickly. That February the Germans unveiled a new weapon, a small radio-operated tank that carried a one-thousand-pound explosive charge. It could be remotely driven near a selected target and detonated, causing substantial damage. It proved slow and cumbersome, however, and very vulnerable to our antitank weapons.

In March 1944, Cassino was reduced to rubble under a concentrated aerial bombardment. In the spring of 1944, the Allies increased day and night bombing raids, and targeted just about anything that would slow down the Germans. The enemy moved their troops, artillery, tanks, and supplies mostly during the night. It didn't help, because every move they made was reported to the Allies by the partisans. The Germans had an unbelievable supply of antiaircraft batteries and were unfortunately very often successful in hitting their targets. Downed Allied bombers and fighter planes were scattered all over the European countryside. I happened upon hundreds of downed aircraft throughout the war.

The terrible war went on, but the news and rumors were often good and getting better. What my dad had predicted was happening. The German troops were spread too thin and were now retreating on the Russian front. The Russians captured thousands upon thousands of German prisoners, who would experience the horrific treatment that the retreating Germans had once levied on them. German losses on the Russian front were enormous, and they now recruited all the men they could in Germany as well as in their conquered countries. The Germans lowered the draft age, and boys of occupied countries became immediately expendable to the Nazis upon turning fifteen. Many of the soldiers we killed or captured toward the later years of the war were just scared young boys or unwilling older men.

In the Low Lands of Belgium, a warrior named Major Jim led the FFI. He was a very successful and recognized leader in the F10F Sector III, and was well known as a battle-hardened officer. He commanded acts of sabotage that seriously hurt and delayed the enemy. His Underground Resistance force ambushed and destroyed enemy patrols, which helped us to accumulate weapons and ammunition. The price paid for such accomplishments was very high. Hundreds of his participants were caught and summarily executed.

Mr. Gossens, the same family friend who had rescued me from the Krupp Steel Company by enrolling me in the Red Cross, introduced me to the FFI and Major Jim. My particular branch was part of the F10F Sector III under Major Jim, and was very active in the East and West Flanders of Belgium. Our unit was to ambush and attack enemy patrols, and to sabotage their convoys, railways, and military installations and communications. Most of our weapons were British, plus some German backup weapons that we recovered from attacks or ambush raids. We had to learn and train very quickly. The FFI informed and trained us well, and we were routinely reminded of the consequences should we be caught. We were eager to serve our country and die for this cause, which we all believed to be right and just. The unity among our group was strong, and we felt as though we were playing a role in history. After my job with the railroad, my specific job with the FFI was in explosives and how to use them properly. I learned the ins and outs of plastic explosives, TNT, and Pentolite. The training I received was geared primarily toward sabotage missions, and I developed into a very effective demolition expert. I had already learned to disable German machines with alternative methods. I could cripple trains, trucks, tanks, commanders' cars, motorcycles, etc. with what looked to be an ordinary lubricating grease but was actually a certain abrasive compound that quickly wore out any parts to which it was applied. Always at night, we entered German parking garages or lots that were guarded but too large to be guarded properly. This type of mission required something or someone to cause a distraction for the guards. The typical diversion consisted simply of two attractive girls walking by and starting a conversation with the guards. These girls were Underground Resistance friendlies, so they were putting their lives on the line for the mission. Once the guards were preoccupied, we slid into the lot and applied an abrasive lubricant to u-joints, engine oil, or in brake fluid. This is where our training paid off, as we could apply our special lubricant to a large number of vehicles very quickly and effectively. Our actions were responsible for thousands of disabled Nazi vehicles—we hoped when they needed them most. We intentionally were never around to witness the fruits of our labors.

We always felt that freedom wasn't such a far-fetched idea, and each mission felt like a step in that direction. While we had much success, we were working against a behemoth, and we didn't dare celebrate yet. This period of hope and purpose did bring with it much difficulty. We had to stay alive. The Germans would just as soon shoot you as look at you. The Underground Resistance had begun hearing reports of an upcoming invasion attempt by the Allies. The location and date were kept quiet until the last minute to avoid any potential problems. In preparation for the invasion, the leaders in London had drawn up detailed plans for the Resistance fighters that called for the destruction of the railway systems, cutting off specific roads, sabotaging power stations, and capturing fuel and arms depots. The need to slow German troop movement was imperative for the invasion.

Retribution was part of the German fear-spreading policy. Germans lashed out violently when there was rebellion amongst their empire. The FFI was created with the sole purpose of disrupting the war machine by any means necessary, and thus was directly responsible for thousands upon thousands of civilians being executed as retribution for acts by the FFI. Nazi protocol called for fifty civilians to be executed for each act of sabotage by the Resistance. But, the movement toward the goal of liberation would never be allowed to slow or stop, no matter what the cost. Each member of the FFI knew this consequence up front and still never questioned his or her motives. When we lost a brother, we used this loss as further motivation and as reminder that our liberation would cost lives and sacrifices.

Meanwhile, daily and nightly, hundreds upon hundreds of Allied bombers attacked Germany's main cities and industrial centers. The destruction was increasingly massive. The Americans bombed by day and the British by night. We noticed, however, that the bombing raids intensified at the beginning of June. We witnessed the increase in aerial activity and knew it was preparation for something big.

We gathered around our illicit radios to listen to messages from the BBC.

Finally, on the evening of June 5, the French language services sent out a series of sentences, meaningless to the Germans, that were in fact messages directing specific resistance groups to prepare for the invasion. In Normandy, Resistance fighters felled large trees across roads to impede the Nazis. Bridges and lock gates on canals were exploded, and trains careened off the blown rails. The Resistance planned over one thousand railway cuts. The SOE dropped additional equipment such as weapons, explosives, ammunition, and some food, and often SOE agents were dropped off or parachuted by the British Moon Squadron.

As a result of these events, there was mass confusion in the German ranks. The Underground destroyed large areas of the main roads and made them impassable. Easy methods of communication had been interrupted, supplies delayed or destroyed, troops rerouted and sooner or later derailed. The Nazis were feeling the impacts of our efforts and the anticipation of the Allied invasion made many of them begin to question their German strength.

During the months leading up to D-day, I was in Langerbrugge, which was a small town located a few miles Northwest of Ghent harbor. We noticed a large number of German troops loading up and moving out in haste. On June 6, there were several German navy ships in the harbor that were attacked furiously and repeatedly by low-flying Allied planes. I couldn't see what was going on from where I was, but could tell the planes were British. The manner in which they flew suggested they weren't on the defensive, either. Later in the day, we found out what all the commotion was about. It was D-day! We could feel freedom around the corner. We felt a renewed hope and determination to see victory. The word spread like wildfire and gave every man extra energy and vigor. Every step we took now held more value and weight. We each wanted to do all we could to assist the cause.

My witness to D-day, when the Allies landed in Normandy, was limited only to Langerbrugge with the FFI. We were aware the Allies would land someday and somewhere in France, and the liberation from the German occupation would start. We also knew a lot of good men would die for our freedom—my thoughts were constantly with them because I knew the hell they would be going through.

D-day Cometh

In England it was 0930 hours. General Eisenhower had paced the floor all night waiting for each new report to come in. There was no doubt now that a foothold had been achieved on the Continent. Although the hold was slight, there would be no need to release the message that he had quietly scribbled just twenty-four hours before.

In case the Allied attempt was defeated, Eisenhower had written: "Our landings in the Cherbourg—Havre area have failed to gain a satisfactory foothold and I have withdrawn the troops. My decision to attack at this time and place was based upon the best information available. The troops, the air and the Navy did all that bravery and devotion to duty could do. If there is any blame or fault attached to the attempt, it is mine alone." Instead, at 0933 hrs (0333 hrs. New York time), a far different message was broadcast to the world. It read: "Under the command of General Eisenhower, Allied naval forces, supported by strong air forces, began landing Allied armies this morning on the northern coast of France."[1]

At 1015 hours, the phone rang in Field Marshal Rommel's home in Herrlingen, Germany. The caller was his chief of staff. The purpose: the first complete briefing on the invasion. Rommel listened with a sinking heart. It was the day he had been waiting for. The one he had said would be "the longest day." Although there would be months of fighting, it was clear to Rommel that the game was up. It was only mid-morning, yet the longest day was all but over. By an irony of fate, the great German general had been on the sidelines during this decisive battle of the war. All Rommel could say when his chief of staff had finished was, "How stupid of me! . . . How stupid of me!"[2]

By nightfall on June 6 there were 150,000 Allied troops ashore on the European mainland and thousands more on their way. It was the beginning of the end of World War II; Germany would capitulate in less than a year. Those who fought on the beaches of France that day changed the course of nations. For some 4,400 American, British, and Canadian servicemen, this day of terrible glory would be their last. The number of casualties of Germans is sketchy at best, but records indicate that between four thousand and nine thousand Germans died during the invasion.

The much-vaunted Atlantic Wall, which Hitler had believed to be a masterpiece, was crumbling before them. The beachhead was only five days old when the Allies established their own air bases there, alleviating the necessity of bringing planes across the Channel from Britain. The battles in Normandy grew fierce, because German resistance was growing in direct ratio to the Allied successes.

While the landing in Normandy was taking place, in hundreds of villages and cities patriot forces were rising against their oppressors. Every success of the Underground Forces or FFI was a gain for the Allies, and even though it took place hundreds of miles from the official front, they were all part of a great battle for the liberation of Europe. Deportations and executions of many suspected Belgian patriots had been shrinking our force of fighting men, and those left were few indeed, fighting against the mass of the German Army with all of its fine modern equipment. But the FFI had one thing the Germans could not match: a real cause worth fighting for.

As the war progressed, food shortages caused widespread starvation for the civilian population. The destruction worsened due to daily bombing. In their retreat, the German artillery torched most cities with incendiary shells, and in some towns, the main roads were closed and accessible only to the retreating army. There were checkpoints on every road leading in and out of the towns.

The Germans were very well aware of the underground fighters' resolution and knew the patriots would never give up or surrender. The enemy was clever, suspicious, and relentlessly searching for us. A lot of the ambushes we carried out were silently executed with knives, hatchets, and strangulation in a determined effort to stay quiet. We also had a good network of communication that kept us well informed and busy.

On June 26, 1944, the radio announced the capture of the Port of Cherbourg, and the Allies turned their efforts to other sectors of the Normandy front. The BBC announced that the mighty Russian forces on the Eastern Front of Europe were driving the Germans back in retreat. The Allied armies in Italy were closing in on the Germans from the Southern Front.

Hitler, who had feared a two-front war, was now in the giant nutcracker of a three-front war. In desperation, ten days after the first invasion in Normandy, Hitler hurled his long-heralded secret weapon from hidden launching sites in France and the low countries of Belgium and Holland. German Buzz bombs and V-2 missiles rained on London and landed on our cities anywhere and at anytime and without warning.

In July 1944 the French cities of Caen and St.Lô fell to the Allies, and in effect decided the fate of the Germans in France. On August 25, 1944, Paris was liberated. What an exciting time for the French and the Allies! Hitler had given the orders to blow up and burn every government and historical building, every museum, church, subway, and bridge. The Eiffel tower also was to be destroyed. These orders remarkably couldn't be carried out because of the swiftness of the Allies. What the world would have lost had the Allies arrived later!

Freedom was indeed around the corner. We knew the Allies were gaining and approaching our Belgian borders. Our field telephones and radios kept us informed of the battles and the Allied progress toward key cities and harbors like Carentan, Isigny, Montebourg, St. Lô, and Caen. All sources reported the German losses were enormous as they retreated from France and Italy.

One problem we faced on a daily basis was wear and tear on our equipment. In battle, our boots were our most prized possession, even though they were worn through and caused the most problems. A common practice on the battlefield was to acquire better gear when the opportunity presented itself. An opportunity presented itself with each enemy we killed. The Germans were known to have superior clothing and weaponry for battle. My FFI uniform consisted of what I had brought from home. Our FFI-issued boots were nothing more than laced-up work shoes made from rawhide. These shoes were causing many of us problems. They would never stay dry in our environment and thus created thousands of cases of trench foot and frostbite.

Trench foot is a painful condition caused by prolonged exposure of the feet to damp, unsanitary, and cold conditions, which if left untreated, leads to gangrene. I had been in need of boots for a while when I happened upon a dead German with the same size foot as myself. Knowing he would not be in need of them anymore, I borrowed his nice dry boots and likely saved my feet. Shortly thereafter I replaced my thin and worn jacket with a German-issued replacement, which incidentally was much easier than finding matching foot sizes. I had to be extra vigilant when not with my squad, as I could easily have been mistaken for a Nazi. I had removed the badges and medals to help avoid potential confusion. The Nazi soldier who had previously worn my coat had been shot in the chest several times, so my jacket came sporting a few holes in the chest. We soldiers were always looking for a way to stay dry and warm, and borrowing from the enemy wasn't a crazy notion. This included weapons when ours became disabled.

Several weeks later, while a few of us were on a mission in the border town of Menen, we began to see faint flashes and hear distant explosions from artillery attacks and bombings. We knew the Allies were approaching the border and us. We also realized that we were in the middle of an ongoing battle. Usually, when we completed a mission, we hid ourselves in preselected safe barns, homes, or hedgerows, while we waited for instructions from headquarters. We very often had the assistance of Belgian patriots who were overjoyed to help us hide. This day we had lost communication with our unit; the previous day we had lost two underground fighters and our field phone when a hand grenade hit them. We had alternative plans but still needed specific instructions and information before we moved. Until we figured what to do next, we decided to hide in the patriot's old barn for the night. Next day, one of us would slip out to connect with our unit. However, according to our guard, around 0200 hours, enemy troops arrived at the farm and immediately overtook the farmhouse. They parked their tanks and vehicles under the trees for cover. They kept us awake all night with their continuous communication jabber and by running the tank engines in rotation to charge up the batteries and save fuel.

In the morning we searched for a way out and realized we weren't going anywhere for a while. We learned quickly of our precarious predicament. We were surrounded by an SS Mechanized Panzer Battalion, which included tanks, artillery, and numerous trucks with plenty of infantry. They combed the grounds and entered the barn in search of clues that would surely give us away. We had hidden in the second-story loft of the barn, but as the Nazis inspected the barn we overheard them wondering aloud about a ladder to the loft, which we had pulled up with us. They made plans to retrieve one as they stabbed the hay bales with their bayonets and checked every corner and angle of the ground floor, postponing their search of the inaccessible loft.

By their remarks we knew these soldiers were very upset about our sabotage, where we mined the roads, installed booby traps, blew up the rails, and messed up their communications. The soldiers outside were so close to the barn that most of the time we could hear every word of what they were saying.

We needed a way out: five of us were pinned down with no escape apparent. We couldn't move north, east, or west, or we would surely run into German troops, supposing we escaped from the barn perch. The only chance, we decided, was running south toward the French-Belgian border. We were cut off from our unit, practically out of explosives, ammunition, and food, and had very little water. Our best bet was to stay hidden until the Allies hopefully approached close enough, and make a run for it. Our days-old intelligence told us that the Allies were headed north in our general direction. We needed that to still be true. We left our backpacks and unloaded tools, lunch kits, blankets, and anything that wasn't absolutely necessary. We did not leave our Sten guns with extra clips. For backup, I took my 9 mm. Luger pistol, my combat knife, and four hand grenades. Our southerly escape route would not be an easy one.

There was no right time to run through a wide strip of pasture covered with mines and barbed wire, which was referred to as no-man's-land. We knew the SS could easily pick us off as we escaped, but couldn't just run because we needed to pay attention to the mines, avoid trip wires, and find a way through the barbed wire. We stayed in that hideout and listened for sounds of the Allied artillery and infantry fire. We couldn't stay hidden in the barn much longer, because some SS moved in during the night to the southwest part of the barn, also waiting for the Allies. Before daylight we gently lowered the ladder, quietly eased down and crawled away from the barn through a ditch. We knew the Allies were close when the nearby SS artillery and tanks opened fire on them. We had to take advantage of the confusion to move or face our enemy up close. We waited for the hand signal from our point man and fanned out toward the Allies. The Germans opened fire on us as soon as we cleared the barn. We ran as hard as a human knows how to put some distance between that barn and us. We gave the Germans five moving targets to shoot at. I guess we surprised them when we threw our hand grenades at them and returned fire while running, jumping, rolling, and crawling through the barbed wire, mine, and trip wire obstacles. After several minutes of running, the Allies began to return covering fire. We were caught in the crossfire and felt the tracers, the bullets and pieces of shrapnel, rocks and dirt flying all around us. When we got to within one hundred yards of the Allied tanks and infantry that were approaching, we noticed something. A soldier walking next to a Sherman tank was talking on a field telephone and signaled us to hit the ground, which we did. I guess we were in their line of fire. Once the Allies had a clear shot at the enemy, all hell broke loose. The tanks were coming straight at us followed by the infantry. What a sight! It was actually happening right on top of us! The firing by the German contingent was indescribably loud and furious. When the tanks passed us, being exhausted, we stayed on the ground until ordered to get up. Several men screamed orders at us in German "Hande Hauf!" (Hands up!). We looked around and took count; only three of us survived. Of the three, one of my friends had been hit and was in serious condition. He was taken to the field hospital where he died that same night. We didn't think we could make it, but two of us made it with cuts, bruises, and many shrapnel injuries. I had survived once again, but barely.

The incoming Allied force spoke German because they knew we couldn't speak Polish. Besides, I was wearing the same pair of borrowed German boots and a German leather jacket that I borrowed from that dead enemy. The soldiers we met were not British, but were from the Sixty-Ninth Polish Armored Division fighting under British command. They spoke German well, which made it possible to communicate with them. They were not surprised when we told them we were Belgian FFI fighters, because they rescued several French FFI Maquisards in a similar predicament. We were questioned briefly and went to the nearest field infirmary where they took care of our cuts and bruises. One piece of shrapnel injured my left elbow, but the bone and the tendons were not damaged. I had a nasty burn caused by the heat of the shrapnel. After it was cleaned and dressed, the corporal escorting us asked what we were planning on doing. We explained that we had been separated from our dwindling unit and now, considering the circumstance we found ourselves in, asked if we could merge with his force. He chuckled at our eagerness. He said he liked us Belgians and that we were welcome to fight alongside them. He after all needed some men to assist with the locals and their dialect. The corporal sent out word to locate our missing unit and to bring them in alongside them. He asked about the severity of our wounds. We assured him that we were fine but were in dire need of water. He knew we were also hungry, dirty, and tired, but recognized that our spirits were high. We were ready to continue the fight because we were now part of the liberation and finally with the Allies! Unfortunately, only two of us made it through that dash through no-man's land.

My unit was never ófficially located, but I learned later on they joined up with a Canadian force entering Belgium. The fighting went on with the Panzer Battalion during the course of the night. The rifle fire slowed as night fell, but before sunrise the battle started all over again. Finally, after a day and a half, the Germans retreated as our much larger force drove them out. We were cleared by the Allies and treated with respect and care. A Polish tank commander handed us what looked like a large sandwich, but it was more than a sandwich. It was a thick and tender grilled steak between two thick slices of buttered toast! I don't know how and where he got such an incredible gift, but I never had a sandwich like that one again! We ate it while moving on, but it was a nice change from our K-Rations, stolen raw eggs from chicken coops, raw vegetables taken off the field, or German field rations taken off dead soldiers.

When the British and Canadians captured the French town of Abbeville from the Germans, the massive Allied armies crossed the border of Belgium at Hirson on September 2, 1944. The Americans entered the Belgian towns of Mons and Namur, while the British approached from Tournai. The goal was to work the Allied forces into the outskirts of Brussels, the capital of Belgium. I moved on and fought with the Polish Army toward the north part of the Flanders. I helped by translating information from the Flemish population that spoke Flemish only. The locals were able to share solid intelligence from their days with the Nazis. We entered the town of Kortrijk, where for a couple of days we ran into strong opposition. We finally pushed the Germans out and moved to the town of Isegem next. The Nazis fought as though they would never surrender, but luckily we were now equipped to kill every last one of them. The enemy hated to retreat and never seemed to give up, and we very seldom overtook a block or a street without having to fight hard for it. In their retreat, the Germans mined and booby-trapped everything. We had to deactivate mines, clear roads, houses, buildings, and deal with every dirty trick left behind by the fleeing Huns. We liberated several small towns and their neighboring farms, which had been abandoned. The animals we discovered on these farms had not been fed or watered in months. We were witness to grotesque scenes of malnutrition and starvation. When we could, we tried to locate water or food for them. These suffering animals received whatever help we could muster, but there simply wasn't adequate help available. It was difficult to witness their situation, but regardless, we held a much higher regard for these animals than we did for our Nazi counterparts.

My newly joined fighting force consisted of a small group of multinational people coupled with the larger Polish Army. We approached the town of Deinze, a province in East Flanders, and received strong machine-gun fire from several fortified concrete bunkers located on a nearby farm. We couldn't tell how many, but they sure made a racket and fired constantly. We had cleared the town fairly easily, but this ordinary farm was defended by what seemed like a handful of Germans with machine guns that included my least favorite, the MG-42. The MG-42 was also known as Hitler's Buzz Saw, which spit out a tremendous twelve hundred rounds per minute. We went back and forth with them for over an hour and finally silenced most of them with mortar fire and a few of our own hand grenades, but one Nazi proved especially hard to kill and kept returning fire. He seemed to be in full panic mode, shooting everywhere in the hopes his bullets would hit us or scare us away. We finally landed a grenade in his vicinity and took him down. He had made his last stand at the edge of a large bomb crater, in which we found another injured SS officer holding an empty Luger in one hand and his guts with the other. He wasn't going anywhere but was still alive and strong enough to curse us. Nearby lay a young dead Hitler Youth gunner who had been hit twice in the head. We interrogated the mortally wounded SS officer and asked if that young boy had been ordered to protect him, to which he yelled back that it was his duty to do so. So I replied that it was my duty to cripple him some more and raised my pistol and fired a shot into his shoulder. He screamed out in pain. I then reached down and ripped off one of his many medals that read "Für Schliesien," after the Battle of Schliesien for which he was awarded for his bravery. I explained to him in German that he wasn't going to mislead young boys anymore. He was very vocal and cursed us on and on. He told us that we don't know what's coming for us. He concluded what would be his final words by telling us that we were all going to die. A Polish soldier then shot him in the other shoulder followed by the knee. We left him there in agonizing pain. Someone finally killed him minutes later just to shut him up. We checked the other four SS gunners and took one medal and the Luger pistol from the SS officer as souvenirs.

I couldn't believe that I had survived all the horrors still in one piece and that it now seemed likely I would make it back home. I happily learned that the Polish army I was fighting with would be heading toward my hometown as it continued toward Germany. As we worked our way toward Ghent, we were approached by many of the newly liberated locals who continued to ask us if we were the ones who liberated them. They were in search of someone to hug and thank. They had waited a long time for this day, and they would not be denied this celebration. We certainly welcomed their affection. My hometown Ghent was finally in sight, and although much of it lay in smoldering ruins, seeing it still brought a sense of relief. I hadn't been back in nearly two years. Polish, Canadians, and British fought their way toward my hometown, which was finally liberated by our Polish Army on the southwest side, followed by the Canadians and the British on the southeast part. Civilians poured out to greet us with absolute joy and tears of happiness. Every person who was able came out to confirm that it was real. They told us that the Germans evacuated a few hours before we arrived. The people of my hometown appeared near starvation when we moved in and were physically worn out by the period of occupation, but they mustered a joyous celebration at our arrival. I still had a job to do, but I desperately wanted to see my parents and make sure they had survived.

While I was talking with civilians getting information, Sergeant Vitol Komar from my adopted Polish army came by in his jeep and asked if we were close to my home. He said we could check it. I took him up on his offer and we headed off through a town that showed vast destruction. We made it to my street not knowing what to expect. The anticipation of seeing the house was incredible. Then there it was! Our home was slightly damaged by an artillery shell that angled through our roof and exploded in the neighbor's house. The neighbor luckily wasn't home when it happened. My home remained intact, as did the front door, to which I still had a key. I walked to the door with trepidation and pushed the key into the lock. As I turned the key and entered, my small snow-white pet wolf was first to meet me. She didn't seem to recognize me due to my extended absence and thus barked ferociously at me. I noticed the empty German cots lying everywhere in the entryway. I rushed in and found Mom and Dad sitting startled in the kitchen. I had totally surprised them. My mother burst into tears upon seeing my face and we exchanged hugs for a good while. Dad's face was lit up with joy to see me as well. Arm in arm, we checked the rest of the house. My parents were very happy to see me alive. It was so good to be home! On that afternoon, to my surprise, my sister came home under bodyguard escort. She also was in the FFI, and had worked in downtown Ghent in the secret Underground Resistance office for the past two years. This was all complete news to me. Our reunion was heartfelt and joyous in the highest order. My family was now free! Unbeknownst to me, Lucienne had been secretary to Major Jim, who had commanded my underground unit. I stayed around town for a couple of days checking on friends and family. We lost several members of my family, we would learn, including my cousin Suzanne who had helped stranded Allied pilots make their way back to England. When these pilots were shot down or crashed, her group would assist them in an underground railway of sorts to escape capture and get home. Once the pilots made it to the ocean, the English used speedboats and fishing vessels to transport them across the English Channel. Suzanne was arrested by the Gestapo after she was discovered hiding one of these survivors and jailed for her Resistance efforts. She was badly abused by the Gestapo and German Police there. We learned later that she was transferred to the well-known death camp of Auschwitz. She was hand-selected for experimentation by Auschwitz's resident devil, the Nazi physician, Dr. Josef Mengele. Dr. Mengele used Suzanne and many others for his personal experiments. He and his cohorts surgically removed Suzanne's breasts and reproductive organs without the use of anesthetic. Mengele wanted to see how these women survived after these sadistic surgeries. She understandably did not survive these horrors, as our family was made aware after the war through extensive notes left behind by Mengele. My other cousins Gustave and Theo had been arrested and executed for activities related to the Belgian underground. Gustave had been a captain in the Belgian Army. Our family also gained a few new members during the war by the special miracle of birth and survival during Nazi occupation.

After the Allied armies liberated Ghent and the civilians had time to acclimate themselves to their newfound freedom, we began to organize much useful intelligence. The people were more than willing to share any and all information they thought could assist us. We located a few Nazi leftovers this way. A few days after liberation, we were led to a group of children who told us a story about smelling food and seeing smoke in the large park in Ghent. The Polish squad, including myself, immediately drove to the park to investigate.

My sister Lucienne, 1945

As the kids had described, we searched and discovered a large underground bunker with air vents protruding through the ground. There was no smoke at that moment but upon closer inspection, we could hear the unmistakable sound of Germans speaking below ground. We didn't know why these Germans remained when their entire force had retreated days earlier. I, being the only German speaker in our immediate squad, began by banging on the air vents. In German, I screamed down the air vent that we had liberated the town of Ghent and they were ordered to drop their weapons and come to the surface immediately. To this, they made no reply. On second command, I told them that if they did not surrender immediately we would pour gasoline down the air vents and burn them out. A Polish soldier then grabbed a gas can off the back of a jeep and began pouring it down the air vent. He then used his Zippo lighter and lit the gasoline on fire. Shortly thereafter, a door in the earth burst open and out scrambled two dozen screaming and scared German soldiers with hands raised high. After listening to them explain, I learned that they knew of the German retreat from Ghent but their orders were to remain in the bunker and await further instructions. Those orders obviously never came. They were taken into custody by our men and marched away from all the civilian traffic that had gathered during this incident. I did not accompany them and learned later that they were all shot at the far end of the park.

I received permission from my unit to have a couple of days off in Ghent. I needed to spend some time with my family. My parents invited two Polish soldiers and three Canadians to stay with them, and we had a great time celebrating together. Dad had some fine wine left in his cellar after the Germans had picked over what they wanted, which helped the lively international party in French, English, German, and Flemish conversations. The British and Canadians stayed with us for a while and made good use of our cots in the downstairs hall and entrance. It was good to be with them for that short while.

We had a great time relaxing, but unfortunately a couple of days later the celebration was over and our orders called us back to action. I was satisfied with my family's condition, so I left my comfort zone to get back into the Allied effort. The last night, the Canadian Signal Band gave a surprise concert celebration at the Music Hall in downtown Ghent.

The Belgian population went wild when liberated. It was a great moment for all. There was a mixture of nationalities present in our towns and homes. The American, British, Canadian, and Belgian flags were flying everywhere. The restaurants didn't have much to offer, but cafés, bars, pubs, and civilians opened their doors and most of the population opened their homes to the Allied troops. Able-bodied citizens pooled their resources and cooked meals for the soldiers with the little food they could find. The gesture was more than enough for any of us. They welcomed the troops with the sincerest gratitude, which nearly always ended with tears and hugs. This was a moment of tremendous joy for me.

In their retreat, the Germans left a hidden battlefield surprise that caused the Allies a tremendous hardship. A new breed of sharp shooters, a group that had originated from Himmler himself called Wehrwolfs, were scattered throughout Germany's liberated lands to keep us from ever feeling secure. As per Himmler's orders, the Wehrwolfs stayed behind and hunted us with orders to kill as many as possible until they themselves were killed. They hid in the ruins of abandoned buildings and on rooftops, firing with great accuracy from their hidden perches. Wehrwolfs sought to kill officers and other high-ranking military, but often killed civilians just to instill fear among us. If we found them, they were executed without mercy. These were diehard Nazis who faced sure death staying behind the retreat to kill as many strategic targets as possible. For this reason, even in liberated lands, we never let our guard down, ever. In our postwar movements we were constantly on guard against these suicide soldiers.

The liberation of Belgium was a milestone victory, but the battle was far from over. The northern part of Belgium was still held by the Nazis, and we could hear the artillery firing to the north. The Nazis still had ample supplies in the harbor of Antwerp and were trying to save it from the Allies. The Allies were having difficulties clearing and taking the harbor, which was of vital importance. The harbor in Ghent had been liberated, however, and ships and dock workers were working hard to get us needed supplies. Nevertheless, Antwerp Harbor was a much more critical asset that significantly aided whoever controlled it. Regaining this harbor was an "at all costs" directive.

The Poles left a small party behind in Ghent to get the railroads up and running, as they needed train transportation to get supplies to Holland for their next major offensive. I remained in Ghent with them and with the American forces working in that harbor. The majority of the Polish force headed to Antwerp, and a large contingent of Belgian Underground Resistance fighters was assisting the Polish Army in this endeavor. This is a fact that is rarely talked about in history books. The Belgians knew how critical it was to the Allied plans to liberate this installation. "Possession of this port, if usable, would solve our logistic problems for the entire northern half of the front," explained General Eisenhower. But the Germans had vowed to destroy Antwerp before leaving it. Preparing to carry out that pledge, they filled five ships with explosives and tied the vessels to Antwerp's docks or quays and awaited the order.[3] If carried out, this order would have rendered Antwerp harbor unusable for the foreseeable future.

Without the SOE coaching, the Belgian Resistance, fully aware of what the Germans were up to, took countermeasures, and some six hundred Freedom Fighters, divided into six assault companies, took the opportunity to secure the Antwerp Harbor. On September 3, 1944, as the Allies came within sight of Antwerp, the Resistance struck hard and made a contribution beyond price.

By September 6 they had taken the Bonaparte, Kattendijk, and Boyers Basins, along with two bridges on the Albert Canal. Antwerp's great harbor and all its installations were delivered to the Allies in working order and almost intact, which allowed the Allied Forces to unload their logistics and pursue the battles.

This event often gets left out of history books. The harbor at Antwerp was a major reason the Allied front was reinforced and was able to advance into Germany.

We were continually assaulted by many V-1 and V-2 missiles that caused a substantial amount of damage. The big danger was the possibility that one of those missiles would hit an ammunition ship in the harbor, which would have caused a chain reaction and a terrible inferno, with military and civilian casualties and massive destruction. Luckily, that didn't happen.

The official history, which mostly omits the Belgian Resistance Fighters' participation in the clearing of Antwerp harbor, recorded that the Polish forces moved into Antwerp, where the Germans forced hundreds of civilians to stand in front of them as a human shield. This cowardly act was used often to slow the Allied advance when the Nazis were pinned down. They knew the Allies wouldn't attack under those conditions. The Polish army began to work around to the sides so they wouldn't hit the civilian shield. They slowly encircled the Nazis and began to tighten the noose. Polish rifles picked the Germans off one by one as they worked toward the middle. The Poles succeeded in destroying most of the German positions without hitting the civilians out front. The infantry slowly crushed the outnumbered Germans and destroyed the enemy's positions as patiently as soldiers know how. The Poles liberated the area with minimum civilian casualties. Since they had no desire to capture the Nazis, every one of them was shot and killed. It took four days of continuous and strategic fighting to accomplish this successfully. This Polish victory was a significant event and greatly sped up the Allies' ability to move into Germany, but their effort unquestionably was benefited in a major way by the Underground Resistance working alongside them.

The Germans were forced out of Flanders, but the fighting lingered on for a few more weeks. German V-1 and V-2 rockets exploded daily in and around our newly liberated towns, and we still had a few of the remaining Wehrwolf snipers to deal with.

As the enemy retreated we witnessed several vigilantes, calling themselves patriots, taking acts of retribution against suspected traitors and collaborators. The lack of any police empowered these vigilante groups, and they had a field day dealing with those they designated as traitors. The executions were brutal and without legal justification. These turkey shoots went on day and night. A few Nazi collaborators tried to buy their way out, but they ultimately faced a public hanging. Hate and revenge were out of control as the carnage went on. Women suspected of collaborating or sleeping with enemy soldiers had their heads shaved and tarred if they were lucky. Collaborators' homes were marked with a large swastika or terrible words. These street vigilantes would often tell people they were part of the Underground Resistance in an effort to validate their revenge killing. For two weeks I was on my own with no official military or country that would claim me. I moved around the city with several other men who hadn't yet found a belonging. I was without command or authority, but my mission was still certain. I would never stop fighting the Nazis as long as there was breath in my lungs. As our small group wandered Ghent, we would find the victims of these vigilantes. We witnessed bodies hanging from trees and light poles or just lying in the street. There weren't nearly enough soldiers to stop it or deter it. This vigilante justice continued until the American Army came in much later and restored law and order.

Part of the Job

After many battles, the unwilling participants who suffered the most were the women and children caught in the middle of the battle zone. Dozens of times I happened upon a situation where women and children were trapped beneath the rubble of a bombed-out building or levee. The compromised levees were especially difficult, as children often got caught in situations where they were at risk of drowning. I had learned to carry a rope that I used to pull many of these children to safety. Quite frequently I would see one of my fellow Allies helping to rescue a woman or child from certain death as we worked our way toward Germany. It was all part of our job, and was among many characteristics that separated us from our enemy. But we did come across many children in Hitler Youth uniforms trapped in perilous situations who received no help from me or other Allies.

The Army

I tried to maintain fighting with the Polish Sixty-Ninth, but there was no way I could convince the Polish commander to let me continue with them as a volunteer. He said they were under British orders and couldn't authorize it. The commander thanked me for the past battles I fought with them, but because of the British command, he had to let us Belgians go. I was told the United States Army was accepting civilian laborers, and so I was introduced to a Lieutenant Miller, who was handling the hiring of civilian workers. He told me they were having trouble communicating with the Flemish dock laborers. English was completely foreign to them, and there was no way Flemish Walloon would be understood by the Americans. I showed Lieutenant Miller that I could help solve that problem if he hired me as an interpreter. I explained that I was educated in four languages and had been a combat interpreter and combat soldier in the Polish Sixty-Ninth Division.

I volunteered to question prisoners and translate their information. I wanted to join the American Army and continue to the heart of Germany. Lieutenant Miller told me that joining the US Army was impossible. However, he took me to see Commander Captain Clark on the off chance he'd allow me in. He wouldn't hear of it and quickly dismissed me. Lieutenant Miller then took me to City of Ghent Acting Manager Col. Joseph Jenkins, who was a big six-foot-seven-inch Texan. The colonel said he didn't want to take the responsibility, but Lieutenant Miller insisted, and asked the colonel to give me a chance as an interpreter or guide. Colonel Jenkins asked the lieutenant if I could speak English well enough, to which the lieutenant said, "Affirmative, sir!" Colonel Jenkins then told Lieutenant Miller to give me a *Yank* Magazine and have me read something loud enough for him to hear me in the next room. I read it loudly with my French accent and after reading a few sentences the colonel hollered: "Alright, Okay, I didn't understand a damn thing he read, but if you think you can use him let's get him on board, but he is your responsibility!" The colonel added I would be paid as a US Civil Service Employee from petty cash and would be considered a mercenary soldier until other arrangements could be made.

I immediately reported to a Major Wilson who said my job was to translate and guide. My direct boss was Sergeant Fortuna, who showed me around and took me wherever I was needed. For several weeks, I translated English into Flemish and Flemish into English. Considering that the war was going on, it was a very easy job to have.

Toward the end of the week, Lieutenant Miller took me to supplies to fit me with an appropriate uniform and combat boots. I drove a jeep and was now a Belgian Patriot and mercenary soldier serving alongside the US Army. I felt a real sense of purpose and belonging. My uniform had a small patch with the words *Belgium* identifying me as a foreign soldier.

Hundreds of American Liberty and Victory Class ships docked in Ghent harbor unloading their cargo of military supplies, which were badly needed at the front line. The American officer's English and the Belgian dockhand's Flemish created a significant hurdle in the work detail. Many problems couldn't be solved unless someone translated. I made myself very available to both sides and thus a very useful mercenary, in a different sense from the usual. There was an overwhelming amount of supplies to be transported by rail and trucks from those ships. I loved the job, which carried a bonus—I ate onboard the navy ships, which had quite amazing food. The naval menu consisted of the best fish, chicken, and beef served with fresh vegetables seasoned perfectly. I had grown tired of eating raw vegetables straight out of the ground, so anything cooked was an improvement.

As a kid, my dream had been to become a naval officer on a large ship and this experience, while not my dream, was certainly a welcome one. The American supply and transportation ships of the Liberty class and the much

Working with the Allies

larger Victory class were modern, new, and reeked of firepower. One could not help but feel the spirit of a military force that had no intention of losing.

Ghent harbor kept the supplies moving toward the front lines. Ammunition and food were paramount for a successful war effort, but gasoline was easily the most precious resource for a victory.

Red Ball Express

With the liberation of Antwerp Harbor, the activity soon slowed down in Ghent and soon their operations would move out toward Germany. I had no intention of being left behind, and in the beginning of December 1944, I asked Major Wilson, who was the commanding officer in Ghent, if I could be transferred to General Courtney Hodges's First Army. He agreed, made a few phone calls, signed the transfer, and told me to report to Major Brown in Vielsalm. I hitched a ride with the Red Ball Express, which was the legendary trucking supply runner for the Allies. I asked to be dropped off in Liége, which was on their way and near the front lines.

The use of a red ball for signaling began as early as the 1800s, with a white flag containing a red ball in the middle, indicating the important ship of a vice admiral. Later, the term *Red Ball* was used by railroads and trucking companies to denote express shipping of perishables.

The French railway system had been destroyed by Allied air power before the D-day invasion to prevent its use by German forces, so until tracks were repaired, trucks were the only way to move supplies. After the liberation of most of Belgium and the race to the Seine River began, there were twenty-eight Allied divisions in the field. Each of these required about 750 tons of supplies per day for offensive operations. At its peak, the remarkably successful Red Ball Express included nearly 6,000 trucks barreling along narrow French highways that had been turned into one-way thoroughfares from which civilian traffic was barred. These roads made a loop from the Allies' forward base at Chartres back to Cherbourg. Drivers—about 75 percent of them African American—were selected from among able-bodied soldiers not critical to the current Allied offensive; in the segregated US Army, black soldiers were assigned to non-combat duties. Some of them had never driven a truck, but were given an hour's instruction and sent into action. They manned the trucks in twos, driving nearly round-the-clock without headlights, one perhaps sleeping while the other drove, although rare attacks by a now very weakened Luftwaffe and by German ground forces may have made sleep hard to come by. The slow-moving convoys were prime targets, but German attacks probably weren't the biggest problem for the Red Ball Express: driver fatigue and field maintenance on the overburdened trucks proved to be bigger issues.

I really didn't know much about the black drivers but got along fine with them. I must admit that occasionally we didn't understand one another because of our language barrier, or perhaps it was my French accent. I had been a valuable member of the Allied force because of my ability to understand many languages, but many funny conversations took place while a Red Ball Express truck driver and I were in the front seat together. We always found a way to explain what we meant and worked it out with a good laugh.

These drivers decided to call me "Frenchy." I told them I wasn't French, but they insisted on it. They protected me and treated me like I was an ally. Time permitting, on a long drive they told me some stories about their families, their country, towns, and history. They had a pleasant way about them and sang beautiful songs that they called soul songs or the blues. Most of them were very religious and talked or sang songs about God and Jesus Christ.

The Red Ball Express trucks were on the road around the clock, and the drivers pressed on without fear or rest. The enemy had the roads and bridges mapped out to the nearest detail, and often, as trucks approached the east part of Belgium also known as Wallonie, the Nazi spotters shared our location. Being close to the front line took guts when you were driving a large truck full of supplies. Nazi artillery shelled the supply trucks constantly, and unfortunately, sometimes accurately. German Wehrwolf snipers aggravated the situation by always trying to kill the drivers. I had the opportunity to ride many times with the Red Ball drivers, and my appreciation for them always grew stronger. I felt very close to these brave men who risked so much and usually never fired a shot. The Red Ball Express was instituted to bring supplies to front line troops. For every gallon of fuel that reached the front line near the Belgian border, five gallons of fuel had been expended delivering it—but it had to be done. When the supply chain was interrupted and supplies, mainly fuel, could not be delivered, major offensives had to be halted by the Allies.

The country of Belgium looked like a big battleground. As I traveled east, I saw many towns that had suffered extensive damage. The battles always took their toll, and as the Germans retreated they tried to lay waste to what remained standing, often leaving little of use. The land was littered with wrecked tanks, trucks, artillery, planes, weapons, supplies, and hundreds of bodies and animals. There was widespread destruction in just about every city and town. Civilians were trapped in this hellish situation and fought valiantly to survive.

American Army

I was dropped off with the First US Army on the northeast of Bastogne, near the German border. The First Army, the oldest field army in the United States Army, had entered the war through the beaches on D-day. A sergeant took me to Major Brown, who was very busy and told me to get a cup of coffee and wait. When he got off the phone, he summoned me and said Major Wilson told him how much help I had been, and said he had the same problems as Wilson. His interpreters knew some French, but information delivered in this

Walloon language caused more problems than it solved. He handed me a folder dealing with Army versus civilian matters and said that he figured out roughly what they wrote, but that some portions were not clear. He also told me he didn't have prisoners at the time and wasn't planning on taking any. However, when the time came, he could always use another rifle. I answered him that this was what I came here for: "To kick ass big time!" He had a good laugh about that and said, "You're speaking my language, Frenchy!" Apparently, my moniker traveled with me. This was one of two Major Browns that I served under during the war. This particular Major Brown had been badly injured in a recent battle and required a steady regimen of morphine. I learned he died shortly after I met him due to a morphine overdose.

German forces remained in control of several major ports on the Channel coast until May 1945; those ports that did fall to the Allies in 1944 had been sabotaged to prevent their immediate use by the Allies. The mangled French railroads, bombed and sabotaged to hamper the Germans, now stymied Allied movements, requiring days of labor to repair tracks and bridges.

Generals Montgomery, Bradley, and Patton each vied to make supply shipments to his own army a priority, but Eisenhower, whose ultimate goal at this point was to capture the industrial heart of Germany in the Ruhr area, prioritized shipments to Montgomery's northern forces.

It is of note that General Montgomery and General Patton had a horrid dislike for one another. Patton's confidence is legendary, and he fought constantly against Montgomery to get what his army desperately needed to fight on. Montgomery, who felt that he should have been the supreme commander of the Allied forces, certainly had no less confidence than his American counterpart, even though his Operation Market Garden (September 1944) had largely been a failure.

While the Allies struggled with supply problems, Field Marshal Gerd von Rundstedt reorganized and stiffened the German defense.

CHAPTER 4

The Ardennes

Faced with a stalled offensive on the Eastern Front but maintaining a defensive line, Hitler decided that his best hope of winning the war was to divide and conquer—separating the British and Americans from their Russian allies. To do this he would attack the forces on the Western Front—smaller in number than the vast Russian army, and overextended in their rapid march across Europe—and sign a separate treaty with the West, so that he could turn back to the Eastern Front in full force.

> The Allied armies were overextended—their positions ran from southern France to the Netherlands. German planning revolved around the premise that a successful strike against thinly manned stretches of the line would halt Allied advances on the entire Western front.
> The German High Command decided by the middle of September, on Hitler's insistence, that the offensive would be mounted in the Ardennes, as was done in France in 1940. While German forces in that battle had passed through the Ardennes before engaging the enemy, the 1944 plan called for battle to occur within the forest itself....
> For the offensive to be successful, the planners deemed four criteria critical. The attack had to be a complete surprise. The weather conditions had to be poor in order to neutralize Allied air superiority.... Allied fuel supplies would have to be captured intact along the way due to the Wehrmacht's shortage of fuel.[1]

We didn't know the Germans were able to plan such a battle, but with the deceiving Germans, anything was possible. A German counteroffensive on such a large front was something we thought was impossible with the arsenal they had available. We were not really surprised, however, when it happened.

I was dropped off in Eupen, Belgium, on December 15, the day before the offensive began. Colonel Jenkins ordered me to be taken there because I had requested to be on the front line. I wanted to be in the action where I could kill Germans instead of merely translating. Many civilians fleeing out of Luxembourg told us of the serious buildup of German Panzers and artillery close to the border, but no one would consider the information reliable. We, the Allies, were convinced the Germans couldn't possibly have the resources to try a major counteroffensive. We were about to find out otherwise.

I had apparently been dropped off right in the middle of something big about to happen, and everyone was retreating. I needed transportation to get out of there. The transportation pool was empty because everyone was leaving in a hurry, and every truck or jeep driving by was already overloaded. After some while, a jeep stopped and offered me a ride. The lieutenant in the front seat asked what I was doing there. I showed him my traveling orders and told him I was looking for General Hodge's First Army, where I needed to meet with a Major Brown in Bastogne. This was the second Major Brown for me. The lieutenant said he was going in that direction and could drop me off.

While traveling, the lieutenant and the other officers in the jeep asked me what it was like during the German occupation. I answered that it was miserable, and I couldn't find anything good to say about the Nazis. I answered many of their questions about my last few years. Their uniforms were adorned with a Screaming Eagle patch, and when I asked if they were part of the D-day landing in Normandy, the lieutenant said they were right in the middle of it and would never forget it. He said it was absolutely unbelievable that they had pulled it off, and he was glad that wouldn't happen again. He asked where I was when they landed in Normandy. I told him I was in the FFI ambushing German patrols, confusing them, blowing up and destroying bridges, roads, locks, trucks, communications, and supplies, and anything else that could delay or cripple them. He asked what I was going to do in General Hodge's Army, and I said that I volunteered as a combat interpreter and probably would be asking prisoners questions and translating the lies they told me. The conversation was lively, and finally I arrived at my destination, wished them the best, and thanked them for picking me up. They were quickly gone, and God only knows what ever became of those men.

The dropping thermometer could mean snow. I learned that the Germans were now back in Belgium, advancing faster and moving closer. The sounds of artillery fire were getting louder. I spoke with a few civilians crossing town, fleeing from eastern villages. They said they had abandoned their farms and animals to get away from the approaching Germans. The civilians had terrified looks on their faces, and the bitter cold was no doubt affecting them. My long jeep ride to Bastogne left me right where I thought I wanted to be, in the mix. I was to find out that this was much more than I bargained for.

The Ardennes covered about eighty miles of the Belgian-German border. The 1944 battle started on December 16, and the Germans struck out mightily. It was one of the coldest, snowiest days in my memory. The First Elite Guard of the Adolf Hitler Armored Division lashed westward and south of Saint-Vith in Belgium; the Elite Guard Armored Division struck north of the town. Simultaneously Von Rundstedt ordered local attacks along the whole line from Monschau to Trier, which was right on the German and Luxembourg borders, to divert the Allies' attention. On the first day of the attack, we had no idea of the magnitude of the German offensive but figured their target was Bastogne. It was a small town, but the crossroads were of incredible strategic value to the Nazis.

In the initial German assault, Hitler's former chauffeur and bodyguard, Sepp Dietrich, led the SS Panzer Army in the northernmost attack route; Hasso von Manteuffel led the Panzer Army in the middle attack route, and Erich Brandenberger led the German Seventh Army in the southernmost attack route.

That December brought frigid temperatures—heavy snow, sleet, and a stinging wind—utter misery for the Allies, who were not equipped for such punishing conditions. Casualties from exposure to extreme cold grew as large as the losses from fighting. The enemy knew and was prepared for these harsh winter days, and had provided not only winter clothing, but also white camouflaged uniforms and helmets that made them very difficult to spot on snowy days.

The Battle of the Bulge

The Battle of the Bulge reads in history as one of the greatest military maneuvers ever put together and ultimately the last great battle that ended the Nazi's place in history. It was the largest and bloodiest battle of the war. I will tell you that war is an exercise in information and communications and reacting to each. The greatest source of information for the soldiers was the infirmaries or hospitals that treated the wounded and dying. Wounded men arrived daily from their various battlefronts, eyewitnesses with news to share.

But we followed instructions as they were given, and didn't know what was happening over the next hill or town. Radios were a luxury. We dealt mainly in probability. *We think the Germans are there, so we will go there.* Nobody stays still for long, so information was always evolving and often old after a day. When I read of the Battle of the Bulge years later, I learned far more information than by my actually being there. Orders were given and we followed. Everything else, and I mean everything, was not made known to us. We felt very much as if we were alone, fighting in our own private wars.

The Battle of the Bulge started on December 16, 1944, at 0430 hours, when the enemy made their move from the east, and we became aware when the

German artillery began firing in rapid succession.

The sky was gray and the temperature was dropping. Major Brown described to us the situation and said that the German assault was being considered serious. The Allied troops were facing the dreaded SS Hitler Panzer Army. The men comprising this army had their beginnings as Hitler's personal bodyguards and thus were highly trained, experienced, and ruthless killers.

By 0800 hours all three German armies attacked through the Ardennes. In the northern sector, Dietrich's SS Panzer Army assaulted Losheim Gap and the Elsenborn Ridge in an effort to break through toward the River Meuse.

In the center, von Manteuffel's Panzer Army attacked toward Bastogne and St. Vith. Both roads were junctions of great strategic importance. On the first day of the attack, we had no idea of the magnitude of the German offensive. By the way they advanced, we knew their target was Bastogne.

Finding Otto

Prior to Germany's last major offensive, the First Panzer Division had been directed on a special mission led by Otto Skorzeny, who was called "the most dangerous man in Europe." Otto was successful in infiltrating a small part of his battalion of disguised, English-speaking Germans behind the Allied lines. Their mission priority was to spread rumors throughout the Allied lines, thus creating mass chaos among Allied intelligence. Skorzeny's men were also charged with capturing select bridges that would aid in the German advance. The primary bridges on their list crossed the River Meuse, and were important strategic bridges for both sides. Although Otto's men were not successful in capturing these bridges, the battalion's presence produced mass confusion all out of proportion to their military activities, and their rumors spread like wildfire. Allied forces grew so concerned that they began second-guessing orders, all part of Otto's plan. Even General Patton was alarmed, and on December 17 described the situation to General Eisenhower as "Krauts . . . speaking perfect English . . . raising hell, cutting wires, turning road signs around, spooking whole divisions, and shoving a bulge in our defenses." Checkpoints were soon set up all over the Allied rear, greatly slowing the movement of soldiers and equipment. Military policemen drilled servicemen on things that every American was expected to know, such as the identity of Mickey Mouse's girlfriend, baseball scores, or the capital of Illinois. This latter question resulted in the brief detention of General Omar Bradley himself; although he gave the correct answer—Springfield—the GIs who questioned him apparently believed that the capital was Chicago.

The tightened security nonetheless made things harder for the German infiltrators, and a number of them were captured. Even during interrogation, they continued their goal of spreading disinformation; when asked about their mission, some of them claimed they had been told to go to Paris to either kill or capture General Eisenhower. Security around the General was greatly increased, and he was confined to his headquarters.

Because these prisoners had been captured in American uniforms, they were later executed by firing squad. This was the standard practice of every army at the time, although it was left out of the Geneva Convention, which merely stated that during wartime, soldiers had to wear uniforms that distinguished them as combatants.

In addition, Skorzeny was an expert at international law, and knew that such an operation would be well within its boundaries, as long as they were wearing their German uniforms when firing. Skorzeny and his men were fully aware of their likely fate, and most wore their German uniforms underneath their Allied ones in case of capture. Skorzeny himself avoided capture and survived the war, where his legend only grew. He was reported to have been involved with the infamous Nazi Odessa ratline escape network, which sprang up after the war. This network set up secret escape routes to assist SS members in avoiding capture and prosecution by the Allies, who were actively hunting them down. Rumors of former high-ranking SS members who utilized the Odessa Network periodically make modern headlines; though they continue to hide around the world, their numbers decrease each year.

By December 17 Eisenhower realized that the Ardennes was a major offensive, not a local attack, and he ordered some 250,000 troops to reinforce the Allied line. The Eighty-Second Airborne was also moved into the battle near Liège, north of the Bulge.

By the evening of December 17 the Leibstandarte SS Adolf Hitler Division spearhead had pushed north to engage the US Infantry Division, and Kampfgruppe Peiper arrived in front of Stavelot. As the German plan called for the capture of St. Vith by 1800 hours December 17, the prolonged action in and around it presented a major blow to their timetable. Peiper was already behind schedule, as it took thirty-six hours to advance from Eifel to Stavelot; it had taken the Germans just nine hours in 1940. As the Americans fell back, they blew up bridges and fuel dumps, denying the Germans critically needed fuel and further slowing their progress.

Malmedy

The Malmedy massacre was reported to us shortly after the event occurred. This was about the worst news we could have received at a time when we needed optimism. The news caused the men in Hodges's Army to change their policy and no longer take any prisoners, but to execute anyone we captured.

At 1230 hours on December 17, after seizing a desperately needed US fuel depot, SS-Waffen Lieutenant Colonel Joachim Peiper's battle group, which included 4800 troops and 600 vehicles, encountered elements of the American 285th Field Artillery Observation Battalion. The greatly outnumbered Americans surrendered after a brief battle near Baugnez, but were lined up and shot. Peiper's forces next captured another eighty-four Americans, who were then surrounded by tanks and machine-gunned until the last man fell.

A few of the soldiers feigned death and escaped to American lines, where their accounts of the massacre enraged American troops. Although reports of shootings of prisoners of war occasionally emerged from the Eastern Front, such events were relatively rare. I remember the news hitting us hard. Afterward, it became common for us to execute any German soldiers we captured. After the war, if a prisoner was learned to have been involved in the Malmedy massacre, they went to trial for war crimes.

Conditions deteriorated rapidly as the entire front along the Bulge was swept by a blizzard, and both sides had to use picks to cut foxholes from the frozen ground. The doomed Germans fought more desperately as their dead stacked up like firewood in front of American positions.

Bastogne

On December 18, 1944, the city of Bastogne faced imminent disaster. The Germans were again on the offensive. German divisions had reinvaded Belgium. The Allied commander called a meeting the next day in a bunker in Verdun. An optimistic Eisenhower told his generals the situation presented the Allies with a good opportunity: he believed German forces could be more easily destroyed when they were on the move than when they were dug into defensive positions. When Ike asked George Patton how long it would take to turn his Third Army north to counterattack, Patton famously replied that it would take him forty-eight hours—a claim that no one present found believable. But Patton, once again burnishing his reputation as a military genius, had anticipated his commander's request and had given the order before the meeting ever took place.

That day the morning air seemed colder than the day before. The military traffic, intense throughout the night, continued. For the most part, all the civilians in Bastogne who wished to leave had done so. Those left now were determined to stay, and we certainly were determined to make a stand and hold it.

Early that morning, under cover of darkness, Second Panzer Division soldiers had captured the tiny village of Neffe, along with the small contingent of Americans occupying it. This put the enemy less than two miles from our position at Bastogne. At 0800 hours, German cannons began to fire on us. Unless they received a direct hit, the old stone and brick buildings held up fairly well. The damage, however, was inevitable and increased with each hit. No one lingered in the open for long. We prayed for supplies, as we desperately needed bandages and antiseptics, not to mention food and dry clothing. Our swollen feet made walking difficult; we were afraid they were frozen but dared not remove our boots for fear we would never get them back on.

The Battle of the Bulge began for me when the 101st Airborne Division took up positions around Bastogne. Our mission became to defend Bastogne and await reinforcements. We were severely outnumbered and knew the lopsided odds we faced. As difficult as our situation was about to be, I was content to be just where I was. I had been sitting in a classroom just a few years before, had worked my way through the Belgian Resistance, and now found myself fighting alongside the Allies for the future of Belgium. I wanted so badly to make a difference; I honestly believed that there was no place I would rather be.

We were immediately placed on food and ammo rations, which pained us all. We were only allowed to fire the artillery if the target involved five or more Germans. Anything less and we were expected to engage them with our rifles, pistols, and grenades, albeit as sparingly as each circumstance would allow. Despite continued strikes, we were able to hold the perimeter. The Germans would use smaller, concentrated attacks on selected locations instead of mounting an all-out assault. This poor strategy ultimately gave us a chance. We had to shift men around constantly to defend specific points of attack, which wore us out but ultimately neutralized the Germans' advantage in numbers. My position was constantly being changed, so I never was able to really secure a location. My most urgent priorities were shelter from incoming rounds, dwindling ammo, and fatigue.

I learned that the German commander dropped a message by airplane in the center of Bastogne, addressed to our commander General Anthony McAuliffe. This would initiate one of the more legendary stories to come out of the Battle of the Bulge. When McAuliffe read the message, which demanded the surrender of Bastogne, his reply was simply "Nuts!"

Meanwhile, unknown to Allied intelligence, Field Marshal Von Rundstedt was about to make a last, desperate attempt to change the course of the war. Rushing in the German Sixth Elite Guard Armored Army, a particularly fanatical force toughened in battle on the Russian front, he massed what was left of the best of the German army on a fifty-mile-long line between Monschau Forest and Trier.

The most critical day of the long battle was December 20, when the German advance pushed back the Allied line between Wiltz and Malmedy—the "bulge" in the Battle of the Bulge. The Allies retreated from St. Vith in order to form a large defensive position on its outskirts.

The frigid temperature grew yet colder, much to our dismay. Each night the Germans would creep out and dig new foxholes that were closer to our outer perimeter, until they were within earshot of our defenders. This is an unnerving feeling, I can tell you, as I held a perimeter position several times.

Thursday, December 21, at around 0430 hours, I was ripped from a nap by screaming Germans, gunfire, and several cannon blasts. The screams, I gathered, were our enemy trying to locate their own. The fog was so dense I couldn't tell whether a Nazi was right beside or right in front of me. I kept turning my head from side to side, trying to peer through the mist, as my brain seemed to be playing tricks on me. Everything seemed to move when in reality nothing was really moving. I felt a pain in my stomach, probably from hunger and sleep deprivation. I knew if given the chance I could sleep for a week. The pain in my feet was excruciating, but I desperately wanted to stay on them and keep them moving to avoid frostbite. With the coming of daylight, the shelling increased.

The American drive to end the German siege began on December 22. Patton's divisions approached from the south, and the Eighty-Second Airborne and the defenders of St. Vith began to push back against the German advances. Bastogne saw some of the heaviest fighting. But while German troops continued to batter the town, most of the force had skirted the town and was now some fifteen miles past it. Completely surrounded, the 101st, the Ninth Armored, and some miscellaneous troops like me held the town for five days.

One day a soldier came by with a printed sheet that he said came directly from the top and would give our morale a boost. It was written by General Patton and was making its rounds to all the Allied soldiers. It was a prayer Patton addressed to the Almighty just days before Christmas.

"Sir, this is Patton talking,

The last fourteen days have been straight Hell, rain, snow, more rain. More snow, and I am beginning to wonder what's going on in Your Headquarters. Whose side are You on, anyway?

For three years my chaplains have been explaining this as a religious war. This, they tell me, is the Crusade all over again, except that we're riding tanks instead of chargers. They insisted we are here to annihilate the German Army and the godless Hitler so that religious freedom may return to Europe.

Up until now I have gone along with them, for You have given us Your unreserved cooperation. Clear skies and a calm sea in Africa made the landing highly successful and helped us to eliminate Rommel. Sicily was comparatively easy and You supplied excellent weather for our armored dash across France, the greatest military victory that You have thus far allowed me. You have often given me excellent guidance in difficult command decisions, and You have led German units into traps that made their elimination fairly simple. But now, You've changed horses in midstream. You seem to have given von Rundstedt every break in the book, and frankly, he's been beating hell out of us. My Army is neither trained nor equipped for winter warfare. And as You know, this weather is more suitable for Eskimos than for Southern Cavalry men. But now I can't help but feel that I have offended You in some way. That You have lost all sympathy with our cause. That You are throwing in with von Rundstedt and his paper-hanging god. You know without me telling You that our situation is desperate. Sure, I can tell my staff that everything is going according to plan, but there's no use telling You that my 101st Airborne is holding against tremendous odds in Bastogne, and that this continual storm is making it impossible to supply them even from the air. I've sent Hugh Gaffey, one of my ablest generals, with his 4th Armored Division, North toward that all-important road center to relieve the encircled garrison and he's finding Your weather much more difficult than he is the Krauts.

I don't like to complain unreasonably, but my soldiers from the Meuse to Echternach are suffering the tortures of the damned.

Today I visited several hospitals, all full of frostbite cases, and the wounded are dying in the field because they cannot be brought back for medical care.

But this isn't the worst of the situation. Lack of visibility, continued rains has completely grounded my Air force. My technique of battle calls for close-in fighter-bomber support, and if my planes can't fly, how can I use them as aerial artillery? Not only is this a deplorable situation, but, worse yet, my reconnaissance planes haven't been in the air for fourteen days and I haven't the faintest idea what's going on behind the German lines.

Damnit, Sir, I can't fight a shadow. Without Your cooperation from a weather standpoint I am deprived of accurate disposition of the German armies and how in hell can I be intelligent in my attack? All of this probably sounds unreasonable to You, but I have lost all patience with Your chaplains who insist that this is a typical Ardennes winter, and that I must have faith.

Faith and patience be damned! You have just got to make up Your mind whose side You're on. You must come to my assistance, so that may dispatch the entire German Army as a birthday present to Your Prince of Peace.

Sir, I have never been an unreasonable man, I am not going to ask You for the impossible. I do not even insist upon a miracle, for all I request is for four days of clear weather.

Give me four days so that my planes can fly, so that my fighter-bombers can bomb and strafe, so that my reconnaissance may pick up targets for my magnificent artillery.

Give me four days of sunshine to dry this blasted mud, so that my tanks roll, so that ammunition and rations may be taken to my hungry, ill-equipped infantry. I need those four days to send von Rundstedt and his godless army to their Walhalla. I am sick of this unnecessary butchery of American youth, and in exchange for four days of fighting weather, I will deliver You enough Krauts to keep Your bookkeepers months behind in their work. Amen."[2]

The Answer

Acting Division Commander Anthony McAuliffe had arrived in Bastogne via the Normandy invasion, where he parachuted in commanding the 101st Airborne Division. He was an easygoing leader who was well liked and had our respect. I saw him but a few times, and those times were always brief. We never engaged in direct conversations. Yet this man gave us strength and a formidable strategy to last through one of the most famous of all battles of

World War II. Commander McAuliffe was our beacon of strength at a time when our lives needed it most.

My stay in the Bulge was anything but comfortable. The ability to keep one's weapon in working order was always priority number one, followed closely by not getting shot. My weapon changed multiple times while fighting in the Bulge. We were obviously taught to use the weapon we had been issued, but often during the course of battle, our weapons were rendered useless for any number of reasons. When this dreaded moment found us, we searched for whatever weapon was closest. This weapon change could be facilitated when a soldier in your company was killed and no longer needed his weapon. Your new weapon could also be from a dead enemy soldier you happened to come across. When a German soldier's weapon became available and you knew how to operate it, it became yours. The heat our weapons generated from spitting out bullets was immense. An intense firefight could create a tremendously hot barrel. This heat could warp the weapon's barrel if you got caught in a prolonged battle, and this became an instant problem for a soldier. The muddy conditions that existed everywhere presented challenges, as well. A barrel full of mud or mud in the mechanisms could easily jam the weapon. As our lives and mission were on the line, we did our best to keep our weapons working, as the alternative was often your death. During the Bulge, my American-made M-1 Garand, dubbed the greatest battle implement ever devised, began wearing out from the constant abuse as it delivered deathblows to the Krauts. The barrel at one point glowed from the heat it was producing. This intense and repeated stress to my rifle finally rendered it useless. I needed a replacement. One of the dead Krauts lent me his German-made Mauser 98, which held more bullets in its clip than the M-1. The Mauser lasted only a brief few days and was damaged when I set it down to throw a hand grenade. The enemy returned a grenade, which landed close enough to send earth and mud showering down on my rifle, and a rifle lying in the mud isn't worth picking up. Then came the FN (Fabrication Nationale) FN-L; this 30-caliber Belgian weapon had a twenty-bullet clip, which was far superior to the eight-round clip of the M-1 and bested the design of the Mauser. I felt more effective with this weapon, which was a far cry from my early Sten Gun. The British Sten Gun was widely used during my time in the Underground for the simple reason that it cost around seventeen dollars apiece to create. The barrel of a Sten Gun constantly required replacement after concentrated use because it warped. Most supply dumps included extra barrels for just this reason.

The city and battle zone remained blanketed in fog. Men complained mostly of being frozen and having wet feet. The numbing cold was lowering their pain tolerance. But all was not totally dark. There was good news from east of town. Our counterattacks had been somewhat successful, and many small German units were surrounded near Neffe and Bizory.

In late afternoon the 101st Airborne had to abandon Sibret and Assenois to the southwest. While running across Bastogne to take a new position, I could see the extensive damage done to the town by the constant shelling. Destruction lay everywhere. A few disabled military vehicles sat abandoned here and there. Many buildings showed signs of destruction. Luckily, no fires were reported at that moment. The day ended with the sounds of explosions and gunfire.

On Friday, December 22, the shelling of the town had not completely stopped during the night. The days and nights of constant battle were taking their toll on my squad and me. The cold and the fog did not improve. But a breeze had come in and made the air easier to breathe. Even with the constant smell of war, there were still things to be grateful for.

It had snowed heavily the night before. The cases of frostbite continued to increase. I went to the field infirmary to be treated for frostbite every two or three days. When you were able to see a medic, you might receive a small morphine injection to help you with the pain. If the pain wasn't too severe, they would gently massage and warm your feet. I was able to receive this treatment several times, and I believe this allowed me to leave Bastogne with all my toes still attached. The more severe cases were sent to our field surgeon when amputation was the only option.

The sunrise brought improved visibility over the previous day, and the temperature was stabilized just above freezing. A few biscuits and some coffee sufficed as breakfast and lunch. With the onset of daylight, the noise of battle increased, and mortar shells again fell on the town. Incredible rough fighting continued in this frozen miserable landscape. Bastogne was a sea of agony. We were growing thinner by the day. We knew very well the situation before us. We stood outnumbered, outgunned, surrounded.

In our foxholes we tightly hugged the ground. Sometimes during the shelling one of us would receive a direct hit and disappear instantly, but those casualties were surprisingly few. Each shot we took was carefully considered: we couldn't waste a single bullet. We received help from others behind us moving in to support our positions.

When the Nazis mounted a ground assault, German bodies would pile up in front of our foxholes and sometimes fall in on top of the defenders. The Germans at times would have to climb over their dead and wounded just to keep moving forward. The puddle of water inside my foxhole was forgotten during these attacks, and my boots repeatedly became soaked. The nighttime raids were the most difficult for us, although sometimes a shell that hit a building nearby would emit enough light for us to see a German we hadn't previously seen.

It was cold day after day, and each day seemed harder to endure. If we had dry socks and boots, it would be more bearable, but I guess then we wouldn't be able to stay awake. I fought sleep and death almost interchangeably. My sheer determination to stay alive and help my fighting brothers was all I had to go by. I knew that if I didn't shoot that Nazi he would have no trouble shooting me.

Then on Saturday December 23, we witnessed a miracle: the sky cleared. The heavy overcast skies had kept our planes grounded, but now new orders went out and a squadron of P-47 Thunderbolts began bombing and strafing the Germans near Bastogne. The order had been to help clear the path for Patton's Third Army to reach us. This gave all of us renewed hope for rescue—and maybe even a supply drop. That much-needed drop happened around noon that day and elicited another attack from our enemies. The Germans responded with as much cannon fire as they could muster from the perimeter. I was told the rations were quickly dispersed, but as I was in an exposed position was not able to enjoy any. A team of surgeons had also made it in to Bastogne by way of glider and quickly found their hands full with wounded. What we didn't know but learned later was that the Germans were experiencing the same shortages of fuel, ammo, and food that we were. They just had so many men that it wasn't easily discernable.

It was bitter cold that Sunday, and we remained exhausted. Living on rationed morsels of food and coffee was catching up with us. We were quickly using up our reserves. We were convinced that massive help was on the way, and we knew we would be victorious. We were keenly aware that Patton's Third Army was now battling to relieve Bastogne. There was some serious praying going on in those foxholes. Then we became the target of a Nazi fourteen-inch railway gun and its incredible power. This giant cannon, built by Germany's Krupp Company, had been outfitted for the railroad, so it was transportable. Its range of twelve miles was so vast that few locations were safe. When it was fired, everyone took notice. Where the shells landed, entire buildings collapsed and disappeared into craters. We simply prayed not to be on a point of impact. The blast left no windowpanes unbroken within a two-hundred-yard radius. This new weapon caused the Allies a great deal of worry. Luckily, it was ridden with mechanical issues and not yet mass-produced. Our infirmary was destroyed by a cannon's direct hit, which killed most of the wounded inside. We received another ammo resupply which allowed us to shoot more frequently and worry less about conserving bullets. We returned fire as quickly as the Germans advanced on us, which was often. This Sunday was as bloody and wretched as any other day here, but something seemed to be happening that caused the men to get excited. I never learned what caused this but I only assumed help was coming. The German assault seemed to lose some of its steam, and we were able to relax a little more than we had in any of the previous days of the siege.

Merry Christmas

Monday, December 25. Merry Christmas! There were plenty of uncut Christmas trees around, which were very lacking in decorations. No presents this year except for the enemy shells exploding around us. I can't brag about the Christmas concert of rifle fire, machine guns, mortar, hand grenades, and heavy artillery. It was deplorable. I hoped I would be able to keep my hearing. Every day an explosion nearby would render me deaf for a brief period of time. I often remembered seeing my commanding officer giving orders, but I couldn't hear a thing. I could see his lips moving but I had been temporarily deafened by a blast. I would remain alert and kill anything that ran toward me from the perimeter until someone told me different. This would always be the most memorable Christmas I ever had, but it lacked a single pleasant moment.

The final German attack against Bastogne was launched that morning. There was utter destruction of German men pouring out toward us. Our brave men who clung to their dugout positions with everything they could muster repeatedly repelled the German advancements. The men of the Third Army were on the way, and we had to hold this town.

We had survived so much and the Germans now seemed to be growing desperate. The temperature was falling again. Light snow began to fall. We were shelled throughout Christmas night without end. The Nazis were steady in their resolve to capture Bastogne at all costs.

In addition to the shelling around 2000 hours, German airplanes began blanketing Bastogne with B-1 Elektron-Brandbombe incendiary bombs. The initial explosion was rather lackluster, but the bombs dispersed a white phosphorous chemical that ignited after impact at such hot temperatures that all nearby wood structures and combustible materials burst into flames. These German bombs left absolute destruction wherever they landed. We were getting the Nazis' best show, and still we held our ground. The fires created by these incendiary bombs now became a heat source for the frozen soldiers. When the opportunity presented itself, we would get as close as we could to the flames to bask in their chemically engineered warmth.

Tuesday, December 26, another clear sky. The battle had raged all night. I went to the infirmary for my frozen feet that were hurting more than ever, and I was having increasing difficulties walking. The nurses told us additional medical supplies were badly needed. I regularly and carefully got out of my foxhole in a semi-crawl and moved around a bit just to try and get warmer. It seemed to help a little. We fought to stay alert. We fought to stay covered from enemy fire. We fought to stay warm. At times, death seemed an easy way out of all this suffering, but I did not want to die. I shared the same attitude as my division: we could not allow the Nazis to gain an inch on Bastogne.

But that day, at 1650 hours, help arrived in the form of General Patton's Thirty-Seventh Tank Battalion of the Fourth Armored Division. Our saviors had arrived! As the battalion pulled up to the 101st Airborne's lines, General McAuliffe drove to the perimeter to meet them. Captain William Dwight of the Fourth Armored asked the general how he was, to which McAuliffe famously answered, "Gee, I'm mighty glad to see you!"

Next day, December 27, snowstorms engulfed the Ardennes area. The battle tide had turned, but nonetheless raged on. Each of us defending Bastogne longed for the day when we could leave our foxhole for a change of scenery. Patton's force was bringing that day to us.

We now had reinforcements, which greatly improved our morale and our resolve to never give up fighting. The Germans, now heavily outmanned, were forced back from Bastogne and into a defensive position. The 101st expected to be relieved but was instead given the order to resume the offensive. I was finally relieved after the new battalion arrived, and I was incorporated into one of the many divisions of the American First Army. I trudged happily away from Bastogne and the worst experience of my life. My ability to walk away from Bastogne left me shaken to the core. I felt extremely fortunate to walk out. Was I truly lucky, or was someone else looking out for me?

My first destination after my departure was a tiny nameless military post where I received some medical care, followed by a much-needed shower. I looked as pitiful as a man could look. I was covered in my own filth and smelled worse than death. Gunpowder does not wash off easily, and I had been coated with it for weeks. I had several times used puddle water to clean dirt and gunpowder off my face, and it was likely that it was more urine than water. My long-awaited shower came from a tank truck, which dispensed fresh, clean, and frigid water from the nozzle. This was not a shower one could enjoy. It was taken in haste, since the outside temperature matched the water temperature. I hurriedly finished scrubbing off the battle and transitioned to controlling the shivers. I was then outfitted with clean clothes. The best reward of all this was the new warm socks. My feet so appreciated the socks! I knew the war wasn't over, so I was back in circulation as quickly as I had dropped out to bathe. The battle of Bastogne ended any chances the Germans had of reaching the harbor at Antwerp, which was their primary goal. This effectively ended the Nazi offensive effort and put them in a full defensive posture. Now, it was merely a matter of time before the capitulation of Nazi empire.

On January 16 the First Army returned to Bradley's Twelfth Army Group. The battle moved on and our forces were reequipped. My aching feet now had renewed strength. The frostbite medicine, the dry socks, and the dry boots undoubtedly saved my feet from surgical removal. The icing on the cake was when they issued waterproof boots and winter coats, which while very late in arrival were well appreciated. We finally were able to walk in the mud and water and keep our feet dry.

In the Battle of the Bulge, 89,500 Americans were killed, with between 67,200 and 125,000 Germans killed, missing or wounded. The number of Belgian civilians who died, were wounded, or suffered while caught in the middle of Bastogne cannot be known. They were wonderful countrymen who perished while holding onto a glimmer of hope that liberation would meet them.

In a strange twist of fate, Joachim Peiper, charged with Germany's last military hope in the attempt to avoid surrendering the country, fell into Allied hands and would spend twelve years in prison for war crimes in Belgium. He evaded war crimes charges in Italy because of insufficient evidence. The respect Der Peiper had garnered from his SS peers helped him to obtain his release from prison after time served. After his release from prison back into a world in which he was not celebrated, Peiper went to work for Porsche in its technical division. He got promoted to lead the auto exports division to the US, of all places, which he was prohibited from entering because of his wartime criminal conviction. His criminal record eventually couldn't be suppressed any longer. When it interfered with Porsche sales, he was forced from his position. He found employment again at Volkswagen, again through the help of former SS members, but he had a short run there and ultimately moved to France. It was here in France, working as a book translator, that Peiper finally paid for his crimes. On July 14, 1976, unknown assailants broke into his home and shot Peiper to death, and then used Molotov cocktails to burn his house to the ground. No suspects were ever apprehended. The assailants were suspected to be Communists or former members of the French Resistance who ended Peiper's life on France's most famous holiday, Bastille Day. In the charred remains of his house was found part of a book Peiper had begun about his experience in Malmedy.

Hürtgen Forest

We were told that the Hürtgen Forest was fifty square miles of dense conifer forest broken by few roads, tracks or firebreaks with no place for vehicles to operate. The Ninth Infantry Division of the First Army previously fought there during the fall of 1944, losing 4,500 men in one particular three-week stretch of battle. At one point, the regiment was losing a man and a half for every yard gained, and they gained less than five miles total. In September, when the Allied First Army initially crossed the German border near the dam of the Rur River, intelligence discovered the dam was only thinly defended. The Allies believed they needed to capture the Rur Dam since the water from the reservoir could be released by the Germans, swamping any forces operating downstream. The American commanders decided that the most direct route to the Rur Dam was through the Hürtgen Forest. Had they acted on the dam earlier than they did and from a different path, the drive to the Rhine might have succeeded months before it finally did. Instead, setbacks and Germany's fierce defense of their homeland made the battle for the Hürtgen Forest the longest single battle in US Army history. The loss of Allied lives in this battle sent the Allied commanders reeling.

I arrived in February 1945 after those initial offensives had failed, and received orders to move on with the Ninth Army, which had been ordered to the Hürtgen Forest with the mission to take Schmidt, a village on the other side of the forest that sat beside three roads on the far side of the Kall River valley.

The forest was located about forty miles southeast of Aachen, just inside of the German border, and was the target of the First Army and General Hodges. I joined the First Army with a simple transfer so as to continue the fight. The West Wall of the German defense ran through the forest. Large artillery bunkers and many smaller concrete pillboxes, plus log and dirt bunkers, were scattered throughout the ribbons of concrete and steel antitank defenses, which were part of the German border defenses. German artillery managed to destroy many of the dense, tall trees. They shot off the tops of the trees to create serious ground clutter that was difficult to fight in. It was almost impossible to aim at a moving target, because you lost your target before you could aim and fire. The Germans had built elaborate bunkers and foxholes where they were patiently waiting for us. The only way to advance was by saturating the ground with mortar fire, hand grenades, and heavy machine gun fire. The Hürtgen Forest would prove a horrific place to fight. The firs were thick and rugged at the approaches to the Cologne plain. The lowest branches of the firs started close to the ground, and each fir interlocked with its neighbors. At the height of a man standing, there was a solid mass of dark, impenetrable green. But at the height of a man crawling, there was room, and it was like a green cave, low-roofed and forbidding. We were aware of the "West Wall" which was the German border defense that twisted through the forest, with two parallel belts of pillboxes and log-and-dirt bunkers several miles apart and virtually invisible among the trees.

The debacle of the Hürtgen Forest was due in part to the Allied commanders, who had their minds made up to go through it. You'd put a division in there and they got chewed up. They'd pull them out and put another division in and same story. Hope was not a terribly powerful word to us there. We operated in absolute confusion amidst the filth only a forest can accommodate. I vividly recall the tremendous amount of dirt I picked up inside of my clothing, which didn't help matters. It had been over a month since I had seen my last frigid shower. I was not alone though. The suffering for both sides was tremendous and would later be considered unnecessary.

As newcomers in the forest, we were advised to remain standing and hug the tree trunks when we heard a shell coming, in the hope that the tree trunk would provide at least a little protection; lying flat on the ground only created a bigger target. The Germans were using a technique called tree bursts. Tree bursts consisted of artillery shells that were timed to explode before they hit the ground or in the trees so as to rain down splinters and hot metal shrapnel upon us. We learned quickly to hug those trees. The pine needles that blanketed the forest floor disguised trip wires and five different kinds of mines. You couldn't find a safe spot. Men were falling everywhere.

Sometimes you were firing backward and sometimes you were firing forward. Everything was all mixed up. After a couple of days, you didn't have any food, and our enemy cut off the approach to our chow line. When we finally got out of the forest, by retreat I might add, there was a small solitary old log cabin being utilized as an aid station and it surprisingly contained both German and Allied critically wounded. There were no other available options for these dying men. This seemed an anomaly in the entire process of war, with our medical team helping their wounded. Human compassion was the overlying factor. Doctors from both sides were here, working to help one another in one of the true humanitarian spectacles of the war. They were bringing all the wounded into that one log cabin near the Kall River. Many of the surviving men who emerged from the forest did not talk with anyone, but rather just sat and looked at you very straight and unblinking with an empty expression on their faces. I remember getting out of the forest and walking away from it in disbelief. I didn't know where I was going but wanted to get away from the hell I just left. The Germans had the whole countryside mapped, and left soldiers down the firebreaks, knowing those were our only escape routes from the forest. The paths of least resistance would lead you into Nazi guns, machine guns, hand grenades, field mortars, and other horrors waiting to snatch your life from you. When I joined the First Army, I received the lucky order to face this challenge.

Fighting in the forest would go on for nearly three more weeks. One officer counted fifty shells that fell around him in ninety seconds. To top it all, it rained most of the time, and the water ran into the foxholes. The men slept in it, aggravating their cases of trench foot; many came down with pneumonia. Then the snow came, wet and wind-driven, and it fell on the men and into their food and into their coffee. There were no battle lines. No "tide of battle," but one big bloody mess of gunfire, explosions, and misery. Surviving it was some sort of miracle.

When we captured Germans, which wasn't often, we would seek out the highest-ranking man for questioning. Several times the captured Nazi exhibited aggressive behavior toward us even when staring down the barrel of a gun. I, along with several other German-speaking Allies, noticed how they bragged to us about their power and their new weapons. Many times we were warned about the coming battles. Nazis emphasized that we had a big surprise coming. I personally enjoyed getting right in their faces and ordering them to shut their mouths! I ordered them to only answer our questions.

Although our casualties were small compared to those the Allies suffered there in the fall, when relief arrived I was more than grateful to receive orders to pull out. A forward observer, trained to accompany the lead platoon of attacking infantry and call in artillery on enemy targets, said, "The Hürtgen Forest was the worst progression of war I had ever seen."

All three corps of the Ninth US Army would finally fight their way to the west bank of the Rur, on the other side of Hürtgen Forest. None of our soldiers dared cross it because the enemy still controlled the Rur Dam. On February 10, the Allies finally captured the Rur Dam, but the Germans had jammed its floodgates open the previous day. The resulting flooding of the Rur Valley delayed the Allied advance to the Rhine for two weeks, until the floodwaters receded on February 23.

So many men died to take those fifty square miles of forest, and those who lived spent so much time desperately digging holes for their own protection during the battle. Despite the best efforts of the soldiers, there were relatively few burials. I learned later that when the snows melted in the spring, hundreds of bodies and parts of bodies appeared on the forest floor. The stench no doubt was unimaginable.

Reproduction Farms

It was around the end of the Hürtgen Forest debacle that we learned of a new horror being committed by the Nazis upon their own people. The Nazi war machine ran as an efficient and advanced operation, albeit for all the wrong reasons. Efficiency and technology were vital to their early success. Hitler was keen on empowering his troops and increasing their destructive power. Hitler found his perfect partner in Himmler, who was the mastermind of many atrocities. Our underground intelligence had gotten wind of a particular Himmler creation called Lebensborn. We grew to know them as Reproduction Farms. The farms were originally set up in Hitler's hometown of Braunau Am Inn as homage to the Führer. A large requisitioned park was developed with a hotel and hospital, which contained the best of everything available to the German people. Himmler filled the development with German girls ages fifteen and up who were put through blood and ancestry background checks to ensure their pure bloodlines. The Lebensborn's purpose was as a rest and relaxation location for SS leadership. The women's sole purpose there was to do the bidding of their superiors and to get pregnant. It was considered an honor to become pregnant by a German officer. This selective breeding was run by the Race and Settlement Central Bureau and would honor and reward the mothers of male babies. This German creation was cast as a solution to help solve the male population decline Germany had been experiencing from its war. These females were kept pregnant or in service to their assigned SS officers.

End of the Bulge

The Battle of the Bulge officially ended when two large American forces joined on January 25, 1945. Aftermath casualty estimates from the battle vary widely. The official US account lists 80,987 American casualties. British losses were estimated at 1,400, and estimates of German losses ranged from 60,000 to 100,000.

By early February 1945, Allied lines were roughly where they had been before December 16. In the east, the German army found itself unable to halt the Soviet juggernaut. German forces were sent reeling on two fronts and never recovered.

Over the Rhine

American troops broke into Germany on January 29, 1945. By March, Germany had been invaded from the east by the Russians, with US and British troops attacking from the west.

A milestone was reached when the First Army's Ninth Armored Division reached the Rhine at Remagen early in March. They were surprised to find that German attempts to destroy the bridge had failed, although it was under continued attack.

The US Navy joined in the fight. The sailors, working in coordination with army command, launched their armored boats into the river a few miles above Remagen in order to transport the First Army and its materiel across the Rhine—the first time the river had been crossed by a foreign invader since Napoleon. Enemy fire from the far shore was intense, but it was fiercely returned by our men in the boats. That is how I crossed into the land of the devil.

The Allies were again on the offensive, but the Americans were short of in-theater reinforcements. The lack of able bodies caused General Eisenhower to offer infantry positions to enlisted Negroes who were in service units but were not allowed to fight. More than 4500 volunteered, with some taking a grade reduction in order to qualify. They were incorporated into both the Sixth Army Group and the Twelfth Army Group, and it is partly due to the excellent record in battle of these unselfish men that the American military finally recognized their capabilities.

It was still cold and muddy, but my feet were looking and feeling much better. Dry socks and waterproof boots helped a lot, and it looked like I would keep my toes.

Every inch we moved closer to Berlin, our infantry battalion (around one thousand men) encountered more and more German resistance. The roads between towns were mined and purposely cluttered with tree trunks and heavy foliage. Hitler had given orders for his men to stand and fight till the last man.

But the battles inside Germany were much smaller and noticeably different from our previous battles. We were routinely charged with clearing a town or village from pro-Nazi resistance. Oftentimes, our jeeps would drive around detailing orders over a loud speaker to any potential enemies. The announcements called for all Nazi resistance to move to an open area without arms and surrender. These orders were seldom followed, and thus required our intervention.

The majority of these resisters were civilians who refused to recognize the end of the Nazi reign. I found myself involved in clearing the towns of Raffelsbrand, Vossenack, Schmidt, Hürtgen, and Kammerscheidt of these resisters. Our bullets, mortars, heavy machine guns, flamethrowers, half-tracks, and grenades often came into play to dislodge our enemies, depending on the situation. For the most part, we went house to house, street by street, to ensure that the pro-Nazis were dispatched. We would take the house by force, usually smashing in the front door with the butt of a rifle. The intent was not to preserve the integrity of the front door. Sometimes we used explosive devices when the doors were very sturdy. We entered very carefully and on full alert. Most homes were vacant. If occupied, we could tell if the occupants were hostile or not by their reaction to our entry. If the occupants gave any negative feedback or hostility, they were summarily shot. We were very careful to preserve non-hostile civilians, however. Often the occupants hid in the basements, which were prevalent in Europe. We learned that the Nazis considered us a more hospitable enemy than the Russians. When we threatened to shoot anyone not surrendering, Germans didn't always take us at our word, since we were known to be more civil than the Russians. Many Nazi holdouts met their deaths because they expected us to capture them and not shoot them.

Despite the numerous pockets of resistance, most of the civilians seemed to realize they were headed toward total occupation. As their homeland was being completely destroyed, they finally realized that Hitler had lied to them. Germany was being hacked to pieces and lay in crumbling ashes. Her military spirit was being crushed and broken. She must now learn to live in peace with other nations or die.

As the Third Army overran the German salt-mine town of Merkers, they made a marvelous discovery. Deep in one of the mines was a strongly constructed treasure house in which were concealed, under heavy guard, the treasures of the Reich, stolen from many countries. More than $100 million of pure gold ingots and millions of dollars' worth of German, British, and American currency were found. Priceless artistic and literary masterpieces from all the museums and libraries of eastern, southern, and western Europe were recovered. Ancient manuscripts and paintings by Vermeer, Rembrandt, Titian, and the moderns were discovered. Many more of these bunkers of stolen treasures would begin to surface as the Allies marched through Germany. It had been quite easy for the Nazis to acquire them. It would take many years and extraordinary measures to get most of the treasures back to their rightful owners.

FDR

On the tragic day of April 12, as American troops were gaining new triumphs, they and their nation were stunned by a tragic loss. Their Commander in

Chief, Franklin D. Roosevelt, while tending to some paperwork and posing for an artist's portrait, experienced a massive cerebral hemorrhage and slipped away a few minutes later. Allied officers and enlisted men alike were startled by this news. They could not believe it when it came over the field radios in the German night. Many of them had seen the president in Casablanca two years before, when he reviewed American troops, and to all of them, whatever their politics, he was their commander in chief. In tanks and half-tracks, in planes and in foxholes, men bowed their heads. Soldiers wept openly. They had lost their leader in action, but they had not lost their cause. The war was going on, and they would wrest the victory that their fallen leader had so long and carefully planned.

Twenty-four more days and the American troops would erect a memorial to their fallen commander in chief, which would help his name live through the centuries. All he had worked and died for would become a living reality. It would be engraved on the tablets of history through the ages in seven letters—VICTORY!

Surrender

On May 7, 1945, all German forces unconditionally surrendered. The war in Europe was over! We could finally stop and reflect on the past months and years of suffering and honor the ones who gave their lives. They were my heroes. My parents would miss me if I didn't return, but I was single and didn't have the same concerns as the soldiers with families. I didn't have a wife and children waiting at home like many of my fellow soldiers.

I must admit that the battle of Bastogne was a life-changing experience. My previous experiences in the Belgian Resistance were serious, and the battles I fought in as a mercenary were heavy prices to pay. I will though always consider the Battle of the Bulge to be the most horrific experience of my life; likely most everyone else who participated did so as well. I never threw as many hand grenades or fired as many shots as I did in those eight days in Bastogne. During the battle, we captured very few enemy regulars, and as far as I was concerned, the SS didn't deserve a chance to survive. Seventy years after the war I still haven't made up my mind about the German regular army. I assumed most of them acted out of fear of Hitler, because they knew they would be killed mercilessly if they disobeyed. What we did to them was important and necessary. I also obeyed orders, as I didn't have any choice. I imagine the Nazis were no different in this regard. War is war . . . but murder is murder. We killed the enemy because they wanted to kill us. We didn't murder the enemy. I know the difference, and I always will.

I received my dismissal papers in June 1945 as my service in the Ninth Army had concluded. My status as a mercenary was complete. I finally received a chance to call home to check on my family and to tell Mom and Dad that the war was over.

That is when my parents informed me that I had received a draft notice from the Belgian Army. I would be summoned in the coming months. Belgium began its long and bumpy road to civility by implementing a draft to create an armed force with which to protect its cities and people as well as to keep order. On the journey home, I spent several days at the town of Bad Godesberg, where I translated for the Nazi prisoners and the Allied guards. The journey home wasn't easy for me. My mind raced with thoughts about my future. I desperately wanted to rest and recover, but I had been involved with the war now for five years and I didn't know how I would make it as a civilian again. I finally made it home and the reunion celebration was very grand. I have not experienced a greater joy than celebrating with my family and countrymen. People came from everywhere with the best they had to offer for the party. Tears of joy and tears of happiness lasted for three days. Belgium was ours once again! I was very happy to see my family and gorge on some delicious food. My thin frame needed the nourishment. Everyone treated me as a hero, which was nice. I liked the attention very much. After more than a few months at home, though, my mind began to wander again. I didn't know why, but I knew I was not happy. I was not comfortable being home. I had grown so used to combat and its lifestyle, I wasn't ready for it to end. I wanted to be back in uniform. My rest and recovery had helped immensely, but the remainder would have to wait. My nation needed me as much as I needed her. I didn't want to wait for my draft call up, so I happily enlisted in the Belgian Army in November 1945. I met many surviving Belgian soldiers who had escaped the initial German invasion when they were rescued from Dunkirk in 1940. They were now reactivated into the Army, along with many like me.

CHAPTER 5

The Belgian Army

1945-1952

Leaving the US Service wasn't easy. My life was irrevocably altered by the ideologies of Adolph Hitler. By the grace of God and incredible sacrifices of millions, I was witness to the greatest triumph of good over evil that the world had ever seen. I, for some inexplicable reason, was one of the lucky ones, for which I was eternally grateful. I would carry an everlasting bond with this period in history and these men and women.

The Belgian army was practically wiped off the map by the German invaders back in June 1940, but some Belgian soldiers had escaped through the miracle of the Dunkirk rescue. After the liberation, Belgium immediately experienced political problems. Politics had been a problem long before World War II, and thus was nothing new to our countrymen. The socialistic belief system seemed to have achieved a strong foothold once the country had been liberated, and many demanded the end of the Belgian kingdom. I knew the country had problems with its French and Flemish-speaking populations, which had no intention of mending their broken bond.

King Leopold III, the official ruler of Belgium, had remained in the country after surrendering the Belgian army to the Germans on May 27, 1940. He vehemently refused to evacuate as his ministers had urged and therefore was captured and placed under house arrest by the invading Nazis. He spent the entirety of the war locked in the Royal Palace of Laeken in Belgium, then in Saxony, Germany, and lastly in Austria, where he never came to terms with the Germans. He was finally liberated by the US 106th Cavalry in early May 1945. After the war, Leopold abdicated his throne due to a majority of support for his son Baudouin. Baudouin was too young, though, and lacked the necessary training and education to assume the responsibility of leading the kingdom. Leopold's brother Charles served as Prince Regent until Baudouin was installed as Belgium's fifth king in 1951. Leopold had lost the favor of his

In Koln, after the war

ministry and countrymen for many reasons, including his marriage during his imprisonment to a baroness who was considered out of the royal line. He lived the remainder of his life in exile in Switzerland.

In Belgium, the king was not just a politician but also a military leader. He studied in a military academy where he was educated in political and international affairs. After his training, when he was capable of being a king, he assumed the responsibility of leading the army, air force, and navy. He studied political and international law and consulted his government to find solutions to internal and international problems.

Our country had fought and survived under the adage of "Unity makes strength," which remains the Belgian motto today. Now, faced with rebuilding nearly from scratch, half of the country opposed the other. It was inevitable that with a strong new socialist faction, we were doomed to have serious problems. We could have chosen a unified peace but were now facing problems everywhere we looked.

Rebuilding Belgium

The retreating Nazis had ransacked each and every town it passed through. Anything of value was taken or destroyed. The devastation was everywhere you looked, and the prospect of rebuilding this once great nation of Belgium seemed impossible. The Belgian government quickly returned from their voluntary exile in London. The first order of business was to find someone they could trust to lead the rebuilding effort. They reinstalled the federal police to instill order and peace—or at least create the perception. The government installed American Colonel Jenkins as the manager in eastern Flanders. He was a powerful man who had a reputation for being hard-nosed and getting the job done. Power plants were made a priority, as electricity and natural gas were a necessity. The endless devastation that could be cleaned up was hauled to city dumps by a never-ending run of trucks. Businesses that were able and willing began to open their doors again. The nighttime was a nervous and dangerous time in the cities, because vigilantes were prevalent. Any persons known to be associated with anything Nazi were under constant threat by any citizen wanting to exact revenge. The most shocking move in the rebuilding effort was the Belgian government's decision to ship their German prisoners back home and not utilize them in the cleanup and rebuilding.

The Belgian army boot camp started with ninety days of combat training, including thirty days of medic training. The medic training was a new twist. In 1946, Belgian combat soldiers had to be able, to a certain extent, to bandage themselves or help other wounded soldiers or civilians who needed help. Medics took care of the serious injuries. I benefitted from this training years later, as I was able to bandage my own kids with their cuts and scrapes. Obviously, I didn't need the combat training, but our new military needed to be working as a coordinated group and following the same orders.

When I completed the basic training, I requested an assignment as an interrogator or translator. My division was Flemish-speaking and, of course, our officers spoke only French. The army recognized my past military experience and promoted me to the rank of corporal acting sergeant in order to communicate with the troops. There were advantages, such as I never pulled KP duty or stood guard. I was better paid as a sergeant and had my uniforms custom tailored.

Toward the middle of 1946, my division left Belgium and traveled to the British Zone of Occupation in Germany. The war was well over, but there were still vigilante shootings and acts of sabotage to deal with. There remained Nazi holdouts that would not accept their defeat and continued to harass the occupiers.

While we were patrolling one day, a member of our squad strayed from our group and encountered a Wehrwolf's sniper bullets. He was shot three times before we could repel the aggressor. We dragged our man to relative safety and began to assess his condition. He was bleeding badly from the upper torso

In Koln, 1947

and in very poor condition. He was in need of a blood transfusion as soon as possible. Our medics, lacking time to transport the patient to a medical facility, asked us who had a matching blood type. Our blood types were listed on our dog tags for ease of discovery. I happened to be nearby and a match. The medics called me over and I sat down next to my wounded friend. Without hesitation, they rolled up my sleeve and found a vein in my left arm. They plugged an intravenous needle into my arm, then plugged the other end of the tube directly into his arm, a direct blood transfusion. My blood flowed freely into his body in a steady stream, and I was hopeful it would prolong his life so his wounds could be treated. My blood wasn't enough, though. It wasn't long before medics decided to end the transfusion, as the wounded man was too far gone. My blood wasn't enough to save him, and he passed away there in front of us.

Many months earlier, I crossed the German border with the American Army, and now I was crossing it as a Belgian soldier. Our division traveled by military train to the Dutch border town of Maastricht, which was a British checkpoint. The British not only controlled the British and Canadian armies, but also the Belgian, Polish, Dutch, Norwegian, and Luxembourg armies. We crossed the border into Germany in the late afternoon, and immediately had to deal with several beggars needing food and black marketers selling food and various things. When they saw the brass lion on our black berets they backed off, knowing they couldn't expect anything from us. We gave food and candy only to the children.

Germany was in apocalyptic ruin. Some of the streets had been cleared, but nothing was being rebuilt yet. The de-Nazification had begun almost immediately following the war. All remaining factories were closed down or destroyed. The plan was to rebuild Germany into a light industrial and agricultural country under strict guidelines and assistance. This took many years to implement and required much intervention and manpower. We essentially were taking a country that had been reduced to the stone age and giving her resources with which to start a rebirth, all the while fighting against numerous holdouts that wanted to kill us.

Right after the war, when the Allies occupied Germany, the currency was in occupation money, but the black market transactions were mostly done by the exchange of goods such as cigarettes, coffee, silk stockings, and all kinds of canned food. One could get just about anything on the black market. Of course, most of it had been stolen out of the ruins of abandoned homes, mansions, castles, factories, and office buildings. Postwar spoils were available everywhere, but getting any of it through the British checkpoints was very difficult.

From the border we traveled by Belgian army trucks toward the Rhine River and arrived in the middle of the night at the Cologne (Köln) Central Station, which was still in very bad shape. There wasn't much transportation available except for the military trucks and jeep car pools. Just about all the bridges across the Rhine River were destroyed and replaced by temporary pontoon bridges. The town of Cologne was in ruins, and the countryside was still littered with scattered war material. Women and elderly people were stacking bricks on both sides of the streets for miles in every direction. They looked defeated, hungry, and tired. Do not misunderstand me when I describe my hate for the Germans, but there were a lot of decent German civilians who hated Hitler's policies but had little choice but to follow. Hitler and the Nazis made it simple: If you don't support the Führer, then you are an enemy of Germany and must be punished or executed. A lot of good people out of fear of the Gestapo closed their eyes to the horrors of the Nazis.

It sounds heartless, but I was glad to see them suffer. I wanted them to crawl and beg, which they often did. Yes, at that time of my life, after experiencing the occupation of the Nazis, I couldn't help hating them. I felt they deserved what happened to them. I couldn't forgive them for what they did to my country, my family, and to the rest of the world. They were supposed to be an advanced race, able to see right from wrong, and should have recognized the suffering they were supporting.

When we questioned the German civilians about the Nazi crimes, they denied knowing anything about them. This pattern of feigned ignorance would infect Germany as its citizens tried to break ties with its past. They were very reluctant to talk to us, but their behavior suggested they knew what transpired in the concentration camps. I saw what the Nazis did to people who opposed them. I knew about the concentration camps, especially in Belgium. Everyone knew the camps existed, and there was no way anyone could ignore it. Many concentration camps were scattered all over Europe. We had three of them in Belgium.

Later, we crossed the Rhine at Mariaburg, via Deutz, Kalk, and Brück, and arrived late that afternoon at our destination in Bensberg. It was a beautiful little town with some castles, a large monastery, and a fortress downtown. The fortress looked more like an old castle and was located in the highest part of town, which overlooked the whole area. The British Provost (MP) now occupied the fortress called Schloss. Our barracks were on the grounds of a large new monastery a couple of miles out of town that was requisitioned by the Belgian army. We arrived at our barracks in Bensberg around two or three in the morning and were hungry and tired. We stopped by a military kitchen where we saw a large butcher's block table loaded with sandwiches, and we could smell coffee. We asked the cook if we could have some of those sandwiches and coffee. He gave us the okay but said to wait until he had beaten the bugs out of the sandwiches. He wasn't joking! As he hit the sandwiches, we saw large roaches running out the corned beef sandwiches and falling to the ground. For a few seconds we froze, but we were so hungry that we grabbed the sandwiches and most of us ate two of them. Nobody complained or got sick from that meal; no doubt the strong coffee killed any remaining living roaches. I still think about those sandwiches every time I see a roach or eat corned beef.

The monastery was an incredible place to be staying and a far cry from traditional camp. The monks there had begun returning to their ancient monastery. The new monastery luckily hadn't suffered much damage and was built out of beautiful white marble. There were numerous statues of saints also sculpted out of solid white marble. I wondered which church or building in Europe they were stolen from. We had been hearing stories of SS officers disguising themselves as monks to hide from prosecution in the monasteries. The SS officers luckily stood out like a sore thumb to the trained eye. Actual monks in this monastery, as part of their religious custom, had long beards. When a monk was noticed to have a rather short beard, it became a matter of investigation. We ordered each suspect to strip to the waist and raise his left arm into the air. We were looking for any tattoos on the underside of the man's left arm. If the monk in question was tattooed on his left arm, then he was immediately taken outside and shot. The monks were not in the habit of tattooing their blood types on their left arms as the SS were. This tattoo

The Bensberg Monastery, where we discovered Nazis posing as monks

allowed German medical personnel to identify a wounded SS soldier's blood type with ease. The tattoo allowed us to weed out dozens of SS officers hiding amongst the monks.

Germany was a beautiful country before the war, and every so often we would find traces of this beauty. The small towns often offered the closest glimpse. The majority of the larger towns and cities were in absolute ruins. Most of the cities looked like ghost towns. In 1946, when I crossed the River Rhine for the second time on our way to Bensberg, I noticed much less destruction, but this countryside was still badly scarred and showed many signs of battles.

One evening after the great meal we checked in with our unit, the Eleventh infantry battalion, who ordered us to patrol the surrounding woods. There had been reported gunfire and suspicious activity for a long time, but the German police didn't do anything about it. We discovered why. We found several German civilians murdered for collaborating with the Allies. We went into high alert for snipers, booby traps, and mines. We were told that earlier in the morning, the main road had been mined and strung with wire, which had decapitated two soldiers in a jeep. Exploding mines killed three other soldiers nearby as well. This scenario played out repeatedly in occupied Germany. The Nazis were defeated, but we still found ourselves fighting them.

Patrols went out day and night searching suspected homes, castles, and all sorts of barns and sheds. Some of those castles were fairly modern but some unbelievably old. The old castles were still occupied by descendants of royalty or other elite and looked like what you see in the movies. They still displayed armors, shields, swords, and flags showing the family coat of arms.

We fought through many ambushes and were lucky when we located and destroyed a stronghold of fanatic Nazi holdouts. We lost many men during those supposedly peaceful days after the war. Every mission we were sent on came with the risk of ambush. The Nazis had brainwashed their countrymen so severely that they were willing to give their lives even after an unconditional surrender. We were happy to kill them, but often the risk outweighed the reward.

A few months later we were ordered to move to Köln (Cologne), where we faced the same problems. The whole town was in ruins, which gave the Nazi holdouts great hiding places. Unreliable sources gave us information that led us often into an ambush and the unnecessary deaths of more men. The Wehrwolfs knew they didn't stand a chance if we found them and gave us hell while they could. Our orders were to clear the enemy out regardless of the situation. It's never easy to kill a man who puts little value on his own life.

Yupe

While on patrol in Koln, we spotted a German man trying to hide and attempting to run away from us. He looked suspicious, so we chased him. We caught up with him very easily because he was limping badly. We were right behind him and screamed at him to stop. When he turned around, we saw a terrifying fear in his eyes. Exhausted and hurting, he fell to the ground. We helped him up and asked him why he was running. He could hardly speak and was trembling. After calming down, he told us that he was German and had been a political prisoner. He had been looking for his family for more than a year. He had no way to research their whereabouts, so he simply searched town to town and building to building. He was hungry and had no place to go. His name was Yupe. We decided to take him with us for a good meal and rest. The more I looked at him, the more I saw the sadness and despair in his eyes. When we arrived back to camp and washed up before the meal, Yupe pulled his sleeves up to wash his hands and I couldn't help but notice the terrible scars and open wounds on both arms. We questioned him about the scars and he told us he had been tortured on several occasions. He explained how he had been hung with butcher's meat hooks by the tendons of his arms and by the tendons of his legs. Some of the meat hooks left permanent open and stretched holes, which were badly infected. No wonder he was limping when walking or trying to run. Our battalion decided to adopt Yupe and took him to our army hospital. When released, he stayed with us where we could help and feed him. We told him we didn't expect anything from him, but he wanted to help and said he felt like helping us now that he was one of us. While on patrol, he stayed back at camp and did some of the chores. It gave us great satisfaction to see Yupe recover.

Yupe seemed happy with us and it was good to have him around. His health was improving some, but he still suffered from infections and occasional fever, and was very anemic. We asked him constantly to slow down and rest and always reminded him that he wasn't expected to do anything. He insisted on helping where he could. He was a good man whose life was stolen from him by the unforgiving power of the Nazis.

Our resolution strengthened to hunt down these die-hard SS soldiers still hiding in homes, barns, sheds, cellars, caverns, forests, hills, and ruins. It was hard to believe the harm they could inflict on their own people.

A few months later our battalion moved to Bonn, Germany, a town on the banks of the Rhine River where Beethoven was born. Bonn had not been too badly damaged and therefore became the capital of West Germany. There was a nice and very large park right on the banks of the river Rhine, which was occupied previously by high-class Nazis. We visited Bonn University, which had been damaged by many explosions and was in the process of being repaired.

Blumenthal

We moved into the military barracks in Bonn and looked forward to sleep, food, and rest. A couple of weeks later, however, we were ordered to Blumenthal to escort a convoy of ambulances transporting surviving political prisoners back to Bonn. The victims were being rescued from a hard labor camp in Blumenthal nearly a year after their discovery. They couldn't leave sooner because they needed to recover from their starved conditions and injuries. They were in very poor health, and most of them were probably not going to survive. These people had lost everything meaningful in their lives, and most of them had lost the will to live. One special German mother and her two daughters survived four years in that hard labor camp. The reason for their imprisonment was the mother's refusal to honor and salute her Nazi husband. After their release from the hospital, Mutty and her two daughters lived in Bonn in an upstairs apartment and worked in the laundry room of the local hospital. One day, one of the daughters told me her SS dad sent them a letter to let them know he survived and was going to be released from a prison camp soon. He somehow had been able to locate them. He was sending threatening and frightening letters, in which he warned them that he couldn't wait to get back to them so he could beat them some more. I told Mutty and the girls not to worry, because we would be there to protect them. They told us what he was capable of and warned us that he was a cruel and vicious man. We comforted Mutty and her girls, saying he was the type of person we liked to encounter. We posted guards and informed the German police of what was going on. I was not in town a few weeks later when the husband showed up at the apartment drunk, angry, and shouting threats at his wife and kids. The Belgian guards were at top of the stairs to the apartment waiting for him.

My handsome brother-in-law, Don Farnsworth

When he finally reached the stairway leading to Mutty's apartment, the guards ordered him to stop and leave. He yelled, screamed, and was raging mad. He was warned a second time to stop and to leave, but he kept on coming up the stairs. One of the Belgian guards opened fire and killed him. There was no contest from the German Police, who testified that there was no other choice. We were glad for Mutty and her daughters, who were able to sleep without fear at last. Mutty's two young daughters were typical tall, blue-eyed, slender German beauties named Erika and Brigit. Brigit had become pregnant by an American GI and had a little baby girl. The GI had promised to return for her and their daughter, but that day never came. Erika suggested to me that we become more than friends, but I was not interested in anything more than helping her. As pretty as she was, I was aware of the difficulties it would present to me upon returning home. I realized that she probably saw me as a ticket out of the hell she was living in.

Germany had a huge problem with the black market for many years after the war. The German police were not trustworthy, so we kept them under watchful eye. We were never really sure if they were former SS or not. They patrolled with us and assisted in apprehending black marketeers. These German police were extremely tough on suspected black marketeers. They would harass them and beat them when they were caught. The items we confiscated were often very expensive items stolen from abandoned or unoccupied buildings.

In 1946, my sister Lucienne married an American Master Sergeant named Don Farnsworth and moved to the American Zone of Occupation in the town of Bremerhaven, which was in the northwest part of Germany. My parents went to visit them shortly after. While traveling by train on the Northern Express, they came through the British Zone of Occupation where they had a one-hour layover in the Central Station of Cologne. I had made arrangements to see them during the layover. Transportation in Germany was not a problem if you had cigarettes, coffee, or nylon stockings, which were highly sought after. I asked around and found a fantastic deal to travel first class in a rented Mercedes Benz with chauffeur in uniform. The transportation was fantastic and the chauffeur was pleasant. I brought along a friend and we enjoyed all this comfort and luxury for a whole day at the cost of only one carton of Lucky Strike cigarettes.

I enjoyed every minute catching up with my parents. They were very glad to see me. I brought a few presents for them and they brought me fresh breakfast rolls, pastries, and Belgian chocolates. The visit was very good, but too brief. We hoped for an hour layover but the schedule changed, and we had less than thirty minutes together.

When I got back to camp I put the rolls in a tight bag secured inside my helmet and hung the whole thing off the ceiling light with a thin rope. I was sure the rats wouldn't be able to get to them but two days later, to my surprise,, something had devoured most of the center of the rolls. The likely culprit was a mouse because the rats we lived with were too big to handle the thin rope.

On an early morning, after I finished rotating the guards, I stopped by the military kitchen to sit and enjoy a cup of hot coffee when one of my on-duty guards suddenly walked in, apparently abandoning his post. I asked him what he was doing walking away from his post. He didn't bother to answer me and helped himself to a cup of coffee. I ordered him to put the cup down, stand at attention and answer me. I asked him again why he left his post and what he did with his weapon. He retorted rudely that his rifle was outside. I told him to put that coffee down and to instantly return to his post. He threw the coffee across the room and ripped a fire-ax off the wall. He broke into a rage and swung the ax through the back legs of my chair, which caused me to fall backwards. Before I could get up, he swung the ax again, barely missing my head. I grabbed my 9mm out of my holster, aimed at his kneecap, and fired a

Me after the war, about 1947

shot through his leg. That dropped him to the floor screaming in pain. As he dropped the ax, it barely missed my face. A couple of guys rushed in to help and tried to make sense of this scene. They called the ambulance and rushed him to the hospital in agonizing pain. The shooting was investigated, which found me in military court. The case concluded quickly, and my attacker was sentenced to ten years in the military prison for abandoning his watch and weapon and attempting to kill a superior officer.

On another occasion, the British brought me before the military court and accused me of unnecessarily killing a Nazi. I had been given orders to guard a resting train full of weapons and ammunition. An unknown German approached the train and I ordered this man in German to stop. I ordered him once more with added emphasis, and he again ignored me. He got within a few feet of me at which time I shot him. The British contested that I should have tried another way to stop the man. The military court quickly ruled in my favor and dismissed the case after hearing the details.

In November 1947, I came home for a three-day visit while escorting a supply convoy going through my hometown. I had not been able to let my parents know of my visit and hoped it would be a surprise for them. Since the convoy was traveling near my home, I was dropped off at the nearest intersection. It was very late at night when I arrived, and luckily I still had the key to the front door. I was unable to sneak up on my parents because our little wolf dog again announced my arrival. After a short visit, a bath, and a shave, I went to my old room and was stretched out in my bed at last! It was so good to be home. I awoke at eight the next morning and was ready to do something different with the little time I had left. After breakfast I engaged in some good conversation with my parents, and in the afternoon I decided to surprise my grandmother, who was living in a Catholic Convent retirement home for women who had retired from government positions. I checked in at the entrance and asked a nun to see my grandmother. She lived on the second floor where the nun asked me to wait while she went to get her. Grandmother appeared on top of the stairs and greeted me with a smile. She then informed me that this was not my scheduled day to visit her. She said that today was my Aunt Mimi's day and that she was just about due to arrive. I told her I was leaving the next day and that I had not seen her for more than two years. She said she was sorry and wished me the best of luck. She didn't leave me any options, so I left. That's the way my grandmother lived her life—as a former school principal, with discipline and very little affection or love.

On my twenty-first birthday in 1948 I was back in Germany on a mission with the Belgian army in the Drachenfels Mountains of west-central Germany. I was struck by the magnificent beauty of these mountains and later would often find myself thinking of them. The image of them became a place of solace I created in my head to escape some of the horrors around me. I remember thinking about our mission and how it would be sad to die on my twenty-first birthday. My birthday had little meaning to the Belgian army. There was no birthday recognition of any kind in the Belgian service. This particular mission turned into a very dangerous birthday surprise for me. We had two squads or forty men with us and had been sent to investigate machine gun fire reported in the deep forest. As in most missions, we were not enjoying ourselves. We had covered a good portion of forest when we came upon a large hidden castle. This castle had the classic stone walls, towers, and surrounding moat. As we came into view, Wehrwolf snipers fired on us from the towers. We learned that a former SS officer owned the castle and he was ready to defend it with his own personal army. This Nazi hadn't paid much attention to the German surrender and seemed hell-bent on defending his castle against any Allied forces. Through sheer patience, determination, and several hours of firing, we finally took out the Wehrwolfs, which allowed us to gain closer proximity to the castle. We then utilized our grenades and machine

The Drachenfels Mountain, where we encountered a Nazi resistance pocket inside a count's castle

guns to blast our way inside. This old castle was straight from medieval times. The stone walls were adorned with shields from different eras of Germany. There were swords and lances hanging everywhere and two shields over the entrance bearing the family coat of arms. Many historical flags from different clans over the years filled the rest of the wall space. It took a lot of time, but we finally managed to kill all enemies inside. We succeeded in our mission and eliminated a hidden SS hornet nest, but lost three good men doing it. This was an extreme example of the Nazi holdovers and their undying devotion to the Nazi cause. Once they had made up their minds to die for their cause, then our only option was to oblige them. In each case, we had to expend precious lives and resources to exterminate these fanatical holdouts.

R&R

Months later, I was off for a few days in Ghent and decided to call some buddies for a drink. I met with Paul Berkenbosch to catch up on things. Paul was a longtime friend who had been sent to a concentration camp for speaking up against Hitler during the occupation. He was picked up unannounced by the Gestapo late one evening and disappeared from my life until the war ended. He had been sent west to the coast of France. His particular prison camp was a hard labor camp. He spent every waking hour helping to build the Atlantic wall in Normandy as part of the German Organization Todt. The same wall that Allied forces had to scale on D-day. He suffered long and hard under the brutal conditions and had nearly been worked to death during his imprisonment. Several times he told me that he had hoped death would take him away from that life. After his liberation, which was sooner than most prison camps due to its western location, he received excellent treatment from Allied doctors. He seemed to have recovered sufficiently to live a normal postwar life. I always felt at peace in Paul's presence. He was appreciative of the life he had been spared and cherished each day. Paul and I became great friends after the war ended. The stories we exchanged were reason enough to get together when we had the chance.

1949

In 1949, I was surprised when I was temporarily discharged from the army. I said temporarily because I wouldn't receive my final discharge until I reached the age of fifty, per Belgian law. The Belgian army could recall me at any time for any reason. Meanwhile I would remain in the army reserve, and once a month I had to spend a weekend at the army barracks to train at the firing range and attend various meetings.

I thoroughly enjoyed my first extended leave of absence in May of 1949. I called my parents from Brussels to let them know I was on my way home. My mother asked me what she could fix for my homecoming supper and I requested a big potato salad with sliced hard-boiled eggs, bacon chips, shredded lettuce, mushrooms, little green peas, parsley, and real mustard and mayonnaise dressing. This was my favorite meal prepared by my mother. I remember that particular salad as tasting especially great as it was coupled with my joy to be home. That first week off went by fast, but it was eventful. Things looked different after being gone for so long. I remembered streets being wider and boulevards longer and larger. My chronic absences over the years caused me to miss the rebuilding and growth of my home. I often found that places from my memories had disappeared or been drastically altered, undoubtedly by war.

Marcel Cerdan

While on temporary discharge, I had the good fortune to spend some more time with my old bomb-making buddy Bernard as well as some other friends. We often visited our favorite bar in downtown Ghent, which featured a large dance floor and a Wurlitzer, an early version of the jukebox. Our lady friends accompanied us on occasion. Lily, whom I had seen only briefly, loved this place and made it hard for me to keep up with her. She loved this scene and wouldn't leave the dance floor. Jazz and swing music owned the place and the drinks were flowing easy. During the German occupation, jazz music was banned, which sent it underground. Even so, it seemed to flourish in secret more than ever. After the war, swing and bebop were at their peak. This particular bar was known at the time as a pickup bar. It certainly was the place

The greatest French boxer of all time, Marcel Cerdan (right).
Photo by Hulton Deutsch/Corbis Premium Historical Collection/Getty Images.

to have a good time.

One particular night while we danced, a fellow unknown to me kept attempting to dance with Lily. He appeared to have it in his mind that he would steal her away. After his advances became irritating, I tapped him on the shoulder and asked him to quit dancing with my girlfriend. He replied that if she wanted to dance with him then he would have no problem dancing with her. I countered, "I will not tell you again to stay away from her." He smiled at me and turned back towards Lily with little interest in my suggestion. I stepped to the bar and grabbed my drink, then promptly marched over, got his attention, and threw my beer in his face. This I imagined would teach him the necessary lesson. The next thing I remember, I was lying outside the bar on the ground bleeding from the face. Lily held my head as she explained that the man who punched me had knocked me over a table then under the next table where I stopped, unconscious. She, with the help of my friends, dragged me out to the sidewalk. After I composed myself, I became angry and pronounced to all who would listen that I was going in there to knock that guy out. Bernard, who had witnessed the entire event, began to howl with laughter. He explained that I should reconsider. "Why should I?" I demanded. Bernard, amidst his continued laughter, informed me that the offender was a man by the name of Marcel Cerdan. I demanded to know who the hell Marcel Cerdan was. He answered that Marcel Cerdan was in fact the current middleweight boxing champion of the world. This effectively changed my mind in regard to any recourse. I did go back inside and bought a beer, which I offered to Marcel. He thanked me and I apologized for spilling my beer on him. I did though respectfully request that he stop dancing with my girlfriend, to which he kindly agreed. I ran into Marcel many times after that, and we developed a brief friendship. Algerian-born Marcel had turned pro at the tender age of eighteen in Morocco, which was part of French North Africa. The year prior to his fist meeting me in that bar, Marcel had beat Tony Vale to become World Middleweight Champion. Marcel would lose his belt shortly after to legendary American boxer Jake "The Raging Bull" LaMotta when he separated his shoulder during a first round knockdown. Even then, Marcel was able to last into the tenth round before his trainer threw in the towel. In route to the rematch three fights later, the plane in which he traveled across the Atlantic to New York crashed in the Azores, tragically killing all on board. Marcel was thirty-three years old. He is still considered by many the greatest French boxer of all time.

Back and Forth

Western Germany had been seeing escalating problems requiring additional military interventions. For some reason, the British had relocated their troops in large numbers back to the homeland. The Polish and Belgians were to fill the void. Things had improved a little by then, and the German rebuilding had shown some steadier progress.

The Belgian Army called me back into service because of the departure of the British. Once back, I received the sad news that Yupe had developed a physical problem from which he couldn't recover. He had so many internal and external scars that never healed properly. A sudden infection shut down his liver and kidneys, and he died. They told me he didn't die alone, and that several of our guys were with him at the hospital and at the funeral. The Belgian Army honored him with a military funeral, with his coffin draped with the pre-Nazi German flag. Yupe's sad life influenced everyone who knew him. It always kept our resolve strong to rid the earth of Hitler's flag bearers. The evil that caused Yupe's unimaginable suffering would always be defended against by the powers of good. I like to imagine he found comfort working with us, and hopefully we gave him some semblance of the family he lost and so desperately needed.

In November 1950, while still in Germany, I was on short leave from a mission toward Hamburg when I had a bad accident while riding a friend's Harley. I was riding on a German superhighway in the middle of the night and noticed several leftover patches of snow and ice, which were tricky to ride on. I saw a fairly large and long bend ahead of me and decided to switch lanes. When I accelerated to reach the high side of the road, I accelerated on a patch of black ice, lost control, and went over the top lane into the safety barrier. That is all I remember, because something knocked me out. An American truck following me saw the accident and picked me up and took me to the nearest hospital. I woke up in a German hospital while they were patching me up for a transfer to a Belgian Army Hospital. I had internal problems they couldn't deal with. So I was placed into a temporary body cast that completely immobilized me and was transferred to a Belgian Army facility. I was diagnosed with cracked ribs, hip, left arm, leg, and a left eye that needed immediate surgery. There must have been at least a dozen military patients in the dormitory, and a lot of painful jokes were exchanged (laughing while you hurt is painful). Weeks went by during which I endured a very painful recovery, but made many friends. When I finally got out of the body cast I was transferred to rehab, and three weeks later, I had sufficiently recovered and returned to duty.

Being of able body again, I was ordered to return with my outfit to Belgium after the new year began. Before I returned to duty I was told I had two weeks' furlough, which I used to visit my sister Lucienne and her husband Don. Lucienne was a secretary to one of the American generals during the war, and Don was a master sergeant who was in and out of this same office. Their office interaction sparked a romance that ended in marriage. They lived happily in Bremerhafen. I had a wonderful time on this visit. We loved going to the firing range, where Don's war collection of pistols, rifles, and machine guns kept us very busy.

I was temporarily discharged again at the end of 1951, and somehow things were not the same in Belgium. The politics were bad, the elections of officials showed a strong trend toward the Humanistic Alliance, and the idea of the new world order was introduced by the Benelux Alliance as a solution for the future European Nations' Alliance. What this all amounted to was a misguided country, and one that I no longer felt at home in. People seemed to have lost their Belgian identity.

I started my civilian life all over again. Jobs were hard to find and hard to keep, especially in between army recalls. I landed some good jobs and then because of recalls, lost them. I was struggling financially and was ready for a big change. I regretted the irreplaceable loss of my youth and my education. I went back to school, which was in the same building it was in before the war. Instead of sitting in the classroom, I picked up the class materials and completed the courses at home. It didn't take long to earn the Belgian equivalent of the GED. I needed this to gain access to most jobs I wanted.

One of the temporary jobs I procured was as chauffeur for a furrier. I worked for a friend who was working for his family. His family had actually made a pot full of money during the war selling furs to German wives or girlfriends of German officers. I drove a top-of-the-line black four-door Chrysler and chauffeured two or three beautiful models around to show the furs to the customers. This wasn't a bad job, and it had some wonderful perks, but I knew this was going to end at the next recall.

I didn't get depressed but tried to be optimistic. I desired a job that wasn't behind a desk. I wanted to be in sales, where I was out in the field talking to people. I enjoyed the interaction very much.

PART 3

Postwar
1949-Now

CHAPTER 6

Moving On

During my military service I saw my future in a whole different perspective, and I surely didn't expect the problems I encountered upon entering civilian life. I was disappointed with the pace of life since I had grown used to constant activity in the service. No one owed me anything for my service, and I felt like I didn't owe anyone anything except respect, but I felt a certain emptiness being a civilian again. I felt like I didn't belong anymore. The country didn't have that same warm feeling. Many soldiers returned from the war only to find available jobs had been filled. We were undesirables in the working world. The first thing a prospective employer asked me was, "Are you free from your service obligations?" When I explained that I was subject to recall, I was immediately considered as a temporary employee or a day laborer. There is nothing wrong with being a day laborer, but I felt I could do better. I would need a lot of patience and understanding from an employer.

Cork

As a man in the service, I was used to moving around often and going places, following orders and giving orders. I had more to offer my world than as a day laborer. I felt I could lead men, and I could instruct them. I was able to learn new skills quickly, or at least I believed myself able. All the training and experience I received in the army wasn't helping me enter the workforce any easier. Dad offered me work with him in the family business, which I figured would be good for me. After so many years of absence, it was good to be home for a while. I imagined I would get plenty of rest and relaxation and gain some weight back, but this wasn't the case. As tired as my body was, I was also restless and couldn't sleep well. I was suffering from bad nightmares about the war. The most common nightmares involved explosions. Rarely I experienced the much darker nightmares involving bodies and being shot. I often heard explosions in my sleep. I wasn't able to fully relax and clear my head from what I had witnessed. Sleep came at a steep price for me. I wanted so badly to rest and enjoy a normal life with the new freedom I now had. I had a lot of catching up to do.

I began my job in dad's cork factory, but I knew in my heart that I would not enjoy doing it. I had little interest in making corks, but Dad asked me to give it a try. The cork business I knew had a very complex operation. The kind of workday it required was torture to me. In calibration and triage of the corks you had to have good eyes, pay attention, and be focused for eight hours a day. While dad's factory produced millions upon millions of corks of all sizes, nothing new was ever created. The work was very monotonous and lacked any stimulation. A cork was a cork. I felt sorry for my dad and thought it was good that he was an architect. The creative side, where he could design custom buildings, was a direct contrast to the cork business. I think the cork business by itself would have depressed him. He even learned to regularly incorporate cork into his construction designs, as insulation. He depended on good people to run his cork business, but I discovered quickly that I didn't want any part of it. For the right person it would be a good job. I was not that person. I wanted to create things, and an architect I was not.

I worked for Dad for a very short while, but right from the start, we had problems with the work schedule. I was actually working for my dad, but not working with him. He was the boss whereas I agreed with him and followed his orders and suggestions. I made the suggestion to him that I have a different work schedule so that I had more time off. He said, "There are no exceptions, everyone works together." He wouldn't change our working agreement but did realize that I was unhappy with the arrangement. He suggested representing our firm and finding some ways to sell needed articles besides cork. He suggested the crown cork, which is actually a metal cap; bottling; or even labels, but ultimately Dad could sense my displeasure and recommended that I find a different job that made me happy.

The war robbed me of completing my education and preparing me for the future, but I had learned enough basics to be able to complete whatever program I chose. I had to learn quickly in the army and to do tasks effectively. I liked the army and wished I could have qualified for advancement, but in those days, higher rank belonged to the higher class only. My parents made enough money to elevate us into a higher class but we lacked a title, which was the key factor in attaining upper-class status. A title was handed down rather than earned, so if you weren't born into this class system, you rarely achieved its benefits. In the military position I had attained, I knew that I would not be able to achieve high enough class to earn sufficient money.

As for my adjustment to civilian life, I had a few problems to resolve. It was very hard getting back to a normal routine. I was uptight and couldn't rest. I

My mother Jeanne, 1945

Mom, Dad, and me at home

Belgian Regimental Police, Bonn, 1946

Dragon Class
Some of the happiest times of my life were spent sailing.

wanted to live a normal life and be independent, but that would require a job with a regular income.

After my cork job ended and between the army recalls, I managed to hold several temporary jobs and take short vacations. I rekindled my love affair with sailing, which began when I was a young child. I spent much time on the water sailing on the Scheldt River. I applied to the Belgian National Sailing team through my dad's yacht club. Dad happened to be on the selection committee, and he pulled some strings to get me in. After I was accepted, I began training to compete in the competitive sailing circuit. We competed in the international sailing races in the North Sea, with Holland, England,

My happy place

France, and Denmark. It was a great life except for the pay, which was menial. I could not support myself in this career path. As much as I wanted this life, sailing would have to remain a weekend hobby.

Most weekends were spent at the Royal Yacht Club, where I had purchased, with money borrowed from Dad, a twenty-two-foot solid mahogany sailboat named *Onyx*. We enjoyed our freedom on that sailboat and utilized it as often as we could. The *Onyx* was wonderful, but quickly ran out of space. My old friend Bernard, also a sailor, and I decided to combine our resources and upgrade our sailing vessel. We traded up for a thirty-two-foot Dragon class sailboat named *DB1*, which was formerly owned by the king of Belgium, who never sailed it. I spent as much free time as possible sailing the North Sea to Holland to the north of France and even to Portugal.

Sailing or boating in Belgium was not only a sport, but also a way to travel or move commercial and industrial goods. I got hired on a few large barges and really enjoyed it. The income again was not sufficient to support me, so it wouldn't last. As far as income-producing jobs were concerned, I applied for several commercial art and illustration jobs in local consulting and engineering firms. During the interviews, I told them the truth about my education and employment history. This didn't help my cause. I also showed them my portfolio, which Dad had saved from my childhood. I had added a few new pieces, but my early Christmas cards were part of my collection. One firm commissioned me for several projects that I was able to finish before another army recall. They were impressed with my work and artistic ability, but because of the possibility of recall, could not hire me full time.

The next opportunity came when the American-based DuPont Company interviewed me. They had sent a representative to Brussels looking for a salesman to run their Belgium operation. I was accepted as sales rep for their crown corks and brand labels. I had plenty to do and was on the road Monday through Wednesday, and sold many popular Spanish aperitifs made by the companies Palomino and Vergara. These were exceptionally easy to sell to the high-dollar spots. Only God could have made this possible! I loved this job. I could see myself working at this job for a very long time. The only thing that worried me was a telegram from the Belgian army. After several months, the telegram came just as I feared, and off I went without hesitation. The DuPont Company, in their efforts to stay in business, filled my job. My stint in the army had cost me dearly, and I was powerless to change my situation.

Another opportunity came several weeks later. I met a distributor of high quality and very expensive liqueurs, wines, and cognacs, out of Cadiz, Spain. He was looking for someone to represent their products to individuals, instead of being sold off the shelves in a liquor store. I was introduced to my future boss, who explained all the details of the production and distribution. The whole idea of personal presentation appealed to me. The good commissions were an incentive to work and sell. I carried a leather traveling briefcase filled with small bottles of the products as samples. They outfitted me with expensive business cards and a list of available merchandise with suggested costs and shipping information. I could sell anywhere and at any time. My first sales were through the Yacht and Sailing Club. The product was so good that it sold itself. My clientele were the well-off and the rich. Most of them had known me for quite a while when I was sailing with the clubs and knew my dad because he was on the board of directors of the Yacht and Sailing Club.

I bought a used British Vauxhall, which was a solid four-door, sun-roofed, leather interior car. I felt quite successful riding around in this. It made traveling easier, and I occasionally drove my dad to his cork customers, even though he preferred to travel by train. He had been traveling for so long and so often that the train ticket checker knew him, and would wake him up at the right time and at the right station so he would not sleep through his stop.

So Dad and I went our separate ways in regard to work, but we still had a strong bond, and we didn't let our differences interfere with our relationship. He even became a customer of mine. I found him some very good sherry, which I supplied to him anytime he ran out. Dad even got me some clients.

Now and then we talked about my business, and he was amazed at how well I was doing with my new employment. He began referring his friends to me.

I began having mechanical problems with my Vauxhall and traded it for an almost-new four-door black-and-white Buick convertible. Now I was really comfortable and looked prosperous in my large Buick selling the Palomino products. My opportunities with the ladies greatly improved with this job. I didn't mind sharing my samples with them as we rode around in my Buick.

I made arrangements with Bernard to help me move the booze in case the army recalled me. I would pay him my commission whenever the recall came. This gave Bernard something entertaining to do, and he kept the business rolling. The weeks went by, then came the recall. This time I was sent to Bonn, Germany. I reluctantly gathered my gear and took off by convoy for Germany.

Several days later, while on patrol in Bonn, I noticed a military courier sitting on his Harley Davidson, just waiting. He also saw me and stared at me. I knew him! Something about his eyes reminded me of my worst enemy from my school days. While growing up we got into fights at school, at the swimming pool, soccer field, and wherever else we had an opportunity. We had some serious bloody fistfights that reoccurred for many years because he was Flemish and I was considered French. The two cultures had a long arduous history of fighting, which stemmed from living in close proximity and speaking two different languages. Etienne and I more than likely succumbed to this entrenched custom as children, even though we probably had learned it from our families. Enemy or not, here he stood after such a long uncertain split. I couldn't believe it! It was really my old Flemish enemy! I yelled, "Etienne, is that you?" He got off his Harley, did not answer me, but came straight toward me. I expected he was going to start a fight or at least an argument, but instead, he hugged me! I hugged him back. Things were obviously different now. We were glad to reconnect and had a short but good visit. We promised each other to get together when released from the military. A few months later, after I was back home, I looked him up. He lived temporarily with his parents, who owned a fairly large and beautiful châlet that had a nightclub and a good-sized restaurant. The hotel side had nice spacious rooms overlooking the river. It was a beautiful place in a great setting surrounded by woods, and right on the banks of the Lys River, which was located about twenty-five miles outside of Ghent. I rented a room for a few days and visited with them. We had a great time talking about the school days and the war years. Our troubled relationship had been buried.

A strange thing began happening to me. I noticed that when I was called back by the army and had to quit drinking for that period of time, that I not only missed the product but I also craved it. This feeling caused me some concern. I had numerous friends from the war who had drunk themselves to death, and it had always scared me. I knew I had a tough decision to make, but based on what I had encountered in the war, I had a very strong desire

I loved working for Coca-Cola. Army recall ended this job.

to remain alive. I was not about to become an alcoholic. The lifestyle I had when selling the alcohol was dangerous and reckless, and I feared it would lead me to an early grave. So I made the very difficult decision to quit once I returned from duty, even though I doubted I could replace the lost income. I still believe that this decision had significant impact on my future. My role model in this regard was my uncle Jules, who after his World War I service had the same problem when he was selling high-quality champagne. He had become an alcoholic and nearly killed himself. His decision to quit and move to Canada probably saved his life. I had heard this story many times growing up, and it stayed with me. I really did love the lifestyle this job brought with it, but I felt it was not conducive to a great future.

I called the distributor and gave my resignation. I checked with the engineering firm for whom I made several illustrations, but was told that during my absence they had hired a full-time artist. They said they could use me, however, when they needed additional help.

I hated to part with my Buick but I could no longer afford it. The owner of the Buick dealership gave me a prospect. I sold the Buick to a very wealthy family who wanted it for their teenage daughter's pet lion, Tarzan. I became friends with the family, and occasionally the daughter called me to drive Tarzan around. Liliane told me how her father had business in the Belgian Congo and gave her the lion when it was barely weaned; it just got larger and larger but also sweeter and sweeter. I remember laughing when I saw how much meat it took daily to fill him up. I witnessed personally how he signaled that he was hungry. Tarzan would let out a tremendous roar that no one could ignore. I was glad it was her baby and not mine. The family needed the large Buick to carry the full-grown lion around along with the nineteen-year-old girl. We had to reinforce the suspension and the frame due to the lion's tremendous weight. We also installed a large hook to secure the lion in the back seat. Upon receiving the car, Liliane was delighted, and we immediately took Tarzan for a ride. Tarzan seemed happy in the back seat and often he fogged up the rear view mirror with his warm breath.

On my return from yet another recall, I checked with my ex-enemy friend Etienne, who was employed at the Coca-Cola Corporation. He asked what I was doing and suggested that I should apply for a job with Coca-Cola. He explained what he was doing and said I should meet the boss. As I was unemployed, I applied for a sales position and was accepted. It turned out that I could make a fairly good salary while remaining somewhat independent and have a good amount of fun. My boss Bill Jacquemins was an American. You can well imagine we got along just fine from day one. I had a new Chevrolet truck and was assigned a route partially located in the city that stretched out several miles on a major highway toward Brussels. Customers in the industrial areas became my best clients. Etienne had a different area and route to work, but we drove to the office together and often met for lunch. The main highway on my route to the capital was lined with hotels, restaurants, bars, nightclubs, and many more good prospects. My territory was expanding fast. I liked what I was doing and would win several awards for sales. Within a few weeks of starting, I was promoted to supervisor, with eight delivery trucks on my route. I was now driving a promotional van. I introduced the refreshing Coca-Cola break into the industrial areas and installed water-cooled iceboxes with free Coca-Cola for a month in each of the prospects. During that time the employees received a free Coca-Cola break twice per day. This proved to the management that this Coca-Cola break would improve their production. Then, at night on my own time before returning to the plant, I picked a street and went from door to door inviting the people to taste a cool and refreshing free Coca-Cola. This helped my sales, which grew steadily. I also sold the most coolers and was getting extra commissions. I was making a good living working for Coca-Cola. There was no time to rest at this job, as I stayed very busy. It was rushing, pushing, shoving, selling, and promoting the product six to seven days per week, ten to twelve hours per day. I made a lot of friends and was happy on the job but had not taken that good rest I longed for. I was feeling very tired. You know the kind of tired I am talking about—exhausted and bone-tired.

After work Etienne and I often went to supper at customer's restaurants or at cafés where we played pool, foosball, dart games, bowling, and other bar games. Besides the guys I worked with, my old buddies Bernard, Paul, Jacques, Bill, Gilbert, and Ivan were always ready to go and have fun. This fun did help take my mind off my perpetual tiredness.

Then suddenly, Etienne and I were called back into the service for four months. After a few months of absence from the job, we had to start over again at square one. The Coca-Cola Company held our jobs for ninety days, but we didn't make it back on time, and my job was filled. I really hated losing that job. This same routine of losing jobs to recall went on and on and could continue until I turned fifty and received my discharge.

Life during the postwar years was a struggle. Nothing was normal and everything was changing. Belgium only had a small army, which was called on too often to do too many things that should be taken care of by a federal police force or regular civil police. Recovery was a long and arduous process that required everyone to assume responsibilities they normally wouldn't.

While dealing with my unemployment, my friend Bernard and I signed up for the Zuiderzee sailing races in Holland with our sailboat *DB1*, from the International Dragon class. We participated in the races representing Belgium and the Royal Yacht Club. There were Dutch, French, English, Danish, and Norwegian contenders, totaling more than two hundred, in identical class boats. Bernard and I never won a race, but we never came in last, either.

Then it happened again. While I was off racing in Holland my parents received a telegram from the Belgian Army ordering me to rejoin my regiment immediately. I decided to ignore it for a couple more days while we trained to compete in the races that were happening a few days later.

Three days later, I got home in the late afternoon, picked up my gear, and took off. Etienne had left two days earlier to rejoin his outfit. The reason for the recall was a big political problem which was threatening to erupt in a civil war between the Flemish and French populations. To top it off, we were in the midst of a general transportation strike, which left us without trains and buses. I had no idea how I was going to make it to my unit, which was located in a town called Louvain, about 175 miles from Ghent. All I could do was hitchhike, which wasn't a problem, as I was in uniform. In those days, patriotism was still at an all-time high. I got a ride to Brussels, and there a man and his wife went out of their way to take me to the military fort.

As soon as I reported at the guardhouse, I knew I was in trouble. Three days earlier my outfit had moved out into the Belgian Ardennes. I was questioned by the officer in charge, and after giving me a strong reprimand, he ordered me to take the next military mail truck going out to my company. When I finally got to my outfit, I had some more explaining to do. This time I had to face my commanding officer, who reminded me what accountability and duty meant and of my responsibility to obey a direct order. I knew all this, but I had messed up and had to listen to it. Thanks to my past record, I wasn't disciplined too severely and was able to resume my duties without problems. The problem our division was sent in to defuse was the same culture-differences battle that caused Etienne and I to fight as children. The Flemish and French detested each other, and we were sent in to stop them from killing each other. Our mere presence seemed to keep the violence from escalating.

Less than three months later, things were back to relative normalcy, and once more I went home and had to look for a job. Etienne got off before I did and bought a surplus Jeep and trailer from which he started an ice delivery business, selling to hotels, restaurants, cafés, and bars. He asked me if I would be interested in a partnership. Not having any other prospects, I joined him. It wasn't exactly what I had in mind to make a living, but temporarily, it was a paycheck. Daily we got up at three in the morning, went to the ice factory, loaded the trailer with big blocks of ice, and hit the road to make deliveries, preferably before daylight. It was hard work, and for several hours each morning, our shoulders were very cold and wet. We didn't sleep much because during the day we had to make deliveries and find new prospects. However, our business was slowly growing; we had fun, made some money, and didn't have any inventory to deal with. Best of all . . . we were independent.

All went well for a short while when another telegram arrived, again from the army. We quickly hired someone to handle our ice business. Unfortunately he was unreliable, and by the time we returned he had lost most of our business. Etienne was again discharged from his duty before I was, and told me when I arrived home that he was thinking seriously about volunteering for the war in Korea. He explained that he would get paid while serving, and after two years of duty, he would be released from the army and paid a flat sum of $2,000, which was a lot of money to us. He tried to talk me into doing the same, but I asked him to wait a while before deciding on it. A few days later, Etienne asked me if I would be interested in buying his interest in the ice business or if he could buy me out. He said he wanted to sell the business and had decided to go to Korea after all. I told him I wouldn't want the business without him as a partner, so he sold it. Etienne tried really hard to get me to volunteer, but something kept me from joining. A few days later he left and joined five thousand Belgian volunteers in Korea fighting the Communists. He liked the military lifestyle and was looking forward to the opportunity for action and combat duty. I decided against going to Korea, as I was done serving on a full-time basis. I wanted out permanently, but I didn't have a choice in the matter. I would fulfill my duty to my country as per law, but deep inside me I yearned for a way out.

Two weeks later Etienne was killed on the front line doing what he loved to do, fighting! It made me mad and very sad. It was a great loss for his parents because he was their only child. It was quite a loss for me also. I had a hard time dealing with it. I stayed for a while with his family to help comfort them. Considering how far the two of us had come from our elementary fights to becoming close friends, he was tough to lose. Losing my friend Etienne set me back a notch. I was becoming keenly aware that my life was going nowhere. I was tired of just getting by. I would never make anything of myself on the path that I was traveling.

The vice president of the yacht club had a beautiful sixty-four-foot yacht that was very seldom used. I had been sleeping in my sailboat for a few days as respite from the world and my sorrows. The vice president invited me for lunch and asked how I was doing. I told him I had been resting and staying on board reading books I hadn't read for a long time. He said that I was cramped for space and wanted me to move into his yacht. I told him I didn't want the added responsibility and was doing okay on my sailboat. He explained how much better I would be able to relax in his much-larger yacht. I knew he was correct and finally relented. Talk about comfort and luxury! This was a big jump for my ego, which could only inflate in this type of magnificent yacht.

There was always something exciting going on at the yacht club, and I now had all the comfort I could want. While I lived on the vice president's yacht, I worked on my sailboat. Then I decided to go back to sea. There was a fleet of large trawlers hiring for a twenty days' fishing trip. I checked with my military unit and left them a method of communication with the captain in case of emergency. The crew was informed where we were heading and also reminded that we volunteered for this, but that the catch would be a winner. As usual, there wasn't much rest and the food was lousy, but twenty days later there had been a super catch and the pay was excellent. We ate little more than fish during the trip—potatoes with fish, eggs and fish, beans and fish, and more fish for breakfast, lunch, and supper. It paid very well and provided the needed funds to take another sailing trip. But I wouldn't eat fish again for quite a while.

I waited for Bernard to return so we could embark on our next sailing adventure. Bernard lived in Bordeaux, France, for a while and a few weeks later came back home to stay. This time we took off from Ostende, Belgium, sailed the North Sea to the north of Holland, stopping in the harbors of Hook van Holland, Katwijk aan Zee, Bergen aan Zee, then entered the Walden Zee and docked a few days in the town of Harlingen. We continued toward Emden, Germany. We followed the North Frisian Islands to Wilhelmshafen, Germany, where we visited some friends. On the return trip we had a lot of bad weather, rough sea, and many delays, but it was a great trip that I will never forget. Then we made another short trip sailing south, but were so close to being broke that we had to return home to find jobs. Bernard went home and worked for his father for a while, and I found a fairly good job thanks to a date with a pretty brunette whose dad had a car dealership. Her dad represented the British Nuffield cars, trucks, Jaguars, the luxurious model Rover cars, as well as the Land Rover. The dealership also sold my favorite American General Motors cars. I became a car salesman.

The cars were selling well and I was often allowed to drive the brand-new demos, but I still wasn't happy with my life. I was twenty-five years old, single, and without a good solid future in sight. Selling cars was a temporary job and also a gamble in terms of income.

I was invited to Holland for another international sailing competition in the North Sea. I asked Bernard if he could get free and help me handle my sailboat in the ten days' races. He told me he would be there, and as usual, it was great fun. We didn't win a trophy but did well. We would need a little more training and needed to find a more effective way to trim the sail.

Quite often, Liliane would call me to help her take Tarzan for a ride. I always enjoyed it, and that lion was something else. Evidently he liked me enough and wanted me to wrestle with him before he got in the car. What an animal! Driving around with Tarzan amazed a lot of people on the street.

However, again it was time for a decision. Liliane was a beautiful young girl, but it became more and more obvious to me that she wanted a closer relationship. It could have happened, but she was the daughter of a very wealthy family, and I was not her father's first choice. I would never make the kind of money she was used to. Her way of life and mine were complete contrasts, and I refused to depend on her family to help support her. I had to tell her the truth. I had been making arrangements to leave Belgium permanently, and I was considering moving to United States as soon as all the arrangements were completed. She couldn't believe it. She was thinking that I would wake up to the opportunity to be in her family and was devastated with the idea of me leaving Belgium. She couldn't understand why I would want to leave. I told her she would find a much better choice than I and it was best to end it. I gently disappeared from her life.

USA

In 1949, my sister Lucienne and her American husband Don moved to his home in the United States. Don had grown up in Perryton, Texas. We missed them both very much and corresponded regularly. Before they settled down, they took a long vacation and traveled extensively all over the US. Don wanted my sister to see the beauty of the land before making the move. She was captivated, and after the move, made the suggestion to my parents and me that we join them in the US. They mailed us lots of pictures, which really opened our eyes to the opportunity. We talked about it more and more, but my parents were undecided. The seed had been planted, however, and grew every time the Belgian Army recalled me.

In early January 1952, I brought up the subject of moving to Texas, and asked my parents if they would seriously consider moving to the United States and starting a new life. I told them I needed a complete change in my life and needed a solid future. I didn't have a good future in Belgium, and I surely didn't like the political changes taking place. I didn't recognize the country that I knew and loved. People didn't have the same values as they did before the war. I welcomed learning a new culture and having the opportunity to start fresh. I met many Americans while in the US Army and enjoyed being with them. They were courageous and pleasant even in the worst circumstances. Each of them was proud to serve and loved their country and their respective states. The stories they told were magical to a man of my upbringing. Dad understood that the cork business was not appealing to me, but change to him would be tough. My dad was sixty-five years old and my mother was fifty-five, so a move of this nature would require a herculean effort. They had lived their entire lives in Belgium, and their roots and their other relatives were here. They said that I was the one who needed the change and to go ahead and start my life anew in Texas. I told them if we wanted to remain a family, we all needed to move. I told them I wanted to leave and start a brand new life, but not without them. I would get a job in Texas and help us in getting settled. I corresponded with Don in Texas, who had three sponsors lined up who guaranteed my employment. We talked it over and decided to wait a few more days to think about it. Meanwhile, I was contacting shipping companies to get some prices.

Moving Time

My parents and I had another meeting about our departure to Texas. They had talked about it over and over, and finally decided that being with their children was too important to remain in Belgium. We immediately applied for visas and inquired about the quota limits for the three of us to immigrate to the United States. My parents had to find a buyer for their businesses. They both had competitors whom they contacted, and a deal was made to sell the entities. Besides the business, they had to sell the property, furniture, and their inventory. We had to decide what to ship to Texas and what to liquidate, and do it quickly. It was simple for me because I could easily sell my car and my sailboat, and quit what I was doing at the time. Only a certain number of foreigners could legally immigrate to the US, but my biggest problem was getting permission from the Belgian Army to leave the country for an indeterminate length of time.

While we waited for our visas, I took a quick trip to Germany, this time as a civilian. On the way, I stopped in Brussels, Louvain, and Liège, Belgium, to visit with the families of some of my fallen comrades. I had to say goodbye, and this gave me a sense of closure.

As I was approaching the German border, I remembered how I enjoyed entering Germany in our seek-and-destroy missions against Nazis, and how much I had hated that country. As time went by, however, I found that not all Germans were Nazis and that there were some very decent people living there. The German people increasingly thanked us for liberating them as they began to trust us. I looked up Mutty and her two daughters to make sure they were okay. I visited my friend Yupe's grave. I went to Bremerhafen to visit Admiral Niedermyer and his wife to tell them about my intention to move to Texas. Admiral Niedermyer had rented a room to my sister and brother-in-law, which is how I met him. He had been a very decent person to Don and Lucienne, and so I admired him. He said he was not surprised at my decision. He wished he was young like me and wished me good luck in Texas. Admiral Niedermyer had been a well-respected German admiral who resisted the intense pressures of the Nazis. When the Third Reich came to power, Niedermyer was much too old to serve, so he was for the most part left alone. His previous service to his country allowed him immunity from any service to the Nazi cause. By living in the huge harbor town of Bremerhafen on the Baltic Sea, he remained unscathed, aside from the tremendous bombings the Canadians brought to his town. He was a German all right, but would not conform to the Fascist regime. I am surprised he survived, because many Germans like him were executed.

While we considered all aspects of the move, I took time to visit once more the Ardennes and went back to Bastogne. Most of the town was being rebuilt or restored. The rubble was removed, and a replica of the old town was in reconstruction, because they wanted to preserve the historical construction and looks. The old fortress that had sustained heavy damage was nearly restored, and some of the preserved weapons were on display. The monuments and the church were as they had been before the war. I stopped by the Bastogne War Museum, where I donated my arsenal of weapons and other military equipment I had accumulated from different battlefields. There were several Mauser 98s, an FN FAL, British Enfield rifles, German 9mm Lugers, a P38, Hitler's Zipper MG42, cases of ammo, hand grenades, combat knives, bayonets, helmets, uniforms, medals, and everything else you could think of. All those weapons were accumulated one by one as I discovered them lying around for the taking.

On my return, I visited the large American Military Cemetery in Hamm, Luxembourg, and put on my black beret with the brass lion on it. I saluted my fallen heroes in the manner I thought most respectful. It was a very emotional visit to see the thousands of white grave markers, and to stand at the foot of General Patton's grave. At attention, I gave *Old Blood and Guts* one final salute. As I was close, I went to the little town of Bois. I spent time there in December of 1944 as part of the northeast line of defense held by the 101st and the Ninth. My tour ended in the tourist town of Bouillon, where Bernard and I had enjoyed hunting, fishing, and relaxing.

To my surprise, while on my trip to Germany, we had been accepted

Permission to emigrate

for emigration by the Belgian government. My next chore was to line up a shipping line to accommodate my parents and myself. The popular lines such as the Ryndam, Noordam, the Queen Mary, the Queen Elisabeth, and the Liberty were all booked. Finally, after much effort, I found an opening on the HMS *Heina*, a brand-new Norwegian liner/cargo ship that had first-class fares available for a 26 of March departure. A few weeks earlier, I had applied to the Belgian Army for an extended absence and was waiting for their permission. That permission was granted a week later, but my permanent discharge request was denied.

Our timeframe gave us five weeks to make all our arrangements. We were allowed to ship a maximum of one ton of personal belongings. Except for some of the heirlooms, we sold most of the furniture and gave a lot of things away.

The expectation of leaving the past behind was very exciting for me, but I don't think it was as exciting for my parents, who were still hesitant. My mother cried a lot because of her brothers she was leaving behind. They also were worried about not understanding the English language well, but I reassured them there was no reason to worry because I would be there. Even if my sister and her husband should move away, I would be there. We immediately made arrangements with the Menkes Moving Company, who sent us all kinds of information and restrictions on packing our belongings. The last things I gave away to my friends before shipping out were my Canadian Sten Gun, my last German Luger pistols, my last P38, and a Hitler Youth knife that I had picked up after a battle.

There were several going-away parties and dinners. The Coca-Cola Company gave the biggest party in my honor. The president, Bill Jacquemins, organized a Coca-Cola and rum party, which lasted three days and two nights. There was a complete bar open twenty-four hours during the party, where you could drink all the rum and Coca-Cola you wanted. At night there were several loud bands with much dancing and all the food one might need. My buddies made a huge banner, which they hung above the downtown Main Street reading in large letters: "GOODBYE TEX!" We had parties until the day we left.

CHAPTER 7

Texas

Menkes Moving Company arrived to collect the one-ton crate. Then the day came when we closed the door to our home of twenty-one years. We said goodbye to our neighbors and our old, beautiful, magnificent country. The car dealership I previously worked for provided transportation to Antwerp Harbor for our seventeen large suitcases and us. Trailing behind was a caravan of cars filled with our friends wishing us off. As we arrived at the dock in the harbor of Antwerp, we saw the beautiful vessel *Heina*. We looked forward to our five-day voyage to the new world. We checked our luggage with the porters and were shown our accommodations, which were two very nice and spacious cabins with separate bathrooms. Then I checked out the large dining room, lounge, smoking room, and party room, all very luxurious and new.

It must have been snowing at sea because there was snow and ice remaining on the main deck. They told us the departure would be delayed, and that we could invite our family and friends to come aboard for a while. We had a final going-away party which left Dad and me with a whopper of a bar bill. At 1700 hours our family and friends were asked to say goodbye, and we departed Belgium. It was the final goodbye, and it wasn't easy. There were about fifty passengers for supper that night in the dining room. I looked around to see if I could locate single people about my age, but didn't see anyone I'd be interested in talking to. They were either too old or too young or married.

At the supper table we sat at our assigned seats, and I started with a couple of drinks of Vat 69 on ice. We were in luck because we sat at the captain's table. He was fluent in several languages, and the conversation was lively and pleasant. We had a delicious three-course meal followed by great desserts and after-dinner drinks. The captain told us the ship would pick up additional passengers and cargo the next day in France at the Le Havre harbor.

After dinner, we went to the large lounge for conversation and additional refreshments. Everybody retired early, but I was ready to make a night of it. I was too excited to be able to sleep. I bought a carton of Lucky Strikes and a bottle of Vat 69 Scotch, got a bucket of ice, and went to the lounge. A steward stopped by to see if I needed anything. I told him I didn't need anything but invited him for a drink. He said that since he was off duty, he would gladly join me. We talked about the ship, the trip, the passengers, and the lack of activities at night. We talked about my sailing days, and he appeared very interested. He asked if I would like to come to the bridge and see the map room and the radar room. I remember being fascinated by the detailed maps of the ocean and our route. There was a simple beauty and elegance in these handmade maps that I found appealing. The steward gave me the grand tour, and I was amazed at the latest instrumentation on this ship. He also humorously mentioned that most people would be seasick because of the windy and stormy forecast for the next few days.

The next day we picked up the additional passengers at Le Havre, France, and waited for the high tide to proceed toward the Atlantic Ocean and the United States. As soon as we left Le Havre and made our way in the Atlantic Ocean, the weather changed, and the ship really started rolling and bucking. I was surprised that less than half of the passengers showed up for breakfast and even fewer for lunch. On the second day the weather worsened to cold, rainy, and windy, tossing the *Heina* all over the ocean.

The food on board was absolutely fantastic. There was a good selection of dishes and the menu was elaborate. The storm and subsequent cases of seasickness caused the cancellation of the *Point of No Return* party, but a few of us made up for it celebrating in the lounge. This was a time of joy for me. I knew in my heart that my life would be better now in the United States.

Five days later we entered New York harbor at 1800 hours, and I witnessed the beautiful beacon of hope for so many immigrants—the Statue of Liberty, and it brought tears to my eyes. I became acutely aware of the many immigrants that came before me who felt these same feelings. What this moment must have felt like to them! The customs and federal inspectors came on board to examine everyone's papers. It took another hour to dock, and we finally touched American soil. It was so exciting to me to think what a great adventure was ahead of us! We were expecting to see my uncle and aunt at the dock, but there was no one there to greet us. They lived in Mamaroneck, about forty-five minutes from New York. I called them and was surprised because the shipping company had informed them we would not dock until the next morning. My uncle told me to get a taxi and to meet them at the upper level in the Grand Central Station. We required two taxis and three porters to handle the luggage and ourselves.

Soon we met up with my uncle Jules and aunt Marguerite. My mother hadn't seen her brother for thirty-one years. They must have hugged for thirty minutes. He moved to Canada after World War I in 1921, married my aunt, who had been his pen pal during World War I, and they settled in Mamaroneck, New York. They owned a large drugstore, which served short-order food at a soda fountain.

We were hungry and stopped by his drugstore where we had our first homemade hamburgers with French fries and chocolate malts in the United States. It was delicious! We stayed a few days in New York with them and met some of my cousins. Except for my cousin Ethel, no one seemed to care or wanted to spend any time with us. Ethel showed me around New York and took me to a movie. Grand Central Station fascinated me, and this was saying a lot with all the stations I had seen growing up. The sheer size of the buildings amazed me. While visiting in New York with the family, we made our railroad reservations for Greenville, Texas, via St. Louis, Missouri.

While waiting in the St. Louis station, my dad and I had for the first time a shave and a shoeshine together. We had supper in a restaurant in the station, after which we boarded the Texas Special in the late afternoon.

My New Life

On Easter morning, 1952, at about 0630 hours, we arrived worn and weary in Greenville, Texas, after traveling on the Texas Special all night long through many spectacular thunderstorms. We stepped out of the train to a bright full sun and some of the legendary heat and humidity we had heard about. We were finally in Texas! I was elated to be here, but I could tell my parents were not all that happy. I must admit that it was a long way from the normal conditions they were familiar with. Hopefully the Texas sun wouldn't be more than they could bear.

It was exciting, to say the least. The station was like the ones you would see in western movies with one small ticket window, a small waiting room, and a small loading dock, with a wooden deck all around the building. The luggage cart could hardly handle all of our suitcases. The stationmaster welcomed us to Texas and asked us if we knew someone who could pick us up. They didn't have taxis in the town yet. We could tell that this little town had received its share of rain from a storm. There was a lot of water still on the ground, and it was extremely hot and muggy. The storm had moved out and now we could see that big, beautiful, clear blue sky the soldiers from Texas bragged about.

Soon after our arrival, there appeared my brother-in-law Don. We exchanged hugs and greetings for several minutes, loaded some of the suitcases, and then took off for the house. We told the stationmaster that we would be back to collect the remaining luggage later that day. Don lived about five miles outside of town. Driving northeast on Route 1, we went through the downtown and saw the main square, with the courthouse, a Dairy Queen, drug and clothing stores, and a few more miscellaneous stores surrounded by lots of land. I also remember the town was still caught in the throes of bigotry and racism, because at both ends of the town there was a large sign saying:

"The blackest land with the whitest people."

It sure was good to see my sister again after three long years. We had a good time getting acquainted with their kids, Donald and Janet. We had a lot to talk about, and shared with them news from the family and friends overseas. I told them about the many wonderful experiences we had on our trip. Later on in the day we drove around downtown, picked up the remaining luggage at the railroad station, and met some of Don's friends and neighbors. We stayed with the Farnsworths for two weeks before we found a small place to rent of our own.

The day after we arrived, I went to town to buy some appropriate clothing to work in. This was my introduction to the phenomenon of blue jeans. I was also talked into purchasing several western shirts, a hat, a belt, and a pair of boots. Next, I was introduced to the delicious Texas fried foods and the Tex-Mex cuisine. I had a lot of things to learn and get acquainted with, such as walking in cowboy boots. Talk about a new experience!

Don managed the Greenville Airport, which handled passengers and freight. Central Airlines primarily used the airport; originally they flew DC-3s, which were World War II surplus planes.

One of the main accounts using Central Airlines was a company named Williams Tool & Bit Company, an oil drilling company that was shipping drill bits studded with real diamonds. The owner, Mr. Williams, came to the airport quite often to get away from his office and to pick up packages. We had a friendly conversation about his drilling business, and he invited me to see his plant. He told me he liked Belgium and visited Antwerp on many occasions to purchase diamonds for his drill bits. They shipped the bits all over the world and at great profit to the company. He asked me what I would like to do in Texas and talked about my future. I told him that my early passion was painting before the war, which gave me a desire to work in the architectural engineering illustration field. Mr. Williams was a graduate of Texas A&M University and had many good connections with one of the largest engineering firms in the country, Brown & Root. He could probably find me a job, but it might be in the Middle East. He told me B&R designed and built all over the world. I told him I appreciated the suggestions and his offer to help me, but that I needed to stay close to my parents for a while as I had promised them my help. I would keep looking.

I had not been very successful with my sponsors, because since they had agreed to help with employment, war broke out in Korea. The Korean War made it very difficult for a legal alien to work for companies that had military contracts. My sponsors were Temco Aircraft, General Dynamics, and Central Airlines, who all had military contracts. The sponsors now could no longer help with my employment. My last sponsor was Goff Cattle Company, where I probably wouldn't be a very good hand. I would visit Mr. Goff as soon as I could buy a reliable car to make the trip.

I needed transportation and looked around for a good bargain. I went to a downtown used car lot, where I noticed a 1949 metallic-blue Chevrolet two-door coupe, eight cylinders, with stick shift. It looked like new inside and out and was very appealing to me. Buying that car was quite an experience in itself. There was a small office building in the middle of the lot with several cowboy-looking guys sitting outside in the shade. I said hello and told them I was interested in that Chevrolet and wanted to purchase it. They looked at each other and then back at me as one of them said, "You want to do what to that car?" Then I repeated: "I want to purchase that steel blue Chevrolet car, you know, like buy it." They said, "Young fellow, we don't get too many people like you around here. Where you from?" I told them I just arrived a few days ago from Belgium. One of them said, "That's where my son was during that war over there." I told him to tell his son that I appreciated him going over there to liberate us from the Germans, and he promised to pass along the message. Then I showed the cash I had. One of the men spoke: "If you want to buy it, the price will be $1,050." I replied I only had eight hundred dollars cash. They looked at each other and countered, "Okay, we can do it for $900, but not $800." We walked to the car, started it, drove it, and everything checked out. We went back to the office and told them I really liked the car, but that I couldn't buy it at that price. I turned to leave when they called me back and said, "Okay young man, $800 it is." I gave them half down and asked them to hold the car, and I would pick it up later in the day. I needed to get myself a driver's license. I borrowed Don's car and passed the written and driving test without much effort. Now I was able to see my last sponsor, the Goff Ranch, who had their headquarters in Canadian, Texas.

I set off and drove . . . drove . . . and drove to Amarillo. I spent the night at a truck stop where I stayed in my car close to the front entrance, and didn't sleep much. Before daylight, I took off for the little town named Canadian. I didn't have any problem finding Mr. Goff, because there weren't that many buildings in town. Mr. Goff seemed glad to see me, and we talked for a good while. Then we had lunch and talked with his foreman, who showed me the bunkhouse where I would sleep. This bunkhouse, as it turned out, was full of real cowboys. There was so much loud snoring all through the night that I didn't sleep at all.

Next morning, after a Texas-size flapjack with a side of eggs coupled with a mix of beef and beans, we roped our mounts, saddled them, and picked up saddlebags carrying anthrax medicine and syringes. This medicine had to be inserted through the mouth of the animal and pushed into the stomach. Talk about a mess! Now, I must be honest about roping and saddling my horse: I had a lot of help. Once mounted up, we set out to find the cattle, a ride that covered some nice terrain, some less-than-nice terrain, and some awful terrain. When you found the critter, you had to rope it, secure it, insert the tube through the poor animal's throat, push it through to the stomach, and release the medicine. Then hold the animal until you knew it had swallowed the dose of medicine. Then clean the tube, sterilize it, sanitize yourself, and get back in the saddle for another round. It was some intensely back-breaking work.

It didn't take me long to find out that I didn't fit in the saddle. We were on horseback from sunrise until sundown to treat the cattle against anthrax disease. I didn't get along with horses very well either, and this ranch was run on horseback. Mr. Goff was very nice and patient, but he needed a good hand, which I wasn't. After a week, I told Mr. Goff that I appreciated the opportunity to learn and that I enjoyed the experience, but we both knew that it wasn't going to work out. He wished me good luck and said, "Everything in life has a reason and only the Lord knows the answer to our problems. It is up to us to talk with Him . . . and find out. Now, if we decide things on our own, we most probably will fail."

While I was searching for employment, Don put me in charge of taking care of the airport grounds. Temco Aircraft Company and Central Airlines were sharing the same runways. There were plenty of grassy areas around the grounds to keep me busy mowing. I mowed over hundreds of rattlesnakes, tarantula spiders, and scorpions with those large riding commercial lawnmowers. I knew this was a temporary job, but at least I was earning a paycheck. It gave me a chance to clear my head from all the trash I had accumulated during the war. The simplicity of this temporary work was rejuvenating, and I thought about the war a lot. I couldn't forget the cruelty of humans toward other humans, and couldn't forget my buddies who died. The question that I always returned to was why them and not me? This question began to stir inside of me more and more frequently. Was it sheer coincidence or perhaps there was a higher power involved?

Everybody said that I should get out of town and look for a job in Dallas or Fort Worth or even Houston, because in Greenville, jobs were hard to come by and would be even more difficult for a man in my position. Since Don was employed by an airline, as in-laws we could fly anywhere the airline went for two dollars per round trip. For several days, Dad and I flew around Texas, Oklahoma, and even Arkansas to look for a job. Sometimes we flew off in the morning toward south Texas, to Austin and Houston. The next day we went northwest to Amarillo, Lubbock, and Wichita Falls. People interviewing us were very nice but wouldn't hire us. I got the impression the reason was because we were foreigners and didn't know the language very well.

I took another temporary job in Greenville with the North American Van Lines, located downtown right by the railroad station. The owner, Frank Wolf, asked me if I had experience in moving furniture and appliances. I told him that I moved all the way to Texas from Ghent, Belgium, and was willing to learn the trade. He liked my answer and said: "Well, young fellow, we all need a start somewhere, and it may as well be here. I don't know how long you want to do this, but I will help you." We shook hands, and the next day I went to work. All the employees wore white T-shirts with the company logo on the back showing the silhouette of a wolf howling at the moon. The job wasn't easy, and some days I didn't think I was going to survive. I wasn't used to the hot Texas temperatures, and this was just the beginning of May with humid temperatures reaching 85°F to 95°F. Whatever we had to move came out of a very hot house or apartment and had to be loaded into a hot van. Then we drove many miles in the heat of the day without air conditioning. When we arrived at our destinations, we had to move that hot furniture into a red-hot apartment or home that had been closed for several days. Then, hours later, we drove back in the heat to start all over again the next day. This went on for several weeks before I decided this was not what I wanted to do for very much longer. But I was learning how to move furniture, which was keeping my muscles strong, and the perks were getting to drive a big eighteen-wheel truck called a Big Rig.

My parents and I moved to a two-bedroom rent house on Sail Street in downtown Greenville, which was walking distance to my job. Our neighbors were very nice to us. One of them was Dr. Valencia and his family, who were fun to be with. They were renting a house while their new home was being built. Just about every night the doctor and I went to their future home, which was located fairly close to the hospital, and checked the progress made. They enjoyed dining out in Dallas or Fort Worth, and a couple of times per week hired a babysitter to watch their kids. Every time the doctor went to pick up a sitter, he asked me to go with him to meet the young lady. The babysitters were nice to me and very polite, but weren't interested in dating. Most of them were too young for me anyway. On the occasions when I had a date, there usually wouldn't be another because their parents didn't want their daughter to date a foreigner. It was as if I had the plague or something.

In those days in a small town like Greenville when you picked up your date, you met first with the parents. A date was usually limited to a movie at an outdoor drive-in theater, followed by a cheeseburger and a malt or shake at the local Dairy Queen. By then it was close to time to return the date back home. Luckily, I wasn't looking for a relationship, but the young ladies were nice, very polite, and fun to be with.

Things went well for me at the moving company, but it was time to start looking for a job with a future. I wasn't making enough income with these temporary jobs and was dipping seriously into my savings. Then I had an unfortunate accident on the job. My workmate Slim and I were on the third floor of the warehouse where there was very little light, retrieving a very big mattress. It was a four-story building with twelve-foot high ceilings, and in the middle was a large uncaged (no side protection) freight elevator platform. I was backing up toward the elevator platform, but unbeknownst to me someone had raised the platform to the next floor up. Suddenly I fell thirty-

Me in 1952

six feet through the elevator shaft all the way to the bottom, where I landed on my back. It knocked the breath out of me! I was looking up and saw Slim looking down with the biggest scared eyes I had ever seen. He yelled at me "Is you alright?" It took me a few minutes, but finally I took a long, deep breath. I very slowly checked for movement in my extremities. Everything still worked. I slowly got myself up, told Slim I was okay, and gingerly walked out of the elevator pit. Somebody told the boss what happened, and he came running down the hall, very concerned about my fall. He suggested I see a doctor immediately. I told him a doctor lived right next door to our apartment and that I would mention to him what happened to me. Mr. Wolf then drove me home. However, Dr. Valencia wasn't home, and since I only hurt a little, I decided to forget it. That night I went to bed feeling fairly well, but next morning I awoke in great pain and could hardly move. I called Dr. Valencia, who took me to his hospital, where he examined me and took several X-rays. They incredibly showed nothing broken, but I had several severe internal bruises. He recommended treatments with electric stimulation, which were very painful. A few days later Dr. Valencia released me and suggested I take it easy for a while. I needed to give my body a chance to heal the bruised muscles and joints before going back to work. I took it slowly for the next few weeks. When I became healthy enough to work again, I decided that I needed to find a new job.

Once I was feeling up to it, I went out of town to visit a Belgian expatriate who owned a large shoe factory called *Linda-Jo Shoes*. The factory was located an hour and half away in Gainesville, Texas. The man gave me the grand tour of his plant; then we went to a nearby restaurant and had lunch. It was a very pleasant visit and we talked mostly about the old country. He told me that he couldn't recommend any other place to find a job in his town because his plant was the largest employer. He said that if at any time I needed a job, he would give me one, but he strongly suggested going to Dallas or Fort Worth to find a job with a future.

So I went to Dallas and visited the Belgian Consulate in the hope of getting some advice. The Belgian Consul was absent, which left his second in command to answer my questions and give advice. He was a very feminine kind of a guy. This assistant told me that my best bet for a good job would be to take advantage of my French accent and sell perfume or furs at Neiman-Marcus. He added that those rich women would buy anything just to hear my accent. This advice made me very angry. I explained to him that I knew now what Belgium did with their little mama's boys. I told him I was a man looking for a man's job and that I was sure the last thing I needed was to get advice from him. As I stormed out of the office, he sat there speechless. Me selling perfume!

From the Consulate, I went to the Dallas, Texas, Employment office where the reception wasn't much better. They didn't want to help me and said they wouldn't have anything for "people like me." I asked the woman behind the desk what I was supposed to be like. She insisted I was supposed to be like them, and Dallas didn't have jobs for my kind. That's when I decided to dislike that town.

I had one more contact to check out for a lead in Fort Worth. A few years before I came to Texas, I met Joe Eidson Jr. and his partner, James McFadden Furlong, while on a sailing trip in Europe. We sailed together in the North Sea and spent a few days checking out the coastal harbors. They bought a forty-six-foot sailboat in Sweden and were traveling through Europe before crossing the Atlantic on their way back to the United States. James lived in Houston and was a very likable guy and a very good sailor. However, upon his approach to Houston and while in the harbor, James had his leg caught in the sheets of the mainsail while tacking, and it was severed. It was a serious accident but a blessing that it didn't happen at sea.

Joe Eidson Jr. made an impact on me and told me that if I was ever in Texas, to come see him. I would make good on that invitation soon enough. From Dallas I drove west on what is now called the old highway 80 or Lancaster, and soon went through Arlington, which in 1952 wasn't but two or three blocks deep and about twelve blocks long on both sides of the highway. Soon Fort Worth's downtown buildings came into view. The tallest buildings in those days were the Medical Arts Building at the Burk Burnett Park, the W.

T. Waggoner building on Houston Street, and the Neil P. Anderson Building on Seventh Street. The sun was shining bright and hot as I pulled into town. I continued down to the long Trinity Bridge and could see Forest Park on the left. I liked the drop-off toward the big long bridge and kept on driving toward the Amon Carter Coliseum, where I stopped at a service station to ask for directions to Seventh Street. I decided to stop for a few minutes to cool off. I was hot, tired, and hungry. I went into a convenience store called 7-Eleven, right next to the Seventh Street Theater, and was looking for something inexpensive to eat. I bought a four-pack of day-old Mrs. Baird's sweet rolls and a six-pack of Lone Star beer. I then found myself driving on Bailey Street and ran into White Settlement Road, where I found Rockwood Park and picked a spot to rest in the shade. It was located right by the Trinity River, where a bunch of kids were playing in the river splashing water at each other. I opened both car doors to let in a little breeze and enjoyed my "lupper" (a combination of lunch and supper). Sweet rolls and beer—what a meal!

It was a little after five when I finally worked my way to the Eidson's home. What a mansion! I rang the electric chime and a servant greeted me. I introduced myself and was led to a large library. Soon Mr. Eidson Sr. came and asked what he could do for me. I told him how I met his son in Europe, and he was, of course, surprised to hear how we met. I told him I was looking for a job as an architectural illustrator, commercial artist, or draftsman. He said it would be difficult to hire me because I didn't know the Texas rules, regulations, and standards, but recommended me to check in at the local YMCA and get a room for the night, which I did. In the morning, I went to the Fort Worth, Texas, Employment office where I got a lead for a job. I immediately called the prospect and talked with the owner, who told me to come right over for an interview. It was downtown in the basement of the Neil P. Anderson Building where I met Jay Wilson, owner of the Universal Map and Drafting Company. I had a good interview, during which Jay gave me several tests in calligraphy, pen, ink, pencil drawing, and watercolors. I suppose I passed the test, since I was hired to start the next day. It was a miracle!

I went back to the YMCA for the night and will not comment about my stay, but I can honestly say that I was glad to check out of that place. I found a room with a private bath right across the street from the YMCA, at the old Hickman Hotel. Then, I went to the Federal Court and filed my application to become an American citizen. I also was required to register with the draft board, which classified me as a 1-A, a man fully ready to be drafted. I wanted to have it all done and done correctly, even though I did not want to get that draft notice.

In those days, in order to become a citizen, an immigrant had to file an intention to become an American citizen. I had five long years to assimilate, study English, American history, American government, the Bill of Rights, and the Declaration of Independence. After five years had passed, I would take the citizenship exams, which consisted of an oral and written test. I also had to provide the names of three people who had known me for the past five years and could testify that I was of good moral character. I knew that for the next five years I'd better watch myself and live a good, clean life. In other words, stay out of trouble. At the end of my first week, on July 18, 1952, I drove back to Greenville, where I gave my parents the good news about my job. I then proceeded to pack my bags and move to Fort Worth to stay.

Life in Texas

I was an adult from a foreign country with a particular problem. I had to work and help support my parents, to give them a chance to hang onto their savings. I didn't complete my education in college, yet by another choice I made, I changed my future and profession.

On July 21, 1952, I went to work for the Universal Map and Drafting Company. It was a new experience because I had never worked in a large drafting room with eighteen employees. At first I wasn't very well accepted. Everyone else was younger, and who knows, maybe they didn't like my French accent? There was no doubt that being a foreigner was not a plus in this group. One of the guys working in the group named Jean Capshaw helped me get started and set up with the necessary tools to work with. We got along fine. The other employees seemed to resent me. I didn't let it bother me, as I figured that if I was nice to them, they would change their attitude.

I learned new things such as measurements, US standards, and the use of drafting tools I had never used before. I had been raised with metric dimensions, measures, and mapping of land areas from surveyor's data. Initially I felt lost in another world but overcame it quickly. I was there to learn and learn quickly, so I worked very hard in my training in map drafting.

My first challenge was mechanical lettering, which took practice in order to gain speed. I caught on easily and went by the rule that practice makes perfect. For those who remember the days of Leroy Lettering, this may be a fun thing to remember. I stayed at work and practiced at night while Jay, the boss, was working on his bookkeeping and correspondence.

Mechanical lettering takes concentration and practice. I stayed late at night so I could have time to practice, and didn't have the distractions and interruptions that you get working with office noises. After a few days, the group was friendlier after they realized that I wouldn't be intimidated by their attitude. I learned the main reason they disliked me at first was because the boss and I were quite often having lunch and supper together, and often were going out at night after work. Jay and I were older, more mature, and had experienced things they would never have to deal with. Jay was divorced, and I was single. Both of us served in World War II. He was a captain in the US Army when I was a corporal acting sergeant in the Belgian Army. We shared a powerful history that gave us similar interests.

I regularly ate breakfast at Paul's Café with Jay, which was right next door to the Neil P. Anderson Building. The cafe was a busy place, and most of the time we shared a table with a total stranger. That's where and how we met a Marine Corps recruiting officer and swapped a few war stories and became friends. We talked about life in general, and I mentioned the situation with my parents living in Greenville and the need to find an apartment in Fort Worth. I drove to Greenville every other week and visited with my parents, but didn't intend to continue doing this for very long. I asked the sergeant if I could qualify for the Marines Corps. He said that I would have to pass a rigorous physical test, but that in his opinion I would stand a good chance for enrollment. I went ahead and filled out all the necessary papers and passed the physical test with no problem. They gave me ten days to decide. I liked the benefits, and the job was a chance to see another part of the world. More importantly, if I joined I would qualify to get my American citizenship in two years instead of five. It was a very difficult decision to make. I had just survived a hell of a war and now could make a decision to get into another. I was thinking about my friend Etienne, who joined and was killed within two weeks in Korea. The Korean War was still ongoing. The US government offered an incentive to volunteers that if you served, they would pay you a substantial lump sum upon your return from service. This was a very difficult offer for me to turn down. I really needed the money.

I talked with Jay about it at length and he thought that if I would benefit by it, he could see why I would do it. He asked me to give it a little time before I decided. He said he would hate to see me leave. A few days later, the sergeant recruiter told me he had been thinking about me joining the corps, but didn't think it was a good idea after all. He said that World War II had been rough enough on me, and I should reconsider my intention to join. I thought about it and took his advice. However, just in case I changed my mind about joining, I contacted the Belgian embassy to get the permission to enlist, but was denied permission because of my status in the Belgian Army. That took care of that. I was not a free man yet. With that settled, I knew I needed to make some changes, such as checking out of my expensive room at the Hickman Hotel. I needed to find a reasonable apartment for my parents and me in Fort Worth.

The guys at work told me about a room to rent where several of them lived. It was located close to downtown on Cannon Street, and was a large three-story home with four bedrooms and two and a half baths. Three of the bedrooms held four renters each, with the owner occupying the fourth. We had a good breakfast in the morning, a sack lunch, and supper was on us. It was costing me less than half of what I paid at the Hickman Hotel, but it reminded me of the army. There was no privacy, not much comfort, and not much rest. However, while I was looking for a small apartment, it would do.

Out of the twelve boarders, four worked for Jay Wilson. All of us had cars, so we decided to rotate cars to work in order to share the cost of gas and parking. It worked out great, as Johnny Maughn, Eddie Newby, Tom Nichols, and I became good friends. We worked the same ten hours per day and five to six days per week.

Every month I visited with my parents, who were still living in Greenville. I phoned them on the other weekends so I could stay and rest in town. Occasionally we went to Johnny Maughn's parent's ranch located in Sanger, Texas. We hunted rabbits and coyotes or fished in a fairly large creek. We stretched a net across a narrow part of the creek, and several of us got behind the net, scooping the fish out and throwing them on the bank. I couldn't believe the fast current and the amount of fish we caught in a short time. Suddenly, one of the guys yelled out loudly, "Moccasins!" Of course everyone jumped out of the water but me. They kept on yelling but I didn't know what moccasins were. They finally pointed toward several dark-looking snakes that were in the net and all around me. I leapt out of the water to the bank. I must have utilized some of the luck I seemed to carry around with me as I escaped unscathed. Beginners luck, maybe?

When I stayed in town for the weekend, some of us went to Lake Worth or Eagle Mountain Lake, where we picnicked and went swimming at Twin Points or at Burgers Lake. There was always plenty to do and plenty of girls to entertain. Netball was a favorite game at that time.

Jay Wilson was very proud of his state, and even after I quit working for him, he enjoyed showing me around. He knew the history and was a Texan at heart. We visited art galleries and historical places in town and out of town. A few months passed and I needed more income, so I looked for a part-time job. I found an ad in the paper and got hired by a civil engineering firm named Reeves and Gregory. It was located on Seventh Street in the Jeton's shopping area. Then I found a two-bedroom apartment with one bathroom on the corner of Texas and Lake Street. It was perfect for my parents and me. They could move here and we could save on the rent. Don had been transferred to Bonham, Texas, so Lucienne would be moving away as well.

My parents moved to Fort Worth, and within a few weeks Dad wanted to find a job. He checked with several architectural firms, but wasn't successful in finding one that would hire him. He had always built and designed custom-made buildings and homes, but he wasn't familiar with American standards in construction. The other problem with hiring my dad was the language barrier: since he spoke Kings English, they would have some problems communicating. After several months my dad had an interview with McClure & Company, a home designer, who found a way to use his talents and knowledge. He wasn't paid enough for his work, and half of the time he was paid with hot checks, but he liked what he was doing.

I was working full-time for the Map and Drafting Company, part-time for Reeves and Gregory, and got another part-time job on Sundays with Llewellyn and Company. At Llewellyn, I drew land survey maps and plats for their real estate business. The owner J.C. Llewellyn took an interest in me, as we shared a part of history together. Jack, as he was affectionately known, served as a captain in the army air corps where he commanded a B-24 bomber out of Italy during the war. On a particular bombing mission over Yugoslavia, his plane was shot down by German antiaircraft fire. Everyone on his ten-man crew successfully parachuted out except for his ball gunner. Jack's very pregnant wife Jane was at home in Fort Worth entertaining friends and family during her baby shower when the notifying officer and the chaplain arrived at her door. She was painstakingly told that Jack and his crew were listed as missing in action. Jack's strength and heroic deeds would lead his men for over a month of survival in the German occupied forests of Yugoslavia. Captain Jack eventually met up with the resistance, who coordinated an airplane to evacuate his crew and other survivors. During the boarding process, the plane ran out of parachutes for his crew and thus Jack took a huge gamble and refused to board his men without this safety precaution, even given their circumstances. As the plane took off, Jack and his crew watched as they encountered heavy German fire on takeoff, which brought down the plane, killing everyone on board. Captain Jack would eventually lead his men to the coast of the Adriatic Sea and a friendly fishing vessel, which got all nine men safely back to the Allies in Italy. Jack would be awarded a purple heart for his bravery during his service. Jack ran his business as he ran his life: with honor and dignity. His reputation in Fort Worth was as intimidating as it was successful. I was never without purpose or work on those Sundays at Llewellyn and Company.

I didn't know how long I could keep up this work routine and decided to look for something with a better future for me. I checked out several possibilities on my own and finally went to an employment agency called Babich, who made me an appointment with a petroleum consulting firm called Keller and Peterson.

My interview was with a man named Augie Augustson, who tested my skills in drawing and lettering. I was promptly hired on July 21, 1953. By coincidence it was exactly a year after Jay Wilson hired me. I didn't close the door to working with Jay and occasionally worked part-time for him. This job required a different dress code. The previous job accepted blue jeans, boots, a dress shirt, or more specifically business casual. This new job was classier, and I was required to wear a suit, dress shirt, and tie. It wasn't new to me because in Belgium, as a civilian, I regularly dressed in business suits. I was well accepted by the personnel there and got along fine with my bosses. My immediate boss Augie was very nice and very patient. He taught me most of the graphics and presentation methods used in the petroleum engineering industry. He taught me how to make court exhibits showing many different graphics, maps, and cross-sections illustrating the sub-surface and geological formations that were used for oil field evaluations. I learned how to interpret logs, how to plot all kinds of statistical curves, contour maps, structure maps, isopatch maps, and other engineering interpretations. In those days, most of the lettering was mechanical lettering, done in pen and ink. It was a high-pressure job with a lot of overtime and near-impossible deadlines. I actually didn't mind, because I was single anyway. If working on a project after regular business hours, we had supper at the Petroleum Club, after which most of us went back to work and stayed very late in the night trying to get a head start for the next day.

I wasn't flush with free time but I did find enough to enroll in some night classes at the local university, Texas Christian University. I signed up for government and American history courses as well as other subjects that would help with my citizenship. I wanted to make sure to pass the oral and written examination tests for my citizenship exam. Many middle-aged students shared the night classroom with me as a refresher course for them. However, in each of my classes there were plenty of immature young students who attended for a much different reason. The English teacher, Dr. Woods, was a very strict teacher who wouldn't put up with silly behavior, and often rebuked those who misbehaved. A few of these college kids teased me and made fun of my accent. Dr. Woods overheard this one day and put a stop to it by asking me to say the words or phrases in French, German, and Dutch. Then he looked at the class and said; "He may have an accent, but most of us can't even pronounce or spell correctly in our own language." I remained focused on learning American history and the methods of our government. In those days, our government was very serious about the citizenship rules. One had to prove oneself worthy to become an American citizen. Immigrants had to work hard to learn and had five years to prove their knowledge of American standards.

Being an American in those days was an honor, something to be proud of and cherish. The whole world looked at the Americans with envy. The American dream was a powerful global currency. Things were going well for me; I liked my job, and my parents were happy with the new apartment and multitude of new things to do. The location was very convenient for downtown shopping. It looked as if things were going to work out for us finally. I regularly took my parents by car to grocery stores or to get whatever else they needed.

Most of my time was spent working or going to school. A few months later the workload was getting to be a real burden. The K&P firm was growing, work hours were increasing, and I had problems studying and going to classes. I had no other choice but to drop some of the courses because I needed the overtime pay for the rent, utilities, and other expenses.

Mr. Keller and Mr. Peterson, the partners, met with us to see how they could help with our overload. They knew we were burning the candle at both ends and struggling to meet deadlines. They realized we needed additional help in our department. They hired a young local man named Jack Fikes, who was a graduate of Carter Riverside High School. He was very pleasant man who carried with him an optimistic attitude, which helped a lot. With his help, we could meet deadlines much easier and I could cut back a little on the long days at the office.

Augie was a good leader, and as a team, we achieved great successes at Keller and Peterson. I was really beginning to enjoy the life and promise of a future in America.

Every morning there was an established routine. My boss Augie went for breakfast with the company bookkeeper, Ann Wheeler. When they returned to the office, I went to breakfast with Betty Turner, who was Mr. Peterson's secretary. Our usual spot for breakfast was the Picadilli Cafeteria, Terry's Grill, or Warren's Café. None of these restaurants exist anymore, but the home-cooked food and wonderful atmosphere in those places made for some great memories.

I was still having back pain from the elevator accident and therefore began to develop a limp. Mr. Keller questioned me one day about my accident. I told him the details of the fall and how the pain seemed to be getting worse. He asked me if I considered seeing a doctor, but I told him I couldn't add to the bills I already had. After hearing how it happened, he suggested that North American Van Lines should have paid for it, and that I should get an attorney to help me with it. He recommended two attorneys who had their offices right across the street. After considering my options or lack thereof, I went across the street and read on the door the names of the attorneys as Edson and Jenkins. The name Jenkins reminded me of the colonel I had served under who had been very helpful in my joining the US forces during the war. If this Jenkins was anything like that man, I knew I could get some help. I entered his office and asked to see attorney Jenkins. The receptionist said, "You don't have an appointment do you?" I did not. "But I'll see if he can see you." She went into the office and asked the attorney. I heard him ask her, "Did he make an appointment?" She replied, "No, sir." There were a few words said that I couldn't understand, and then she came out of the office with a smile, saying, "He will see you now." As I walked in the door to his office, there standing right in front of me was the six-foot seven-inch Colonel Jenkins! "Frenchy!" he joyously shouted. "What brings you here?" I said, "Colonel Jenkins, what a surprise and coincidence!" We embraced each other as if we were long-lost relatives. He sat me down and we caught up on each other's lives. I hadn't seen him since he signed the mercenary orders that got me in the Ninth Army under General Hodges. After we had settled down a bit, Colonel Jenkins asked me what had brought me to his door. I explained my situation and the great deal of pain I was having. Jenkins felt that since I had been injured on the job, that it was Mr. Wolf and North American Van Lines' responsibility to pay my medical bills. He agreed to take my case and handled the back and forth with Mr. Wolf, who felt terrible about it, and ultimately his insurance paid my medical bills. Colonel Jenkins had really helped me out of a tough situation. We became very good friends because of our chance encounter, and saw each other often.

Fran

I had not spent much time in communication with God thus far in my life, but I was very familiar with his teachings since childhood. Something seemed to be happening to me spiritually around this time. My life began to seem clearer in its purpose. I began to feel like something or someone was behind all the miracles that seemed to be occurring throughout my life. I seemed to be extraordinarily lucky in that I kept finding my way out of trouble. Good things kept happening that kept me from falling into despair. Then she happened!

My office at Keller and Peterson was on the ninth floor of the W. T. Waggoner building and had two windows on the Houston street side. My drafting table happened to be near one of the windows. While I was thinking about a problem I was trying to resolve, I happened to glance out the window and saw a very attractive young lady crossing the street below. She looked very professional in a black business suit, a white blouse, and black high heels. She walked into the building across the street, and for some reason I looked at my watch and noticed it was time for the coffee break. I couldn't get her out of my mind, and I began wondering if she actually worked in the building she entered that morning. I was hoping to see her again and decided to find out who she was. I had to find a way to meet her!

A few days later, while having breakfast at the Picadelli Cafeteria, I saw her in line ahead of me. I couldn't help but stare at her, which she was totally unaware of. I found a seat a few tables away. I couldn't find the courage to speak with her that morning but I knew now she worked in the area. I made a point the next day of looking out my office window around 0930 hours and noticed that she arrived at our building every day around that time, coming from the building across the street.

A few mornings later, Augie caught me looking out the window and questioned me. "What are you looking at, Lippens?" I was ready to spill my secret, "You see that good-looking young lady walking across the street? Well, I am going to marry her!" He saw her and laughed, then countered, "Fat chance, Lippens!"

So I asked Virginia, the elevator operator, if she could find out her name and where she worked. I soon found out that her name was Fran and that she got off the elevator on the twenty-first floor. That was all I needed to know. A few days went by, and while I was having my regular coffee with Betty, I saw her walk by. I didn't want to talk to Fran with Betty around. More time went by, and it began to seem impossible to meet her. Betty liked the routine of having coffee with me, and I couldn't shake her off. Finally the chance came to

Fran when I first fell in love with her

try to approach Fran when Betty called in sick. I wasn't shy, but in those days, out of respect for young ladies, the direct approach was not always the way to go. As she was leaving the restaurant, I caught up with her and said, "Miss Fran, my name is Jon and I was hoping to meet you and maybe have breakfast with you. Could I join you for breakfast tomorrow morning?"

She said, "I don't normally eat breakfast in the morning, but I guess it will be fine. See you then!" I went back to work and that night didn't sleep well at all. My mind was wondering if she had another boyfriend or if anything else could stand in the way of us. I think I had fallen for this girl.

The next morning, I waited for her in the lobby thinking about what I was going to say or not say. One of the four elevator doors opened, but she was not in it. Virginia, the elevator attendant, said the next one would be it because it had stopped on the twenty-first floor. Sure enough there she was! I said hello and asked if we could try something different and have breakfast at the Warren Café, which wasn't as noisy and busy. Luckily she agreed. It was just around the corner, and I knew my office bunch wouldn't be there. We chatted for a while. I asked her where she worked, and she told me she worked for Rock Island Railroad at the T and P building on Lancaster. Because of my French accent, I guess, she asked where I was from. She said she didn't mind my accent or even the fact that I was a foreigner. We had a good time, but all too soon the coffee break was over. I boldly asked her if she could meet again for breakfast the next morning. She smiled and agreed to. This was the best news I think I ever had. I could have shouted from the rooftops, "I am going to marry Fran! Yes I will!"

During that first week we had breakfast together every day. When Friday arrived I asked Fran if we could have lunch on Saturday; because of my job and my classes at TCU I couldn't date her at night. She agreed to meet for lunch. Fran grew up in a large family house with three sisters, so she knew how to take care of herself. Fran's father had left home when she was younger, and her mother Lera raised the girls to be strong and self-sufficient. Fran respected my military mannerisms and appreciated my attempts at being a gentleman. Fran's friends wondered why she didn't choose an American guy. She told them repeatedly that she thought I was a good person with a tremendous heart, and luckily, her mother liked me. Family was important to Fran, and my journey from Belgium with my family resonated with her. Fran was also very spiritual, which intrigued me. My interests in God only strengthened as I got to know Fran further. She taught me things that instilled in me a desire to learn more. She wasn't like other women I had known. This beautiful woman also came with substance and a strong moral character.

We met for lunch at the Westbrook Grill in the Westbrook Hotel in downtown Fort Worth. The building was where many legendary oil and cattlemen met for their big business deals. The lobby was a mixture of marble and wooden paneling, and the entrance was adorned with a large and beautiful sculpture of Venus. The downstairs grill had a fabulous atmosphere with the same rich wood paneling and plush cushioned booths and warm, indirect lighting. This place was an artistic creation, a perfect place to spend time with Fran.

We had a great lunch and a pleasant conversation. She had some shopping to do, and I had to go back to work. I asked her when we could meet again and she asked me if I would like to go to church with her on Sunday morning. I wasn't about to tell this woman no, and replied that I would pick her up at her friend's house to make it to Sunday school. I actually took three young ladies that morning. I had never been to a Sunday school but thought it was very interesting. As we made our way to the main sanctuary for the service, I noticed that everybody seemed to be happy and was greeting each other with smiles that seemed very sincere. I visited a few churches in my adulthood prior to this one, and this church was more alive than any other church I had visited. I was raised in the Catholic belief that the church required total holiness, quietness, and reverence. If anything had to be said, it had to be in a whisper.

As soon as the service started, the orchestra and choir began singing praise songs. Then the pastor, Homer Ritchie, welcomed everyone and asked to recognize the visitors by the lifting of a hand. I raised mine because I was indeed a visitor. The sermon that day was inspirational and the songs were beautiful. Toward the end of the sermon, the pastor asked if anyone would receive Jesus Christ. Suddenly, several members in something resembling a football huddle surrounded me. They asked me if I knew the Lord and had received salvation. I told them I was new in town and that I was brought up as a Catholic. I said I needed more time to understand what was being taught in the church, and they suggested I meet with the pastor. That night I returned and met with pastor Homer Ritchie, who like me was twenty-six years old. He asked me a lot of questions about my family background, my beliefs, and my hopes for the future. He offered to show me what the church believed and taught. A week later, after the nighttime service, Pastor Homer read several passages in the Bible to me that spoke of the promise of salvation and the forgiveness of our sins. I explained to Homer that I had done many wrong things in my life, and I couldn't imagine the Lord would ever forgive me. He disagreed with my assumption and proceeded to show me step by step how to be forgiven. It didn't take me long to see and to understand that it was the only way I could ever be forgiven. The more I learned, the more I felt like a weight was being lifted off me.

The following two or three Sunday nights, I talked again with Homer Ritchie. I was convinced. On March 21, 1954, in front of his congregation, I asked publicly for the Lord to forgive me of my sins and accepted the Lord as my personal savior in my heart. I knew I was saved and forgiven. The feeling of relieving myself of those burdens was immeasurable. I was not finished, though. I was still haunted by awful nightmares of my years in the war and the hell I went through. I required further assistance from Homer and the Lord.

Fran was certainly surprised but very happy about my decision. I told her that it was the only way I could deal with the past. My parents didn't understand why I became a Protestant, but on the other hand, they didn't believe it made any difference anyway, because they didn't believe in anything. Unfortunately, they were very liberal and very agnostic.

Since I intended to ask Fran to marry me, I visited with her mother months later while Fran was out of town on vacation. I told her of my love for her daughter and of my intention to see if she would bless our union. I told Lera that I knew it was an old fashioned way to ask for a blessed union in this modern world, but thought it was still the proper way to do it. She replied that she didn't know me very well, but that I seemed to be a good prospect for her daughter, and she certainly would bless our union if Fran accepted my offer.

On Fran's return we talked about our future. I felt as ready as I was going to be. I picked her up from the train station and took her to dinner. While we were eating, I asked her if she would marry me. She asked for a few days to think it over, and then she accepted my marriage proposal. I knew it was the Lord's blessing! I was beside myself and told everyone at the office my big news. Everyone was very happy for us. Augie reminded me that I told him I would marry Fran before I even met her. Augie loved my determination.

Getting Married

We looked for an apartment and decided to find one in the TCU campus area so I could very easily walk to classes. The place we picked was located on the corner of Bellaire Drive and Stadium Drive, which at the time was right off the ninth hole of the Western Hills Golf Course (now part of the TCU campus). Our apartment was modest but great, and had a beautiful view of the golf course. There was a large living room, a nice-sized bedroom, a bathroom, and a nice-sized kitchen with dining area.

We set the date for our wedding on June 30, 1954, with the ceremony at her mother's home on South Henderson Street. Homer Ritchie officiated over our simple and beautiful marriage. The cake was as delicious as a wedding cake could be. After the ceremony, we went to the Western Hills Restaurant, where we had a delicious supper and a long visit. Then we retired to our new apartment.

We spent the first day as a couple grocery shopping and relaxing on a lake beach area called Twin Points. We took off a few days and enjoyed Fran's superb meals, as she was a blue ribbon cook. No one could touch her chicken-fried steak with cream gravy, green beans, and mashed potatoes, or her fried chicken with cream gravy and all the trimmings. It didn't take long for me to gain weight and skip a couple of notches in my belt.

Three months later, we received the wonderful news that we were going to have an addition to our family! It was great news and we rejoiced at the idea of having a little one. Fran suffered a lot from morning sickness, and we had to move to a ground-floor apartment because the stairs were too steep and dangerous for Fran.

We found a very nice bungalow-style apartment located on the northeast part of town, on Field Street. There was a large front yard that the owner mowed weekly. We discovered a serious problem with scorpions: they were in the kitchen, the bathroom, and the bedroom. When we got up at night and turned the lights on, they were all over the place. We even found them in our bed and clothing. The owner repeatedly sprayed for them, but they kept coming back. We got tired of them quickly, and with the upcoming birth of the baby, couldn't risk it anymore. We moved to a duplex apartment on Wayside and Cantey, just off Forest Park Boulevard. It had one bedroom, one bath, and a one-car garage. The walls were varnished knotty pine wood, which gave it a very warm and homey look.

We had just settled down in our new place when my lifelong friend Bernard from Belgium came to visit us for a week. He came to see us but also wanted to visit the western part of the United States, which he had read so much about. He went to Colorado, Arizona, Utah, Wyoming, Oregon, and California. While in California, he rented a horse, bought a 30/30 Winchester rifle, a 45-caliber gun with ammo belt, a pup tent, and the equipment necessary to cook and pan for gold. A few months later, he returned to Fort Worth with plenty to talk about and with quite a few good-sized gold nuggets. He had found an old timer who helped him set up camp in the wild, and then showed him how and where to pan. He loved what he had seen and done and made quite a few friends while traveling. He was very impressed with this country and its people. He loved Fran's cooking, especially her Tex-Mex cuisine.

During his return stay, I got the feeling that Bernard was not truly happy with the way his life turned out, and so we talked about it. He had a good business partnership with his dad in a brokerage and commercial insurance company. He had a good future with a good income, but he wasn't the boss. His dad ran the business like a general and thus ordered Bernard what to do, how to do it, when to do it, and where and when to go. The trade-off was that Bernard could afford what he wanted. For example, he owned a German Messerschmit fighter plane, high-priced cars, a forty-five-foot sailboat, and could travel a lot for the business and for vacation. He told me that he didn't know where his life was taking him. He also told me that he would like very much to live in the United States, but that he couldn't give up what he was going to inherit. I didn't know what to say, but I realized the big price he was paying. As unhappy as he was, he would not give up the joy of money and materialism. What he really had was an empty heart and would probably never be happy. His parents were agnostic, and so was everybody else in his family. Status and possessions were the important things in their lives. He was my blood brother, and I loved him anyway. I told him of the turnaround in my life because of religion. He expressed his feeling that religion was a myth, but nonetheless was very glad to see our happiness.

While he was with us, he felt our baby girl kicking around in Fran's abdomen. He thought it was great to feel the baby move. He was happy for us and wished he could stay until the baby was born, but it was time for him to return home. I drove him to Houston the following weekend where he was to board a Likes Lines ship to Belgium. On Friday, we arrived late at night in Houston and rented a motel room for the night. We went out for supper at a steak house where he could one more time enjoy American beef. We then went to the motel and got ready to turn in.

As I mentioned previously, Bernard and I were the best of friends and were blood brothers, but during our growing years we pulled a lot of jokes on each other. That wasn't going to change yet. I thought I'd get the upper hand on Bernard while he was in the shower. So I put some ice cubes in his bed because I knew that he slept in his shorts. I knew he would jump into bed after emerging from the bathroom, which he did. When he made contact with the ice cubes, he jumped straight out of that bed as if he had received an electric shock. He ran around looking for something warm to put on, after which we engaged an ice cube fight. It ended quickly because of the complaints from our neighbors. I knew I would get Bernard's revenge, but I didn't know when and where.

The next morning, we ate breakfast at the motel's restaurant, after which we went to the Houston harbor to check out the ship and load most of his luggage on board. The ship's departure was for the next day in the afternoon, which gave us time to do and see a few more things. We drove around Houston a bit but didn't know what to do or where to go. Bernard came up with the idea to visit the Alamo, but we didn't know where to find it. We didn't find it that day, and I learned later that it was two hundred miles east, in San Antonio. We had a late lunch at a fish restaurant, which had a bar. We spent the rest of the day reminiscing about our youth, the war, the good and the bad, and expressed our hopes for the future. Bernard told me he envied me for having the guts to immigrate to this country. He was right; I was a very lucky and blessed man. We went back to the motel where we had a deeper conversation about my recent transformation through God. I wanted to help Bernard, but he was not ready for the change as I was, so I let it go.

Bernard had mail to take care of in the downtown central post office. In 1954, the main post office in Houston still had wooden floors. There were No Smoking signs all over the place to protect the floor. We decided to smoke our cigarettes inside anyway. While Bernard was taking care of his mail, a police officer approached us and told us to put those cigarettes out and pointed at the signs. As Bernard and I were talking to each other in French, we greeted the officer in French and said: "Bon Jour officer, comment allez vous?" He responded by telling us again in English to put those cigarettes out and again pointed at the signs. In French, I told Bernard that maybe I ought to offer him one of my Lucky Strike cigarettes, but he said he didn't think it was a good idea. So I did, and it was a mistake. The officer took the cigarette to the nearest garbage can and threw it in saying, "No cigarette and no smoking!" and then he shouted, "Can't you Frenchmen understand anything? Do you think this is funny?" I acted puzzled by his actions, and then Bernard offered him one of his Chesterfield cigarettes, which was another big mistake. This time the policeman got completely frustrated and became very angry with us. We could tell that the fun was over. So I walked toward the garbage and threw my cigarette in it and immediately the policeman said, "Yes! No smoking! Throw the damned things away!" Bernard then came up with the revelation saying, "Très bien, Je comprend pas fûmer!" (Very well, I understand no smoking!) The frustrated policeman feigned a smile and walked off saying one more time while pointing at the signs, "No smoking." I think we had our fun and avoided getting into trouble. We mailed the letters and left quickly. We had lunch at another steak house, at Bernard's request, followed by a good final uplifting conversation about our future. At two in the afternoon, I took him to the ship and went on board for a few minutes. I didn't say goodbye but rather, "See you later, old friend!" Somehow we both knew we would never see each other again.

It was a long drive back to Fort Worth, where I arrived around 0100 hours. Fran and I talked a while about the pleasant visit we had with Bernard. I mentioned not finding the Alamo in Houston, and Fran had a good laugh about that. I remember her saying, "Leave it up to a couple of foreigners to be looking for the Alamo in Houston!"

Things were getting rough on the job, and the workload got so bad that I had to quit going to evening classes altogether. I just couldn't find time to study and attend classes regularly. Fran took time off from the Rock Island Rail Road job due to her acute morning sickness. Our apartment smelled of varnished wood, and that made her nausea worse. We decided it would be better to move, and found another apartment on South Henderson Street about a block from where her mother lived. It was a cute large one-bedroom and one-bath apartment.

The months went by, and Fran was getting very uncomfortable. Then on Saturday, June 25, 1955, our daughter Francine was born. All went well at the hospital, and our little baby girl was beautiful. The whole family rejoiced, and a few days later our little bundle of joy was home. The Lord had blessed us tremendously! She became the only baby in the family, which funneled everyone's love to her. Fran's mother was a big help and enjoyed the time being with us. That same year, we bought a small house on 3505 Boyce Street in the South Hills Addition, a half block from Kellis Park. It had two bedrooms this time, still just one bath, a one-car garage, and a great backyard. We enjoyed the neighborhood and made a lot of friends. Most of them were young married couples with kids.

These years were very happy times for us. A few years later, in seemingly military fashion, we moved again to South Ridge Terrace. It was a California contemporary-style home with a large living and dining area and two nice-sized bedrooms. The house had one bathroom, a large kitchen with breakfast area, a very large patio, one garage, and a very nice backyard. Our move was somewhat complicated because I had a very bad infection on my right heel and right leg that was badly ulcerated. Every year in the fall and winter, my foot was repeatedly getting infected, and I had to get it treated by a dermatologist. This was an old problem that had developed during World War II as a result of the frostbite damage to my feet. This particular time, the infection was worse than ever. I was running a high fever and couldn't even stand on my right leg. My dermatologist, Dr. Riddell, was kind enough to come to the house. His diagnosis wasn't good at all. I had the red stripes going up the leg, which was a telltale sign of possible gangrene. Dr. Riddell recommended an immediate amputation. I wouldn't hear of it, but didn't know what to do. Then the doctor suggested a new antibiotic that wasn't cleared by the government yet. This medicine was experimental and still in the trial phase, and had potential side effects that weren't positive. He stated very clearly that he wouldn't be responsible for the result. The medicine could make me very sick or could cause a bad reaction, but it might do what no other medicine had done: halt the infection. Considering my options, I asked him to give me the shot immediately. Lady luck, I knew, was on my side. Several days and many prayers later, my fever broke and the infection lessened. My wounds were cared for, and new skin grew in. My leg was bandaged for a long time and I used crutches, then a cane for many months, but my leg was saved.

Francine was such a joy for us. We nicknamed her Sug, as in Sugar. She was as beautiful as Fran. When I was in recovery, I had much time with her, and she was incredible. Later, after my recovery, most of my days were spent working, so my time was limited with her. I enjoyed taking her sailing, riding bikes with her, and going to the swimming pool at the Convair (later General Dynamics) Recreation Association together. As soon as I got home from work, on the rare days it was early enough, she would be waiting in her swimsuit to go to the pool. Sug loved taking care of her dolls and later the plants around the house. She had early plans to be a nurse when she grew up. She always wanted to be a mother and to take care of children, and one day she would have two children of her own. She doted on them from the moment they were born.

Time Served

There were rumors of war in the African Congo, which was a Belgian colony. Since I had moved to America, I had constantly dreaded a recall by the Belgian Army. I had been lucky thus far, but my streak finally broke. A few weeks later, I received the telegram from the Belgian Army. I was to report for duty immediately. I was now about five months short of attaining my American citizenship. I was married with a child, had a solid occupational record, and had a new life here in this country. I was very sure the Belgian Army would send me to Africa. Many Belgians were dying every day in that conflict. I called our pastor Ritchie and told him what I was facing. He was very concerned and told me that he would get in touch with local Congressman Jim Wright to see if he could help. The Congress was in session at that time, but Jim Wright accepted the emergency call from Homer Ritchie, who explained the situation. Jim Wright told Homer that he would see what he could do. I understand that Congressman Wright immediately called the Belgian ambassador in New Orleans to request a six months' delay for my departure. Pastor Ritchie told me to have faith and to pray that the Lord would make the delay happen. A few days later I received a letter from the Belgian embassy telling me that my request for a six months' delay was granted. You talk about an answer to my prayers!

Five months later, I was informed by mail by the federal court of the day and time I was to appear at the Immigration and Naturalization Court for my written and oral tests. The following week, my boss, L. F. Peterson, testified that he had known me for the past five years and that I was of good

My mom, about 1980

moral character. I also had a letter from my past employer, Frank Wolf, in Greenville, and one from Jay Wilson, who was my first employer in Fort Worth. The examination was very challenging for me, even after five years of preparation. I passed the oral exam and the written exam with flying colors, which concluded the examinations to receive my American citizenship. I was told to be back on the following Wednesday, when I would be sworn in at 1400 hours in the afternoon.

However, precisely a week later, I went to the Federal courthouse to get my long-awaited American citizenship. I stood proudly in the courtroom with many others who were becoming citizens like me. The judge began reading off the names of all new citizens. All raised their hands up and took the oath as administered by the judge. Everyone received their certificates stating that they now were guaranteed the same inalienable rights as every other United States citizen. Everyone but me that is! My name was never called. I had to endure the entire service before I could inquire why. They said they were sorry, but the delay was caused by an error with my name and its spelling. They needed me to come back the following week, at the same time on Wednesday. I was very disappointed, but I had to wait another week.

Our friends Grover and Martha Riddle had organized a huge surprise party for this expected occasion and had invited all of my friends and colleagues. I didn't know about the party, since it was to be a surprise, but Fran still suggested that we should go and visit with Grover and Martha. You talk about a party! I couldn't believe they had done this for me. They had decorated the house with American flags and there was a big tri-colored cake with a big flag and tri-colored balloons. When I walked up to their house, I had no idea I would find so many people there because they had parked their cars in the back of the house and around the corner. They were just as disappointed as I was when I announced the delay in receiving my citizenship. But we decided not to waste the evening and celebrated anyway. It was a great party, and a week later I was an American citizen! I would no longer be subject to Belgian military recalls. I was free to be free. What a feeling!

Our son David was born on March 3, 1965, a few weeks before the passing away of Fran's father, as well as mine. My father, Victor Adolph Lippens, lived a very independent life where he was always in control of the situation. He rarely received medical attention or saw a doctor. One morning, he awoke and wasn't able to get out of bed. He was seventy-seven years old and had no choice but to be taken to the hospital. Emergency surgery was performed, and upon opening him up, the doctor found him riddled with cancers. The doctor sewed him back up and sent him home with two months to live. The prognosis turned out to be accurate. Dad passed away two months later. Fran's father had passed away seven days earlier, from cancer as well. My mother could not handle living alone and decided to live with Lucienne and Don in El Paso, where he had recently been transferred.

David was a good son who was lots of fun to play with. We always found things to do together. When David was old enough, we joined the YMCA and the Indian Guides, where we spent much time engaged in father-and-son activities outdoors. We dressed like the native Indians, rode horseback without saddles, and canoed and fished at Cottonwood Lake. We camped out together, built fires, and hunted together. We once killed a deer together, skinned it, and prepared and tanned the hide, which we turned into a tribal drum. The Pow Wow bonfires were incredible, as were the tribal dances that erupted. Every year, the group selected a new Indian chief, and one year I became Chief Longbow with my brave little sidekick Short Arrow. The years went by, and David became interested in racing cars, racing motorcycles, and chasing girls. He grew too fast, to the imposing size of six foot four inches, with muscles to match. As David grew, I found it very difficult to keep up with him. My body wasn't able to withstand the regular abuses that children's activities elicit. We planned many sailing races together, but the load at my office and my art commissions took up most of my spare time. I will always remember those good times we shared, however. They were indeed a tremendous blessing to me.

Painting

Many years after I moved to Fort Worth, I was introduced to an artist and teacher named Pamela Chapman. I understood that she was a good teacher and expert watercolor artist. I went to visit her and liked her and her work. She had a wonderful studio setup of which many an artist could only dream. I loved her paintings and illustrations and told her that I would like to produce freelance art. She told me she represented a group of well-known artists and told me how to get in touch with them. The only requirements to qualify were passing an aptitude test and being able to afford the expensive tuition. This group of artists were located around New York but were represented by Southern Methodist University in Dallas, Texas. The four-year course would be instructed through correspondence, with the finals given four years later at SMU. She told me the school was founded by an established group of artists called, appropriately enough, the Famous Artists School. One of its founders was an artist by the name of Norman Rockwell. The Famous Artists School had a monthly presentation in Dallas, where one of the teachers would pitch an idea to interested people. The month I attended had the well-known artist Albert Dorne instructing us on *How To Be An Artist*. He explained to the audience that being an artist, as with any other profession, was a gift from God. He said that each one of us had the desire to do something in a different and specialized field, and should accept the fact that God makes it possible for the student or professional to be successful in that profession. Some people are born to be a doctor, engineer, lawyer, banker, cowboy, nurse, plumber, electrician, etc., and are born with that desire and gift. He went on to say that if God created you to be an artist, from an early age you knew in your heart that you wanted to be an artist. You started at an early age to sketch or paint, which I had done since the age of four or five. He seemed to be speaking directly to me.

He explained that when you began your profession as an artist, or began any other profession, you were responsible for your success. He suggested that wherever you go, look around and see everything with a keen, observant eye. Then find a subject you wanted to reproduce in your work. He said that if you study art, you had to choose good, reputable artists and teachers. He, of course, recommended his school. I needed no more convincing.

Now it was up to me. I took the entrance test, which I passed easily and therefore was accepted. It was a tremendous financial burden for us, but I felt it would pay off. The courses were quite difficult, and the teachers wouldn't settle for less than perfection. But I enjoyed learning what I did, and completed the course in approximately three and a half years. I felt myself a very worthy artist, and wanted to showcase my newly crafted talents.

My assignments at work allowed me to use some of my new skills. We were given illustrating jobs called court art that allowed me to exhibit some of my creativity. Our engineers at Keller and Peterson gave us their findings, and we then turned their research into beautiful exhibits of all kinds. I began creating many watercolor and oil paintings, which I hoped to sell. I represented myself at first, as my sales consisted mainly of commissions of well sites. I painted landscapes from places I would see or had seen in my past. Many of these scenes involved ranches and oil derricks. I created engineering illustrations for consulting firms and for court exhibits and for different oil companies. At last, I was able to use my skills as an artist to bring a little money into the house. It was around this time that I painted a landscape of the rugged Drachenfels Mountains. This was where I had spent my twenty-first birthday, fighting the renegade SS officer and his army holding out in the castle near the Rhine River. This painting hangs in my home still today and reminds me daily of that terrible event in that picturesque location. This piece is one of the favorite pieces I ever painted. The beauty of those mountains cannot be ruined by the misery of war. My paintings and illustrations were done in my spare time because work was so busy. I felt I could eventually make a decent living as an artist, but now I needed to feed our family, so I would only paint in the evenings. As much as I wanted to be a real artist, I loved working with people and felt much pride in a job well done.

In 1963, Keller and Peterson decided they were ready to retire and close shop. The incredible work we all had done over the years had made them quite wealthy, and it was assumed they desired time to go enjoy it. Most of the engineers left the company, as they were highly sought after by other firms. Some even started their own petroleum-consulting business.

I had built quite a résumé of work during my time there. I utilized my portfolio, along with my diploma from the art school, to convince General Dynamics to hire me as an engineering illustrator. The art jobs that I did on the side were growing, but not quite enough to warrant being a full-time artist.

My diploma from the Famous Artists School

I did love the General Dynamics job, and it was there I spent the next eleven prosperous years. My job was to paint images of the aircraft we were building or designing. I loved to paint the aircraft in aerial battle scenes. My mind could really soar on these projects. My work hours at General Dynamics were long, to say the least. I began work at 5:00 a.m. and left the building regularly at 10:00 p.m. These seventeen-hour days were very hard on me and my wife and young kids. If I ever had a regret, it was the time I missed with them while I was away at work. The money I was making was good, however, and I had excellent perks. I wore a golden engineering badge, which allowed me access into classified areas and other restricted access sites. As much as I enjoyed the money and status, I was wearing myself out. My home life was almost nonexistent. I left for work before Fran and the kids got up and I returned home after Fran and the kids went to bed. I knew there had to be a better way to provide for my family and have more time to enjoy with them.

In 1974, I had gotten wind of a large, fairly new oil and gas company in Fort Worth called American Quasar Petroleum, which was looking to hire an artist to work in their map-making department. Maps, in those days, were created by hand and were quite a work of art. Computers have since replaced artists in this regard, but the work we churned out took much time and effort and certainly looked it. This new job offered me a manager's role over the engineering illustration department, as well as a higher salary. The hours and social life weren't much better, but I did gain some of my home life back. I was given stock in this fast-growing company as well as a company car. American Quasar Petroleum kept me busy for the next seven years making the most beautiful maps for their business. I enjoyed my time there very much, and I met some very fine people through my daily assignments whom I retain as friends today. The work was grueling, and I loved every minute of it. I was providing Fran with enough money to not worry, and that was all I ever wanted. My paintings took a back seat, but I knew it had to be. I was able to fulfill many commissioned paintings over the years, but they were always completed after work hours.

Sobriety

It was a regular day in 1979 when I made a life-altering decision. I asked help from the Lord to take away my desire for liquor and nicotine. My consumption of alcohol and cigarettes had grown steadily over the years due to my work environment and its associated stresses. It was beginning to interfere with my work. I drank to fill a void in my life. The two things I missed most were spending time with my family—and sailing. These haunted me most.

Nearly every day at 5:00 p.m., all the managers gathered in president Dick Lowe's office to discuss the problems of the day and plans for tomorrow. These managers meetings were regularly complemented with drinks. Once we had completed this daily routine, we would head out to dinner at a local restaurant, or on lucky nights, to the Petroleum Club, where oilmen gathered for evening dinner and drinks. Often after dinner, we would go back to the office to work some more. Work life often enabled this behavior, as cigarette smoking and drinking were as common to me as colored pencils and straight edges. My moment of truth was the result of a hard lesson I learned one weekend evening. I had just completed a commissioned watercolor for a man, when I leaned over the table to reach for something. The ash from my cigarette brushed my illuminating Dazor light and fell on my painting, right in the middle of the sky. I didn't notice it immediately but when I did, it was too late. It had burned the surface enough to ruin the painting. It was a $4,500 commission, and because of his deadline, I didn't have the time to paint another one. It was quite a loss, not only of the painting, but also of the customer. I decided right then and there to quit smoking and drinking at home and at work. Now, it would be only very special circumstances when I would have a drink. I had done it once as a younger man when I opted to leave the liquor sales business, so I knew I could handle it again. It took a great deal more of my will power this time to stay clean, but aside from the rare special celebratory events in my life, I remain free of alcohol and tobacco to this day. I believe my character improved because of this. As a new non-drinker, I would forego the time spent out with the guys drinking to work on my art in my office, which increased my production level. I picked up a peculiar habit that helped me in times of weakness. Occasionally, I would reach into my closet for a large bottle of Scotch that I always kept close at hand. I pulled the plug and lifted it to my face to inhale the aroma in a giant sniff. This has satisfied my urges for the last twenty years.

My painting became more and more prolific. I had developed a considerable group of collectors who were interested in my work. These commissions really helped Fran and me stay ahead of our bills. One of my collectors introduced me to Steve Munday, the news director with *Cattleman* magazine, who showed interest in my work. He wanted to help me, so he wrote a letter introducing me to the owners of large ranches in Texas and all the surrounding states, such as New Mexico, Oklahoma, Mississippi, Arkansas, and Colorado. As a result, I received several invitations to visit these ranches. I saw Texas, Oklahoma, New Mexico, and Louisiana the way most people wished they could see it. You would not believe how beautiful some of those ranches are past the entrance gate. Some were the type that required four-wheel drive vehicles to get around. It was because of this new opportunity that I bought a Jeep Grand Wagoneer.

Artist

I had been painting off and on for years, when time would allow it. The nights, weekends, and occasional office breaks just weren't fulfilling my needs as a painter anymore. My job at American Quasar had me so busy that I figured I would never get real time to dedicate to my craft. When I did paint, I made very good money. I enjoyed selling my originals and commissions. The lithographs seemed to sell themselves.

I left American Quasar Petroleum in 1981 and finally became a full-time artist. I was incentivized to leave by the consulting group that had been brought in to oversee our operations in order to reduce costs. An accountant was appointed to oversee my illustration department, to whom I had to report. This man understood very little of the creative processes that were necessary to create such intricate works for oil and gas maps. He tried to reduce my department staff to help cut costs, and was given permission to reorganize the company. I decided to resign. I couldn't let an accountant make decisions for the art department. The drop in oil prices had set these events in motion, as we had been a very profitable division of American Quasar. I had pondered the idea of painting full-time, and this may have been the blessing I needed to start. I immediately set out painting new watercolors and created one of the most acclaimed works of my career, called *Anticipation*. This painting of a cowboy on a horse watching his oil well sold quickly, as did the lithographs. The oil well in the painting was in fact one of American Quasar's own wells.

Board Road

I sold the original to the American Quasar Chairman of the Board, Wilford Fultz, for $4,750, and 450 limited edition prints that I sold for $150 each. So I painted several more of American Quasar's discovery oil wells, paintings I had little trouble selling. I went on many adventures to capture these wells in their natural beauty. *Panhandle Wildcat* in the Texas Panhandle and *Bobwhite No. 1* in Beckham County, Oklahoma, were two of my more popular creations. A few months later, the president of American Quasar, Dick Lowe, offered to buy the two originals for the company. In August 1980, the principal owners of the company, Dick Lowe, Mickey Schmidt, David McMan, Ted Collins, and I formed a limited edition art partnership, under the name of "Art Ventures Company." I would produce the originals, which would be turned into 450 limited-edition, numbered lithographs. American Quasar Petroleum would purchase 150 prints of each original and also had first refusal on the originals. I was allowed to sell the remaining lithographs.

I painted several originals and their respective lithographs, of which American Quasar bought their quota, but I couldn't sell my remaining stock quickly enough to keep up with the cost of reproduction. The costs to reproduce ranged from $6,000 to $8,000. I couldn't move them fast enough to pay for the reproductions, and I had 3,300 lithographs for sale, with few buyers.

The 150 lithographs of each that were bought by American Quasar were distributed to each partner and investor. The lithographs were printed on a beautiful special paper called Buckeye Limited 100% rag, 90# cover weight, neutral, colorfast, and with a natural finish. I followed up by painting *Guadalupe Peak*, located in Culberson County, which is the highest mountain in Texas at a height of 8,745 ft. Then I completed a painting I named *Breaking Out*, which was another painting of Culberson County, at roundup time. It showed a company gas well in the distance and the well-known Guadalupe Peak and the Sierra Diablo Mountains. *Board Road* in southeast Texas was next.

As well as I thought I was doing at this time, I did have many limitations. For instance, I didn't paint portraits of people or their favorite pets. It was not that I couldn't paint portraits or pets, but it didn't seem to work out for me. The opportunity came before me many times throughout my career, but I very seldom pleased the customers because they claimed that I failed to capture them properly. In these cases, I seldom collected the fee for the commission. I was happy as a freelance artist in oils, acrylics, watercolors, pen and ink, and pencil. I remember the wonderful feeling of independence and doing what I always wanted to do, whenever and wherever.

One of my commissions was for a large four-by-eight-foot oil painting of Aspen trees that captured the leaves turning to gold during the fall in Colorado. While painting the picture of the Aspen trees I visited the Collectors Gallery in Denton, Texas, owned by Mrs. Elaine Court. I showed her my paintings, and she suggested a write-up in the *American Art Magazine*. She obviously liked my work, but exaggerated about my background, education, and accomplishments. Here is what she wrote about me in the *American Art Collector Magazine*:

Fort Worth artist Jon Lippens, a native of Belgium, had his early training in fine arts in Europe. Son of an architect, he learned to paint transparent watercolors, and in 1952, at the age of twenty-five, Jon moved to Texas and settled in Fort Worth. His first jobs were as illustrator and commercial artist, but the lure of the ranches and the outdoors proved too strong. Since 1960 he has devoted his spare time painting in West Texas, Oklahoma, New Mexico, and Wyoming spring and fall roundups at the invitation of the ranch owners. During this time, he has produced oil paintings with knife as well as brush, transparent and opaque watercolor paintings and pen and ink drawings. His works vary from rugged western themes to the picturesque scenery of the East and of Europe. His paintings, which some critics describe as conservative with realism in a traditional style, have risen steadily in value. Jon's original works have sold throughout the Southwest and are currently hanging in a large number of private collections and in galleries across the United States.

Painting gave my professional life so much meaning. I truly enjoyed working for myself, which was something I had never experienced. Prices for my originals ranged from $3,500 to $8,500 and up. I handled all the marketing of my works, which have resulted in representations in approximately 185 galleries in Texas, Oklahoma, Louisiana, New Mexico, Colorado, California, and New York. My originals sold regularly. I was now making much more money selling my originals and the limited editions than I was ever making working for wages. The demand for my artwork was greater than I could satisfy, which was a problem I loved. I painted around the clock. Again I felt as if someone was watching over me and allowing me this perfect gift. These were indeed happy days.

Sky Falling

Then suddenly in 1984, the sales of my art plummeted due to the weakening American economy. I was forced to travel quite a bit to promote the sales of my works. With oil and beef prices dropping, the market for selling art came to a standstill. The majority of my customers were tied to either oil or cattle and ranches. The shock of the economy to my income forced me to go back to work. I had been making a decent living, but I was nowhere near rich. I had no other choice but to try to find a job.

I called oil companies, engineering firms, drafting and commercial art companies, and advertising firms, but none were hiring. One day I had the notion to call my ex-boss Wally Keller to see what he knew. He said he was glad to hear from me, and he knew of an oil company that needed an artist to design and produce promotional brochures and presentations. I went to an interview with Texland Oil and was promptly hired. My job again would be as an engineering illustrator, which kept me busy making maps and oil- and gas-related displays. I had been there for two years and had a stable income. I still painted in the evenings because I truly enjoyed it. Then one day, the vice president called me into his office and sat me down. He told me that my position was being terminated immediately because the bank now controlled the company. I wasn't the only one to be laid off. They also terminated most of the engineers, geologists, and many in the land and accounting departments.

This news came as a complete shock, because the day before, the president told me I was going to have a lot of work for several more months to come. This new development was accelerated by dwindling oil prices, which took down Texland Oil seemingly overnight. I immediately called around to get the word out that I was looking for another job. I called my ex-boss Charlie Croxton at General Dynamics, and an unexplainable miracle happened again. The job I left twelve years ago in 1974 had just opened up again. The man who replaced me when I left to work for Jack Fikes at American Quasar Petroleum had just given his two weeks notice that very day. Mr. Croxton asked if I could start in two weeks, to which I replied that I could start in two minutes. Two weeks later I went to work in the same department: same office, same boss, same desk, same golden badge, same security classification, and luckily, not the same money. Nothing much had changed in my old department except that we had a couple of new young ladies specializing in producing and assembling projection transparencies.

I wasn't a full-time artist anymore, but I was gainfully employed, which was reassuring to Fran and me. My work still remained represented all across the US, and every so often a check with my name on it would come trickling in with my 50 percent commission from whatever sold. Several months after I started again at General Dynamics I was transferred to the A-12 Avenger II project. I shared a cubicle with Bill Creed, with whom I became very good friends. The A-12 Avenger was to be the next technological advance in attack aircraft for the Navy and Marines. This flying-wing aircraft looked very much like an isosceles triangle. The project was different for me because computers did everything. I was trained by the company to use the new innovative Apple computer system, which was great for graphics and engineering drawings. Four years seemed to fly by, during which time we almost constantly worked fourteen- to sixteen-hour days, except for a very few holidays and vacations. I was always very tired, and remember thinking how much longer will I be able to stand it? But the months and the years went by, and then all of a sudden, it was over again. No one could have guessed it, because the government funded the A-12, and they never run out of money, right? But the overruns and delays seemed neverending, and finally the doors were closed on the Navy A-12 project. Thirty-four hundred employees working on the project were laid off. And, of course, I was one of them. We were caught flat-footed with the news because on the previous afternoon we had several meetings where they explained and predicted another surge of work ahead. This was the second time I had been laid off, and I couldn't believe it was happening again. To add to my problem of sudden unemployment and loss of insurance, I learned that because of my contract with the A-12, I forfeited my rights to be rehired in another department at General Dynamics. All I had coming was one week of pay with no severance. What a sweetheart deal!

I earned the classification of a job shopper within General Dynamics, which didn't guarantee steady employment and didn't include company

Bluebonnets

Bob White No. 1

Board Road

Too Young

Thirsty

benefits. I was very disappointed with the management, but there was nothing else to do but to sign up for unemployment and start searching for a new job. I was now a sixty-two-year-old artist looking for a job. What chance did I have to get hired? Everywhere I applied, they wouldn't hire me because they said I was over-qualified or too old.

We consulted our CPA, who suggested going ahead and retiring. I was not ready to make this move, but with my options very limited, I retired from the labor force. At least I would now have time to spend with my paints.

Our Retirement Years

At first I was in shock, but it didn't take me long to get over it. We contacted General Dynamics and made the necessary arrangements. The very same day I signed the papers, I was retired. Retirement was great, but what a change! Every morning, I had to decide what to do with the day. There was a drastic change in our daily activities, which required more planning than I ever expected. I was able to put things off until tomorrow or the day after when I felt like it. I hadn't planned on this hard decision-making, but it didn't take me very long to get the hang of it, and luckily I found plenty to do.

To celebrate my independence, I decided to grow a beard. I consulted with my barber Fran before growing this beard because most of my hair had fallen out or turned gray. Then there was the new dress code. Suits weren't allowed and absolutely no more ties. I had that rope around my neck long enough.

It was around this time in my life that I received a phone call from one of my cousins in Belgium. He told me that one of the Belgian daily newspapers called *La Libre Belgique* was interviewing emigrants and wanted to speak to me. *La Libre Belgique* was published in secret during the Nazi occupation and had survived to become a heavily circulated news source in Wallonia and Brussels. A time was set up for a phone interview. The reporter wanted to know how I was doing and if I liked living in the United States. The interview went on for a while with a bunch of simple, mildly interesting questions. The reporter then shared that he had interviewed a lady living in Belgium who was the sister of an old childhood friend of mine named Jaque Kaplan. My name had come up, which is what led him to contact my cousin. The reporter went on to say he had interviewed Jaque, who now lived in Salt Lake City. I hadn't seen or heard from this man in fifty-plus years. I had assumed he did not survive the war. The reporter passed his number on to me, and I called him a short time later. Jaque had indeed survived the war and was thriving in Salt Lake City. He had made a great deal of money in the stock market. Jaque decided on the phone to come visit me in Fort Worth, and on the day of his arrival I went to the airport to pick him up. I waited outside for a long time and finally went inside where I waited even longer. I continued to go inside and outside looking for Jaque until it occurred to me that he might be doing the same thing. I began asking several strangers if they were in fact Jaque, and on the third try, I confirmed that I had found him. He looked completely different from what I had imagined, but I apparently did to him as well. We had unknowingly passed each other many times without realizing. We spent the next few days together reminiscing and sharing our stories. It was a joyful time for me to find this old friend. Jaque and I remained friends for many years after our reunion.

Now that I was fully retired and fully bearded, I completed several new paintings for a new gallery exhibition I had been invited to. An artist friend in Wichita Falls, Texas, organized an art show in his gallery, called the Compound Gallery. Sid Lambert was not only a very successful architect but was also a great western artist and sculptor. His awesome modern custom-built mansion took up a whole city block and was three floors high. Four other artists from Texas, Oklahoma, New Mexico, and Colorado were invited to show their work. We had a great crowd but didn't sell many of our paintings. At the end of the show, I exchanged an original watercolor of the main log cabin in the Fort Worth Log House Village for one of Sid's great casts of a howling Coyote.

A few weeks later I was invited to show my work at the Executive Suite of the Cowtown Coliseum, where many cattlemen and horsemen were having a conference. At break time they socialized in the lobby, and almost everyone could view my paintings. The organizers and I agreed that this was just a showcase without sales. The paintings could be sold at another time of our choosing. A lot of prospective buyers looked at my work, asked questions about certain pieces, and took my card or brochure. Many people made good comments, and many said nothing at all. As an artist you have to be able to take criticism, or you will have a tough time in this business. I didn't mind the negative comments when they were uttered. I think the worst kind of criticism is indifference. I remember someone making a remark that day: "He doesn't leave anything to the imagination, does he?" I don't know if that was meant in a negative or a positive way. That particular comment struck me as awkward.

Another couple came by several times and looked at a particular painting showing a cowboy sitting on his horse. This horse was drinking out of a shallow stream fed from the water of the Double Mountain Fork of the Brazos River around Post, Texas. After a while, the same lady came back and looked at the same painting again for a long time. Then she introduced herself and asked many questions about the painting and wanted to know about the location of the oil rig in the background. She also asked what the price would be for that painting. I told her, and without hesitation, she immediately told me that they would buy it. She searched in her purse for her husband's business card and asked if I could deliver it next day at their home at 1400 hours in the afternoon. I told her I would be there.

Next day I went to their home and couldn't believe my eyes. This was not a house but a huge mansion. The size of that place covered many thousands of square feet and occupied several blocks. The whole place was unbelievable and very beautiful. Mr. Smith was outside mowing a huge lawn on a riding lawn mower. I sat with his wife by a Texas-sized swimming pool while we waited for him to finish. The landscaping was absolutely beautiful and looked like a botanical garden or a park.

Mr. Smith, president and chief executive officer of the Plumly Lighting Corporation, finally joined us at the pool. He proceeded to ask how long I had been painting, and where I learned to paint transparent water colors with all the fine details. He was very interested in my style of painting, and thus studied the painting for quite a while. He wasn't surprised when I told him that I started to paint when I was eight or nine years old. I told him my dad was an architect and structural engineer in Belgium before the war. He was the one who encouraged me to paint. Mr. Smith said that my work showed the influence and architectural detail that isn't often found in today's art market. He especially appreciated the fine detail in my transparent watercolors. He said he had some wells in northwest Texas that had just been completed. He swore that one of his drilling sites looked very similar to the one in the painting.

We went inside and he asked if I would like to see some other art they had purchased through the years. They gave me a grand tour of the place, which could almost pass for a museum. Each room was differently and beautifully decorated with original paintings and sculptures. When we got to his office, it was decorated with a large collection of trophy animals that he hunted on his many safaris all over the world. Then he showed me his collection of artifacts, which he and his wife picked up while traveling around the world. He actually had special rooms built for each collection. Each nation they visited was represented in separate large rooms. The walls had built-in showcases with special lighting. There were collections of all kinds, with jewelry, original sculptures, weapons, tribal masks, swords, spears, silver, gold, and diamonds. It was beautiful and amazing.

When we arrived in the den, Mrs. Smith had prepared coffee and magically appeared with a black forest cake for the occasion. She didn't have to twist my arm much to eat a second piece. It was delicious. After a wonderful visit, Mr. Smith wrote the check and thanked me for delivering the painting. I told him it was my pleasure and thanked him for selecting my work and showing me all his beautiful collection. On my way out, I asked him where he would find a place to hang my painting. He had a good belly laugh and said he guessed he would have to build another room to hang it. I told him I would be glad to help decorate the walls, to which he replied that he would keep in touch.

CHAPTER 8

End of Days

Life for me never involved many tough decisions. I was always guided
by what seemed right and just, which I now found the answers for in
the Bible. I didn't always make the right move, but spiritually I felt in
the right. My life was irrevocably changed by the war, as it asked more of me
than I ever thought possible. The move to Texas wasn't difficult. The prospect
of a fresh start was powerful. The struggle to make ends meet and the struggle
to make a life all seemed predestined to me. Things for me always had a way
of working themselves out. I had never been rich, and most of the time I was
bordering on poverty, but I never felt sorry for my life or myself. I have lived
a life of purpose and meaning. I had a roof over my head, and my bills always
found a way to get paid. Luxuries weren't a need for me once I understood
the process.

Retirement would have its ups and downs, but then life wasn't done with
me just yet. God's plan for me had more to show. As violent a life as I had
lived, I believed myself to now be a compassionate and loving man of God.
The horrors early on had brought me to this place, and my journey getting
here has made me the human I am.

Fran and I took advantage of the slowdown in business to attend some
religious conferences and seminars with Kenneth Copeland, James Robinson,
Milton Green, and John Wimber. We also took counseling training classes with
the Christian Broadcasting Network, which provided classes to those who were
interested. After many wonderful messages, it became obvious to me that some
people would rather work through God than believe in Him and walk with
Him. I wanted to change that and play a more active role with God.

At the time Fran and I had been visiting the Eagle Mountain Lake Baptist Church and its pastor Jim Hylton. A member of the church, Charlie Carson, mentioned a wonderful place that might be what I was looking for called the Beautiful Feet Ministry. He also reported many good and wonderful things about this street ministry, and I couldn't help but admire his enthusiasm. Unfortunately, I was not interested enough to check into it at the time.

We first met Mike Myers at the Eagle Mountain Lake Church, where he spoke occasionally about his street ministry. I listened to his message, but again, I didn't respond to it. I figured that helping people on the street was not for me. At the time, I didn't have much compassion for the needy. I felt that homeless people needed to get a job or even needed to get a life. I didn't know or didn't understand what the Lord meant when He said that if we loved Him, we should show compassion for the poor and give them help and hope. I was about to learn.

Beautiful Feet

For years Fran and I drove the forty-two-mile round trip to the Eagle Mountain Lake Church, one round trip in the morning and one in the evening every Sunday. When Pastor Jim Hylton's son Randy started a new ministry called the Vineyard Church in Wedgwood, located about a mile from our home, Fran and I decided to visit it. We loved the service, and the location was much better for us. One service in January 1991, Pastor Randy said that we probably wouldn't like what he was going to talk about on that Sunday morning service, but that his message was based on what Jesus asked us to do *if* we loved Him. Pastor Randy said specifically that *if* a Christian claimed to love the Lord, then he would want to quit being just a spectator in church and should instead get out of his comfort zone to do what Jesus Christ had asked him to do. He said that all of us who confess to be Christians, knowing the plan of salvation according to the Scriptures, had the responsibility to share and reach out to the lost, the widows, the poor, homeless, sick, and old, and to those in prison. He also said that we were surrounded by needy souls who were searching for the truth and needed to hear the Word of God. Randy mentioned that a street outreach ministry by the name of Beautiful Feet Ministries would give us the opportunity to do what the Lord asked us to do. His message really got my attention, and during the following days, I prayed and thought about it. I was like most people, living my life without much concern about the needy and those living on the street. It took this message from Pastor Randy to get my attention and touch my heart.

I also remembered that when I arrived here from Europe as an immigrant, I had to get a job very quickly because I was running out of funds. As a foreigner, it wasn't easy to find a job for which I could qualify. In those days, the government didn't believe in handouts to noncitizens. My three sponsors helped me secure a visa but ultimately failed to help me get a job. At first I worked some odd jobs while figuring out what I could do. I was led to Fort Worth, where the Texas Employment Agency helped me find a job in my profession as an illustrator. I could very easily have been unemployed and living in my car or on the street. I saw how easily I could have been homeless had it not been for so many blessings. Instead, it was clear that the Lord was directing my steps and was blessing me tremendously. So I decided to check out Beautiful Feet to see what was going on there.

On Sunday, February 7, 1991, Del Doss and I drove to 1709 East Hattie Street and arrived just as the volunteer helpers came out of the prayer room. At 0645 hours, the Beautiful Feet buses left the parking lot to pick up the children and the homeless. Then at 0715 hours, some of the volunteers broke into groups to go to their assigned tasks. Del went with Mike Myers, and I was going to help Blake Winn visit some old folks in a nearby nursing home called East Park Manors. When Blake and I arrived at the nursing home, one of the residents greeted us and said he was Jimmy Harp. He said he was going to follow us close and would repeat everything we said. He said he was going to be our echo. I didn't know what to think about that, but it didn't take me long to find out. There was also a very unusual young man named Billy Charlesworth who let me know in no uncertain way that he was going to be in control of everything. He told me to sign out the residents who were lined up at the front desk, which I did. He helped me with their names and then told me to load them up. Jimmy Harp repeated my instructions while Blake looked at me and smiled. Billy was lining them up and getting them ready to go outside. We picked up eight of the residents in Blake's van. Jimmy Harp told them to listen to Billy and repeated this many times while he wasn't doing it himself. The whole situation was so very funny and all you could do was to be patient with them, because most of these people were in very bad physical and mental health. It was also obvious to me that they were overmedicated. Several patients didn't really know what was going on and acted like it. However, it didn't take me long to figure out they were very lovable people who needed attention, recognition, and most of all, love. They needed someone to listen to them and love them with compassion.

Blake and I tried to keep the residents together, but the minute they were outside the door, they scattered. Some entered the van while others walked off into the parking lot, not knowing where they were going. As they walked away, a few waved goodbye to the remaining residents as if they were leaving for a big long trip. A few walked toward the street corner and others halfway down the block. As we drove by them, we stopped and asked them where they were going. Some said they didn't know and some said they were going to the store or looking for someone. When we asked them if they wanted to eat breakfast with us at Beautiful Feet Ministries, they immediately were ready to get in the van. Blake told me that when we arrived at BFM, they were to go upstairs into the main sanctuary until their breakfast time, which was at

0800 hours. But when we arrived, Billy, the self-appointed boss, was in charge again and was telling everyone to go in the downstairs dining area. I tried to get his attention to correct him, but he told me not to argue with him and to get in line with the others. I couldn't help but laugh. He asked me why I laughed, and not wanting to hurt his feelings, I told him that I was just happy. I asked Billy again if he would help us to get our guests to go upstairs first until their breakfast was ready. Jimmy Harp repeated it a couple of times just to make sure they understood. I told Billy the reason for them to go upstairs first was that while they were waiting for breakfast, they could sign up for clothing. He thought that was a good idea, and with the help of Jimmy Harp, who repeated the instructions one more time, everyone understood and all went very smoothly.

Beautiful Feet Ministries feeds breakfast and lunch to the homeless every day and incorporates a church service for them. I ate breakfast with them that morning and the food was great. If I remember well, they served scrambled eggs, sausage, plenty of bread, and sweet rolls. Talk about a feast!

At 1130 hours, after the church service, lunch was being served downstairs in the dining area. The residents formed a line and the ladies went first. The food smelled good and was well prepared and very tasty. There was plenty of food for everyone, and after lunch they received the clothing they signed up for earlier. After lunch we took the East Park Manors residents back to their nursing home and signed them back in. When I was about to leave, something unexpected happened. Billy Charlesworth asked if I would pray for one of his friends. I told him I certainly would. As we walked the long hallway toward the friend's room, I was asking God for help because I had never prayed under these circumstances. When I entered the room, I saw a young lady and introduced myself. I only knew that she was sick and asked how I should pray for her. She asked me to pray for her to be healed from advanced stages of HIV and for her soul. The room was kept very dark but I could tell that she was young and very pretty. I asked her if she knew the Lord and if she had the faith that God could heal her. She said she believed in the Lord and had recently received her salvation. She added, with tears in her eyes, that she wished she would have known the Lord years ago before things went wrong, and before she got infected by sharing a contaminated needle while shooting drugs. I held her hand and got on a knee and prayed for her like I never prayed before. I know it was a prayer led by the Holy Spirit. I knew the words I said were not my words but rather the Lord's words.

I prayed and praised the Lord for His presence and finally said goodbye to the young lady. As I turned around to walk out of the room, I looked up at the ceiling where I noticed a very bright glow above the door. There wasn't a light on in the room or a mirror on the wall that could have given that glow. I took it as a sign from the Lord saying that He was right there with us. When I was walking out of the room, Billy was standing in the doorway and showed me several of his sick friends in the hall needing prayers. I prayed for them as best I knew how and when I got through, I felt like I never felt before. I knew right then that this was what I wanted to continue doing. It became clear to me that these people were part of the poor and abandoned sheep the Lord was talking about.

That day something changed in my life. I never before felt such a compassion for the needy and never had experienced the inner joy that came from helping some of the most neglected and abandoned people I had ever known. I had experienced very sad and tragic situations during World War II, but this was in peacetime and in one of the wealthiest countries in the world. Most of these poor people were sick and abandoned by their families and rejected by society. They rarely had family visiting them, but they knew they were loved at Beautiful Feet. I needed this as much as they needed us.

As we drove back to the Beautiful Feet Ministries, Blake Winn told me that very soon he and his wife Linda were going to move to Oklahoma, and he thought I would make a fine replacement. I told him I didn't have a van in which to transport people, but he told me there was a small bus that picked up street people, and I probably would be able to use it. However, I found out that because of my age, the insurance would not accept me as a driver. So I picked them up in my own car, which at the time was my Jeep Grand Cherokee. I nicknamed it the Blue Angel and shuttled the Manors' guests back and forth four or five at a time. It took a little longer, but I got to know them better. I knew in my heart that it was what I wanted to do.

After a few visits with East Park Manors, I met Dee Drechsel, the counselor at the facility, and asked her if I could visit them during the week and teach the Word in the afternoon. She said they would like that very much. We worked out a schedule to see them each week at least once or twice. I started to visit with them and read the Word on Thursday afternoon, and that, by itself, was quite a pleasant experience. Jimmy Harp always repeated every word I said except for what I read out of the Bible. Mary Ann, most of the time, didn't like the subject I was trying to speak about and interrupted me and said what she wanted to hear. She usually wanted to hear only the Proverbs and not the Psalms. She wouldn't quit complaining about it in a loud voice until I quit teaching and read the Proverbs. Patsy didn't like the song I selected but couldn't remember the one she liked best. I called out a few songs but couldn't come up with the right one. It was impossible to keep their attention longer than ten minutes at a time, and by then, they either had to go to the bathroom or said they had to go somewhere but didn't know where. Some said they had to feed their animals, and when they came back, we talked about their animals. Dee, the counselor, was sitting in on most of those sessions and helped me understand some of the problems they faced. I was trying to reach them, which was quite a challenge, and Dee encouraged me to continue. I found out which passages they liked to hear, and noticed they liked questions and answers about God and verses from the Bible. We always did that for a while and then prayed for their needs and their families.

The opportunities for help were endless and everywhere, but Beautiful Feet Ministries was up to the task. Our mission sought to bring the word of the Lord to those in need of it most. They worked fearlessly on the street, going to the shelters and helping homeless in the inner city. The ministry never stood still and was opening new doors and finding opportunities to help the needy and spread the Word. Mike Myers organized neighborhood BBQs and concerts for all to come. Many concerts took place regularly on a grocery and liquor store parking lot, where we shared the Word and provided good food such as hamburgers and hot dogs with all the trimmings. We also had ministry in the night shelters in addition to jail visits, prison visits, and home-to-home visits in the inner city neighborhoods.

There were many surprises when lives were turned around, and it was obvious that it couldn't have been a coincidence. On a Saturday morning when I was mowing the front yard I noticed a car from the water department driving by. A few minutes later it was parked in front of my house, and a large black man got out of the car. He walked toward me with his arms extended and a big smile on his face. He said, "Do you remember me? I am Maurice Davis!" He explained that I had visited with him several months ago and convinced him that the Lord was the only one who could heal him. Then two other men got out of the car. Maurice told them that I was the man who had talked with him before and told him that there wasn't any hope for him as long as he was taking drugs. Maurice remembered that I told him he had to decide if he wanted to die in heaven or die in hell. Maurice learned then that Jesus was right there with him all the time and that He loved him regardless what he did, but the Lord was waiting for his decision. Then Maurice shared that, on the following Sunday morning, while he was sitting on the front steps of Beautiful Feet Ministries with an awful headache, I sat next to him and reminded him that only Jesus could take the drugs away and heal him, and there was no hope for him if he didn't quit drugs. Maurice said that after I left, his heart was pounding in his head and all he could hear with each heartbeat was what I had told him. Maurice said that each heartbeat resounded through his head as no hope, no hope, no hope, and after hours of that, he finally screamed out, "No more drugs!" That day Maurice cried out and asked the Lord to save and change his life. He said the next day he awoke, the desire to get high was gone, and he had been free ever since! Maurice gave me another big hug. It was a good and powerful moment there in my front yard. Before they drove off, I told the other two fellows with Maurice that I didn't change Maurice Davis, but rather Jesus Christ changed him. Several weeks later I saw Maurice once more and he was still doing well. He told me that he picked up the phone and called his estranged family and made arrangements to go back to Michigan where he used to live to get his life and family back.

My mission to bring help to others gave my life a tremendous purpose. I was often called to help others in neighborhoods where I would not normally go. I was never afraid for my safety, which was possibly because of my naivety. My life as a young man in this country was always a struggle to earn enough to survive. I wasn't ignorant, but I didn't grow up with the traditional stereotypes that many accept in this country. People were people to me and not a skin color or a socioeconomic class. I didn't care much about these issues and certainly didn't treat my human brothers differently because of their differences. One particular mission trip took us to a small town in Mississippi, and a new friend of mine named Kenny and I were walking the street seeking people in need of our message. Kenny was technically homeless but stayed regularly at a home sponsored by the Beautiful Feet Ministry. He was always helping in any way he was needed. Kenny had nothing material or familial in his life except God and gave every ounce of himself toward helping others find their way into his kingdom. I saw him every Sunday, and he was always in the midst of helping others. We often prayed together, and he became a valued member of our outreach team. On one route we ran into a gang that considered that area their turf. Once they saw us walking up the alley, we were quickly surrounded. These men were not used to people like us and weren't shy about letting us know. White people weren't welcome in that neighborhood. Kenny spoke first and told them what we were doing there. It was of no interest to them. One of their men said to us, "Shut up, nigger!" Then, their leader approached me and asked me if I was a nigger lover. I responded to him that we were Christians and we loved everyone, including him and his friends. I explained to them about the picnic we were hosting in the park. I added that there would be food and games for everyone. Lastly, I invited them to come and enjoy a pleasant afternoon with their families and the whole town. This I think caught the gang members totally off guard. They excused us and let us head on our way. Before we moved on, though, Kenny innocently said to the leader: "How about a carnation for your sweetheart?" We carried these carnations as gifts for those to whom it might help bring some happiness. The gang leader looked at Kenny for a long time, not quite knowing what to say or do. Then, as politely as he could, he took the carnation and walked off with his friends. We did not have a reason to stay, so we rushed off to the next office building.

The people we met while on missions were amazing. It was a life-changing experience for me to be able to bring about some sort of improvement to these people's lives. I felt as though I was working as God wanted me to. This was in direct contrast to my former life back in Belgium, and I needed to be healed as much as I may have healed these others. I had never before felt as rewarding an experience as I did helping others, and I knew that the demons I may still foster inside me from the war were slowly being knocked out with each soul I made a difference for here.

Going Home

In 1995, Fran and I finally got our chance to return to my birthplace after so many years. We had planned a month's vacation in Belgium and France. It had been forty-three long years since I left Europe, and I eagerly looked forward to introducing Fran to the remaining family and friends who were still living. Honestly, I had really given up on ever returning to my old stomping grounds, but a friend named Don Dickens, who built the drinking water system in the town of Weatherford, Texas, made it possible. He had recently visited Europe and told me Ghent was just beautiful. He thought I should see it again. So on August 1, 1995, Don opened up his heart and his checkbook and paid for Fran and me to go back to Belgium. I was never so excited to travel in my life, aside from the original journey to get to this country. The flight was absolutely smooth to JFK International Airport in New York, where we had a short layover and took a short walk at the airport to stretch our legs. We boarded the flight to cross the Atlantic with the giddiness of children on Christmas. About seven hours later and nine time zone hours ahead, I awoke to the smell of coffee just as we approached the coast of England, followed by a look at the North Sea and the glorious Belgian coast. We landed in Brussels, Belgium, where my cousin Jacqueline and her daughter Lucy were waiting for us. It was really a shock to go back after so many years. I remembered everything being larger. Most things looked as if they had changed and shrunk over the years. Downtown Ghent and its old buildings remained exactly the same as I had remembered, however. The historic structures seemed to be well cared for and kept in perfect shape. As you got away from the old district, you saw modern structures everywhere. Skyscrapers were scattered on the outskirts of town, complemented with many large multistory hotels. I guess modernization was inevitable, but I wish they could have moved these structures out a few more miles. Fran was as amazed as I was. She was seeing all this for the first time and I was reliving it for the first time. I wanted to go home and see the house I had lived in for twenty-one years. When we arrived at the spot, I found it missing. Our home had been remodeled into a parking lot. Next we visited the school of my childhood. It too had undergone many upgrades and modernizations. The Cathedral St. Bavon, where I had been an altar boy, remained intact with few changes, which I found comforting. Fran and I walked inside and saw the large religious paintings and sculptures that adorned this magnificent house of God. We both stood on the same marble steps where I used to stand as an altar boy to keep the incense going during the service. We visited many of Ghent's historical treasures such as the Castle of Gerard the Devil and the Castle of the Counts of Flanders, which were still kept perfect and intact. So many old things throughout the town and country still stood and brought back a flood of memories for me. As we were walking around downtown, we arrived at the outdoor vegetable and fruit market and decided to stop for a visit at a cheese store that used to belong to an old school friend. Not knowing what to expect, we walked in just to see if Jacques Rogge still owned it. His wife Maria stood behind the counter and somehow recognized me. We exchanged heartfelt hugs, and I introduced Fran to her. She immediately called her husband Jacques to let him know that I was there and would be in town for a few days. She handed me the phone. We decided we had to get together, but little did I know that my conversation with him would set some unexpected events in motion. All my old buddies had now been alerted, and everyone wanted to see me. They decided to have a big party.

Just about every night since we arrived in Ghent, we were invited for supper with someone. Old friends invited us, and we always had pleasant visits, with many trips down memory road. Jacques Brun invited us first for a great supper. We had a good time remembering the years at the Royal North Sea Yacht Club, when we raced so many times together and against each other. After a great meal, he showed us his world collection of hotel soaps. He traveled all over the world and picked up a wrapped bar of soap at each hotel he stayed in. His collection numbered in the thousands, which he had catalogued and stored in specially built display drawers. In his extensive travels he probably had accumulated one of the largest soap collections in the world. My old school friend Jacques Rogge and his wife Maria invited us next. Jacque's parents owned the cheese factory, which kept Jacques and Maria busy in the wholesale and retail side of the business. The supper was very delicious and special. It was a several-course meal, each course prepared with different kinds of cheeses. We shared our personal memories about our school years, the war, and all the experiences we lived through and wouldn't ever forget. My buddies and I lived our teen years in a bad and sometimes horrible situation. The war robbed us of our youth, and some of us of our future.

Then we visited Ypres, Belgium, to see another Jacques and his wife Fromonde, who were old sailing friends of our family. Suddenly my buddies decided to organize a big champagne party. As per my deal with myself, I joined these guys for celebratory drinks, and boy did they taste good. I wasn't about to fall off the wagon, but these special moments were allowed. These guys had been in the underground with me and then fought in some capacity with me or with the Allies. After the war, we spent much time together reclaiming those lost years. It was great to see all those guys after so long a time. They could remember many stories and things that I was supposed to have done but somehow couldn't remember. Late that night, after the champagne party, we went to a restaurant where we had a blast, and the party reassembled for the remainder of the night.

My blood-brother friend Bernard and his wife Arlette were the missing ones. I learned from my buddies that they both died mysteriously. I never could find out when and how they died. My repeated inquiries turned up nothing, as no one seemed to know or want to tell me. I don't know why they wouldn't want me to know, but a friend, Paul, told me that I would be better off never to know what happened. I was very disappointed and missed them much.

My friend Gilbert and his wife invited us for a garden party at their lovely home. We talked about the war years a lot. He still had my Canadian Sten machine gun, a German Luger, and one of the many German P38 pistols I gave him before I left. Those weapons had many stories to re-tell.

The next day our friends from Ypres picked us up and took us to the Breskens Sailing Club in Holland, where we met his family for supper. Gilbert's son gave us a tour of his forty-seven-foot yacht, where we had a chat and a drink in the cockpit. I will admit that it was hard being around friends who were drinking, especially given where we were having these parties. The champagne was great, but I considered it mainly for women. If I was going to relax my drinking rules, then I wanted a scotch. Afterwards, we enjoyed a good meal at the Yacht Club Restaurant and drove through the beautiful lowlands of Flanders to their home. It was good for me to see things I grew up with, and the weather couldn't have been better.

The city of Ypres, as well as most of the West Flanders, had been battlegrounds during World War I. Ypres itself had been totally reduced to ruins, and one could not help but see countless military cemeteries and monuments all throughout the town. Museums were full of weapons and equipment left behind by Belgian, British, Canadian, French, and German armies who fought for four long years. Almost all of Belgium was invaded and occupied by the Germans from 1914 to 1918. While these battles were fought in the Flanders, the Americans and French were fighting for us in France. In Belgium, the American flag flies every year on November 11 in memory of the hundreds of thousands of Allied and American soldiers who died for our freedom. The eleventh of November was the date of the signing of the armistice in World War I, with the total surrender of the German Army. This was a national holiday and remains so even after the grander atrocities of World War II. Fran and I visited one of those museums, where we walked through the still-visible trenches of the famous Hill 65, where over one million men on both sides died in their efforts to gain control of it.

Jacques and Fromonde had a beautiful two-story home with a large basement. Their backyard was large, well landscaped, and had a swimming pool. They lived close to downtown Ypres. In the morning, Jacques took us around town and showed us countless museums and buildings while Fromonde stayed home preparing many wonderful Belgian dishes for our lunch. At night, we met with their family for supper in a restaurant in downtown Ypres. The food was never-ending and most delicious. We had a pleasant time together, but a couple of days later it was time to return to my cousin Jacqueline's house to pack for our visit with cousin Jean in France.

The trip going south toward Reims, France, took us through the

Champagne region, which was a beautiful monument to agriculture. My cousins Jean and Monique lived in Reims in an apartment on the fifth floor of a fairly large retirement building. Yes, they were retired, but in a different sense from what Americans are accustomed to. Jean had worked for a large shoe manufacturer that he managed but that the government owned. The government offered Jean retirement in their sponsored building, where he would receive financial aid and very decent housing for the remainder of his life. This was his reward for his successful business practices. He wasn't much older than me, but he was taken care of. His balconies provided a great view of the city and the famous Cathedral of Reims. This structure was originally built in 1211 and was the site of Pope Innocent II's coronation of French King Louis VII. We arrived late in the afternoon while there was a thunderstorm in progress, but the temperature was very mild and the wind was calm. Monique fixed a fine French meal, which was served under umbrellas on their balcony. Each day, we visited historical sites and many of the beautiful parks in the city. The tour of the Champagne region was breathtaking. The countryside was covered with the perfectly manicured vineyards of the large champagne producers who often operated out of historical mansions and castles. We attended several tastings, and yes, I did partake. I enjoyed the walk through their large production plants and caves where they bottled, stored, and aged their product.

We then continued on to Paris, which wasn't too far a drive. We spent many hours walking, shopping, and eating. The tour boat on the Seine River was delightful, as was the lunch in the Latin Quarter. Then as quickly as we arrived, we departed Paris in the late afternoon along the Seine River to Vernon, where my cousin Jacqueline and her family were waiting for us. We stayed across the street in a large, modern, three-story home that was recently built. Their large garden was landscaped beautifully. The family was very curious about my life in Texas and couldn't believe that I had changed my nationality and citizenship. I told them that when I left my old country, it was with the intention to be not only an American citizen but also a Texan. Jacqueline said that she couldn't have done that, but admitted since I was permanently living in America it was probably a good decision. Her strong French pride wouldn't allow her to move. I would never deny my Belgian heritage and all the things I left behind, especially family who no longer were an active part of my life, but America afforded me opportunities I knew weren't possible in Belgium. My life experiences in Belgium were not normal, and not any fault of the Belgian people. We had stood against our enemies in our struggle for existence and emerged battered and torn, but ultimately victorious. I needed a fresh start and a life outside the Belgian military. America was the beacon of opportunity that I so desired.

The French meals were frequent and delicious, and we took our time at the table eating. We didn't just eat. We dined and savored our food over hours of genuine and delightful conversation. The meals were three- and four-course meals that had taken hours to prepare and utilized just about everyone's help getting them put together. Someone peeled the potatoes while another peeled the skins off the tomatoes, or cleaned the fish or shrimp, and so on. It was fun doing the cooking and visiting in their large kitchen, which was built and equipped for big family cooking. We ate all kinds of local dishes with beef, pork, chicken, lamb, duck, rabbit, and fish, coupled with a great variety of vegetables from their garden.

Vernon was our next destination and about one hundred miles from Paris. This small and beautiful town was located right on the river Seine in Normandy. The downtown had been rebuilt to its original beauty from the severely damaged state left by the Italian air force and the German army. They restored the old-style architecture and maintained the countryside, which was still dotted with big estates and many castles. Vernon was where I visited my uncle Gustave after the war for rare instances of R&R. Gustave and I would leave at daybreak and ride through this same countryside in search of a spot to paint. He was a talented artist who painted in oil, while I painted in transparent watercolor. We took off on bicycles with our art supplies and a picnic lunch and had a great time sharing ideas, stories, and life. When hungry, we spread the picnic food out on a towel, opened a good bottle of wine, unwrapped different cheeses and meats, and sliced a fresh loaf of French bread. Those are good memories. It was sad, though, that Gustave's building and paint factory were destroyed by the Italian air force's incendiary bombs, which burned the business to the ground. Gustave never recovered completely from the loss but managed to salvage his business and made a decent living.

The day finally came for our visit to the Normandy coast where the Allies landed fifty-one years earlier on D-day. We left Vernon at about 0600 hours and arrived at Ste. Mere l'Eglise at 0800 hours sharp. We drove along the coast and visited museums, fortifications, and all there was to see on the landing beaches. We went from Ste. Mere l'Eglise to the cliffs of Pointe du Hoc, followed by Omaha, Gold, Juno, and Sword landing beaches. We visited the American cemetery at Omaha, where as an American, I received the VIP treatment. This beautiful hallowed ground brought back a lot of sad thoughts for me, even though this was my first trip to this place. So many good men paid the ultimate price here so tyranny could be stopped. The feeling one gets from walking these grounds is something immensely powerful and moving to the soul. I was able to locate the beautiful grave markers of three men I once knew. I have never been a man of emotion and have never been easily moved to tears, but I placed my beret upon my head and saluted these men with every fiber of my being. I broke down and wept like I have never done before in my life. These tears were more than sadness and hurt, but thankfulness and gratitude to these brave men who had given their lives for the most important cause the world had ever known: humanity. I wanted to remain there for the rest of the day with those who could never leave, and was not ready to leave when it was time for us to go. It hurts as much today as it did then, whenever I catch myself remembering.

We returned late that night to find everyone ready for another great meal, and we had plenty to talk about. The following days we toured different areas in Normandy and Champagne, where we soaked in as much as the days would allow. The countryside was so very picturesque that I wish I had time to paint it.

Our two weeks in France ran out, and it was time to leave Europe. The goodbye was very emotional because I knew we probably would never meet again. We left Vernon in the afternoon for Orley airport in Paris and spent the night in the airport hotel. The next morning we boarded our flight home. As tough as it was to leave, I was glad to get home. While in Europe, we found ourselves missing our good American coffee, cold milk, ice cubes, and ice water.

Little did I know that I would be back in Belgium a year later to visit with my friend Paul Berkenbosh, who was hospitalized in Ghent. Paul had terminal liver and kidney disease and asked me to see him before it was too late. Paul was a close enough friend that I didn't even consider not going. Paul's wife, Mariette, was an invalid who had suffered a stroke years ago that paralyzed the right side of her body. Paul did not look well at all. He was hospitalized because of his illness and didn't have much time left. The hospital allowed visitors only for a maximum of two hours per day. I was grateful and honored that he reached out to me.

After visiting hours were over, Paul's son Pierre and I visited restaurants where I used to eat as a young man. I shared with him many personal stories about his dad that he didn't know. He showed me new buildings in town such as art museums, a new library, new airport, and harbor expansions. One of the most incredible additions was the new electric bullet train, which could travel throughout Europe at speeds in excess of 160 miles per hour. My birthplace had overcome its crippling past to become a leading technological center of Europe, and it showed no sign of slowing down.

When I was young, I had dreamed of being a cadet in the Belgian Navy on board the Belgian School Ship named *Mercator*. This was the one ship I grew up wanting to sail on. I've painted this ship many times over the years in Texas, read the ship's logbooks, and studied its blueprints, but I had never been aboard her. While I was in the service, I learned that the three-masted beauty was dry-docked in Ghent harbor but I couldn't get time off to visit it. That bothered me, since I knew this ship by heart. While I was talking with Pierre, he happened to mention that the *Mercator* was not only available but temporarily docked only about ninety miles away in the port of Ostende on the Belgian coast. I had given up hope I'd ever see that magnificent ship again, but now I was finally going to get to board her. The *Mercator* was 235 feet

Fran and me later in life

long, 35 feet wide, and the tallest of its three masts is 125 feet high. The ship is rigged as a Barkentine model and carries an incredible fifteen sails with a total surface of about 4,800 square feet. Had I been a cadet as I dreamed when twelve years old, I would have surely been drafted into the German army when the war broke out, and the odds of my being here would have been greatly diminished. Walking the ship was a phenomenal experience for me and took me back to my youth, when life was about hopes and dreams on the high seas.

Pierre gave me much of his time during our visit when he was not required to, and I was very thankful for that. Paul's doctor told us that his health had improved slightly, but he didn't foresee a positive prognosis. I had been there for approximately twenty days, and it was time to go back home to Fran and the kids. I had a meaningful visit with Paul, considering the circumstances, and I was very glad to have seen my old buddy. The time we had was not enough, but life for me was back in Fort Worth, and I was ready. Before I left, Paul told me he knew he would never see me again. We said see you later, not goodbye, in the hopes that day would somehow come. The following day I returned home. It was a week later that news of Paul's death reached me. His family and friends held a small and quiet memorial service. If I had known, I would have certainly stayed to the end. But being with my family was good consolation, because this was a tough loss for me.

Retirement allowed me to do some of the things I had always wanted to do and never fully could. I painted now for fun, and, I hoped, to earn a few commissions along the way. I was able to read and study the Bible every day, which made me happy. I think about the war and realize that escaping the war without major medical issues was nothing short of a miracle. I was looking forward to enjoying my golden years, on my terms. My entire life had seemed to be a reaction to events around me and now I wanted to live life for Fran and me.

Breaking Down

It was an ordinary day for me in May 2000. My seventy-three-year-old body was home alone while Fran was visiting with family in California. I was mowing the grass in our front yard when I noticed that I was short of breath. My jaw was feeling funny and tight and I felt like I was having bad indigestion. My neighbor, Martha Salem, who is a retired nurse, happened to be in her yard and saw me in distress. She asked me if I was okay, because it was unusual for me or most people to sit down in the middle of the yard. She urged me to call my doctor immediately. As it was the weekend, I had to wait until Monday morning to see him, then made an appointment with a heart specialist and surgeon named Dr. Vance. After a mild stress test and an angiogram procedure, my heart showed a 98 percent blockage of one of its main arteries and nearly 50 percent blockage in the other artery. Dr. Vance said I would need immediate bypass surgery to avoid serious heart damage or death. I asked him if I had other options available. He said the only other way was to install a stent to treat my narrowed arteries. I opted for the stent, which offered shorter downtime and a quicker recovery. The doctor performed the procedure the next day, without hospitalization. But going forward, I would have to lose weight, eat properly, and exercise regularly.

While on the operating table for the stent installation, Dr. Vance noticed that I was in great pain and asked me about it. I told him that lying still on my back on that hard and flat operating table caused severe pain. I told him the pain in my right hip was unbearable. I asked him how much longer I was to endure it. He said to hang tough, but not to move a muscle. He couldn't give me anything to ease the pain because he needed me to be alert. I had to hold my breath at certain times in order to answer. After the stent procedure, he recommended hip surgery as soon as possible, because the constant pain was not good to have with my heart condition.

The surgery was a complete replacement of my right hip, and was done on September 1, 2000, by Dr. Kleuser at Harris Hospital. Three days later I was transferred to the HealthSouth Rehab facility, where I had to go through the painful task of learning to walk again. Two weeks after the surgery, I was released from rehab and went home. I had a daily routine of exercises, which I did for several months. I was so happy and relieved that I was finally able to lie on my back without pain. It took me several months to recover, but recover I did. I was okay for a while, but my body wasn't feeling normal. I chalked it up to old age. I made my way for several more years with relative ease. Then my world began to unravel. The cancer was diagnosed.

It was April of 2004 when I noticed I was having trouble reading, which was a regular activity for me. I had been reading the Bible on this particular occasion, and it didn't feel right, so I asked Fran if she would read with me to see if she noticed anything peculiar. I read aloud to her, and she said it sounded okay, but after a few minutes of reading, my voice trailed off and seemed to fade away. I had an appointment with our doctor the next week, and when I brought it up, he suggested seeing a head and neck specialist. He took some precautionary X-rays that revealed a growth on my larynx. My immediate thought was why had I ever started smoking, as I knew that was the culprit. I was immediately set up for surgery to remove the mass, and it was sent to the lab for tests. It came back malignant. After the surgery, I was restricted to a liquid diet. Three months later, the cancer came back. I went in for the second throat surgery in August 2004. The cancerous tissue was again removed, but this time I was to begin immediate radiation treatment. Radiation treatments hurt me and made life really tough. The radiation began in 2004 with a seven-week cycle. This seven-week run was excruciating. I could not eat solid foods or swallow without pain. Immediately upon completion of radiation, I began chemotherapy for the next three months, followed by a year of rehab. I was reduced to communicating with Fran through written notes. I dreaded going to the hospital and began to push back against my treatments. I seemed to be sick all the time, and my condition never seemed to improve. This was not how my remaining years were supposed to go. I felt like a science experiment, and my quality of life had diminished significantly. The rehab was effective in giving me my voice back a few months later, which improved my spirits. I became more optimistic about my future and began planning a life worth living. In December of the next year, I went in for a CT Scan and MRI, which I had become quite used to. The reports detailed two cancerous nodules on my right lung. The doctor wanted to do surgery immediately, but I refused. I didn't think I could go through another surgery and recovery of that nature. I had reached my limit and decided to put my fate in God's hands, and it surprisingly made it easier to deal with. My health issues made it very difficult to attend Beautiful Feet Ministries anymore, so it was with terrible sadness that I ended my visits there. I kept making my appointments and was painstakingly convinced to let the doctor remove a large and deep malignant tumor from my left side of my back near the spine. The surgeon decided not to close the hole because of how deep it was, but to let the tissues grow back naturally. Fran was with me daily to clean, disinfect, and apply medicine and a bandage to the wound until it healed. It healed nicely, thanks to Fran's attentive care. Fourteen more tumors on my skin developed and were removed and treated in this manner over the next few years. I allowed these cancers to be treated, as they were not so intrusive.

In April 2008, while carrying something heavy to the house, I felt something tearing or crushing around my left hip joint. For many months I'd had chronic pain in that area, but from that moment on, the pain worsened. I could be standing completely still and my hip joint would pulse with pain. I began to feel acute pain and an intense burning sensation in my left thigh. It was painful to get in and out of the car. When shopping, I used the shopping cart as a walker for a while, and then required the electric cart. Finally in July, I decided to do something about the constant pain. I saw my orthopedic surgeon, Dr. Kleuser, who took X-rays that showed serious damage to the left hip. These hip issues, he suggested, were no doubt caused by wear and tear from my military years. He suggested another hip replacement. I was hoping it would be simpler, because I remembered the pain I experienced when I went through the right hip replacement seven years earlier. I immediately called my heart specialist, Dr. Vance, for an appointment. After several tests, he said I shouldn't have a problem with the surgery and that it was a good idea to have it done. He said the constant stress the pain caused my heart wasn't a good thing.

On September 2, 2008, I had a complete left hip replacement. The surgery was performed at the Baylor Surgical Hospital and was supposed to last around three hours. Due to my enlarged prostate and other complications, however, the surgery lasted an additional three hours, but everything went well.

After a couple of days in recovery, I was transferred to the Harris hospital rehabilitation floor where I would be for about twelve days. The therapy was somewhat bearable, and the therapists were very pleasant and had a great and positive attitude. The nursing staff was very patient, and I can truly say that except for the hospital food, the whole experience wasn't bad at all.

At first, I had many visitors because the entire Bible study class from church and friends from Beautiful Feet Ministries came to see me. My friend and Christian brother David Delfeld came just about every day and volunteered to take me home in his large Ford truck. We got along so famously that he began coming by every other day to take me to walk at the nearby Hulen Mall, where I did my walking rehab. We shared many good times together. David had an exceptional memory, and if he didn't know something, he had the desire to learn it. David worked as a lawyer, and with his exceptional memory he presented a powerful force in litigation. At a large group meal one night, someone asked for the "taters" to be passed. My upbringing had not made me familiar with such a term for potatoes. David, thereafter, referred to me as "Tater." I created the nickname "Bubba" as a reference to his tall stature and imposing presence, which reminded me of a Bubba. We communicate often via Bubbagrams and Tatergrams. A part of me always felt like David or Bubba had been sent to me as an angel. He was an amazing Christian brother and friend who helped me when I needed a friend most.

I was now pain free, but my problem was my age. I have weak ankles and weak Achilles tendons in both legs, and have a problem with my balance. I have become a slow walker. But my hip was recovering nicely, and I felt better than I had in a long while. With the help of a cane, I was able to go and do most everything I wanted to. After surgery, Dr. Kleuser estimated at least six months for a complete healing. Life for me was much simpler now, even with all the troubles I had. I reduced my activities to only those that didn't hurt me, but I began to see much less improvement than I expected. It wasn't the hip; it was the rest of my body that was the problem. I refused to believe that I was getting too old to do some of the things that needed to be done around the house, but I always welcomed some help.

On July 15, 2009, without a warning sign, I blacked out and fell as I was walking toward the kitchen. I awoke minutes later and knew I was in trouble. I took my blood pressure, which showed a pressure reading of 198 with a low pulse of 39. I surely had a problem. I immediately called my heart specialist, Dr. Vance, who told me to call 911. The next day I received a new pacemaker. I began feeling better shortly after the procedure as my blood pressure and pulse regulated. The struggles I had undergone in the military had come full circle, and there was no denying that my body was increasingly breaking down.

I was raising our beautiful American flag on the Fourth of July, 2014, when gravity pulled me backwards and I fell. As usual, I hit the ground hard and had to undergo a bunch of tests such as biopsies, cat scans, X-rays, etc. I escaped the dreaded MRI due to my pacemaker. I hated that MRI machine. The doctors reported some internal hemorrhaging and some more developments. They found four more cancers located in my left kidney, bladder, chest, and right lung. The doctor immediately put me on home hospice and estimated that I had three months to live. This was it! I was directed to begin another chemotherapy treatment within the week. My answer came easily. I had decided a long time ago that I was finished with radiation and chemotherapy. I called the doctor to tell him of my decision, with which he strongly disagreed. He attempted to change my mind, but my mind had been made up. I put it into God's hands, where it always was anyway. A nurse was set to visit me at home three times a week. I was made comfortable with dozens and dozens of pills.

The three-month window came and went. As I sit here pondering the end of this story, I have made it eighteen months past my expected departure from my earthly bonds. I haven't painted in over a year now, as it's just too arduous for me with all the issues I have to deal with. I have most of my mental capacities, which allowed me to begin writing this book. I move slow, hurt often, eat well, and still have good conversations with family and friends when they visit. Fran and I have each other as we walk along with the Lord. He makes every day possible for me as I look back upon my life. I can still get a good chuckle. The things I have done and seen still flow easily through my brain. I often find a program on TV dealing with World War II, and I listen intently to what they say, because I know the real story. I lived it. I have been blessed beyond words. I love this country and wouldn't change a thing about what I did to get here.

I am Mr. Jean Gustave Lippens, but my friends call me Jon.

Postscript

In April 2016, Jon and I had just celebrated the past year of working together on the book. He suddenly got quiet, which was very unusual for him. He shared with me that he hadn't been doing very well. He was very proud of the fact that he had made it almost two years after being given three months to live. He was now bleeding internally, which likely was a result of the cancer's advanced stage throughout his body. Mentally he remained sharp, but it had become painfully obvious that physically, he was slowing down. A few mornings later, Jon woke up with severe bleeding in his urine. The paramedics were called and Jon was rushed to the hospital. He was stabilized and seemed to be his old self. Fran spent nearly every night with him at the hospital. The few nights she went home to sleep, Jon would become very disoriented in his room and uncharacteristically would fight with his nurses and even ripped out his catheter in a fit of anger. After several weeks of this, Jon was moved to a nursing home, as he required round-the-clock care. Fran spent nearly every waking hour with him. Jon's condition began to deteriorate, and he was losing his ability to speak. One evening, Fran received an assisted call from Jon at the nursing home. Jon slowly repeated over and over to Fran, "I love you." This would be the last time he spoke. I visited him a few days later, and I could see the enormity of the situation in his eyes. He seemed to know his time was running out. I talked to him about the book, as I knew he would want to hear details. A few weeks went by and his condition showed no improvement.

It was a Friday morning, May 6, 2016; Jon Lippens quietly took a final breath and slipped away from us. He left behind the woman who saved his soul with sixty-two years of marriage, bringing them four grandchildren and eight great-grandchildren. Jon now forever sails the North Sea in his twenty-two foot *Onyx*, where he always loved to be. He belongs to the heavens now, where his pain and suffering are no more. Sweet Fran does her best without him.

RIP
Jon Gustave Lippens
Feb. 8, 1927
May 6, 2016
US Citizen
Hero
Christian
Blessed

Notes

Chapter 2

1. "Four Belgium's New Stand," *The Winnipeg Tribune*, October 15, 1936, 4.

Chapter 3

1. "Allies Land in France," *The Stars and Stripes*, June 6, 1944, 1.

2. Cornelius Ryan, *The Longest Day: The Classic Epic of D-Day* (New York: Simon & Schuster, 2010), 260.

3. C. David North, *World War II: The Resistance* (Boston: New Word City, 2015).

Chapter 4

1. "Battle of the Bulge," Wikipedia, The Free Encyclopedia, last modified January 23, 2018, http://cs.mcgill.ca/~rwest/wikispeedia/wpcd/wp/b/Battle_of_the_Bulge.htm.

2. Herman Bodson, *Agent for the Resistance: A Belgian Saboteur in World War II* (College Station: Texas A&M University Press, 1994), 219-20.

Bibliography

"Allies Land in France." *The Stars and Stripes*. June 6, 1944.

"Four Belgium's New Stand." *The Winnipeg Tribune*. October 15, 1936.

"Map of the Allied Occupied Zones, 1945." *United States Military Academy*. 1945.

Bodson, Herman. *Agent for the Resistance: A Belgian Saboteur in World War II*. College Station: Texas A&M University Press, 1994.

Bradley, Omar. *A General's Life*. New York: Simon & Schuster, 1984.

Buell, Thomas B., John H. Bradley, and Jack W. Dice. *The Second World War: Asia and the Pacific*. Edited by Thomas E. Griess. New York: Square One Publishers, 2002.

Colley, David P. "On the Road to Victory: The Red Ball Express." [access date] http://www.historynet.com/red-ball-express

Eisenhower, Dwight D. Pre-Presidential Papers. Dwight D. Eisenhower Library.

The Editors of Encyclopedia Britannica. "Pact of Locarno." *Encyclopedia Britannica*. October 13, 2016. https://www.britannica.com/event/Pact-of-Locarno

Friedrich, Kartsen. *The Cruel Slaughter of Adolf Hitler II*. 2011. http://www.lulu.com/us/en/shop/karsten-friedrich/the-cruel-slaughter-of-adolf-hitler-ii/ebook/product-17352621.html

McDonald, Paul F. *A Collar Well Worn: World-Wide Ministry*. Bloomington: Trafford Publishing, 2017.

Military Wikia. "Red Ball Express." http://military.wikia.com/wiki/Red_Ball_Express

Miller, Donald L. *The Story of World War II*. New York: Simon & Schuster, 2001.

Miller, Francis Trevelyan. *History of World War II: Armed Services Memorial Edition*. Philadelphia: Universal Book and Bible House, 1945.

Mitcham, Samuel W. *The Desert Fox in Normandy: Rommel's Defense of Fortress Europe*. Westport: Greenwood Publishing Group, 1997.

New World Encyclopedia contributors. "Battle of the Bulge." Last modified May 20, 2016. http://www.newworldencyclopedia.org/p/index.php?title=Battle_of_the_Bulge&oldid=996098

North, C. David. *World War II: The Resistance*. Boston: New Word City, 2015.

Riley, Jonathon. *Decisive Battles: From Yorktown to Operation Desert Storm*. New York: Bloomsbury Publishing, 2010.

Ryan, Cornelius. *The Longest Day: The Classic Epic of D-Day*. New York: Simon & Schuster, 2010.

Simon, Scott. "The Speech Eisenhower Never Gave On The Normandy Invasion." *NPR*, June 8, 2013.

Stewart, Richard W., ed. *The United States Army in a Global Era, 1917-2003* Vol. 2, *American Military History*. Washington, D.C.: Government Printing Office, 2004.

Wikipedia, The Free Encyclopedia. "Battle of Hürtgen Forest." Last modified January 23, 2018. https://en.wikipedia.org/wiki/Battle_of_Hürtgen_Forest

Wikipedia, The Free Encyclopedia. "Battle of the Bulge." Last modified January 23, 2018. http://cs.mcgill.ca/~rwest/wikispeedia/wpcd/wp/b/Battle_of_the_Bulge.htm

About the Authors

Jon Lippens (right), a purposeful man, suffered through one of history's greatest horrors in Europe and reconstructed his life in the United States. After heroic service in World War II, he immigrated from Belgium to Texas, where, with tireless effort, he created a productive life. He never made a fortune, but his experiences made him rich. America and his art gave him solace from an unimaginable world none should ever experience.

J.W. Wilson (left), an avid reader, art and history lover, and adventurer, was born and raised in Fort Worth, Texas. He is cofounder and currently president of Roxo Energy, an oil and gas operator, and is currently working on his second book.

He and his wife Andrea are both proud alums of TCU, where he played defensive tackle from 1995-2000. They have two children: a son, Ryder, and daughter, Reese.

"Working with Jon was one of the greatest honors of my life."